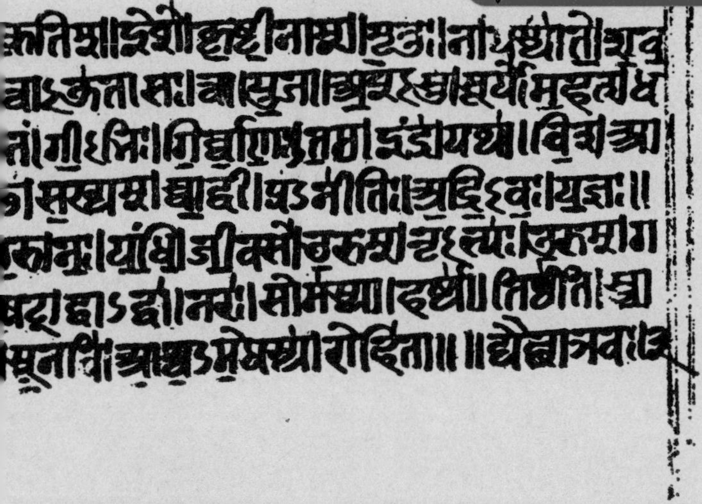

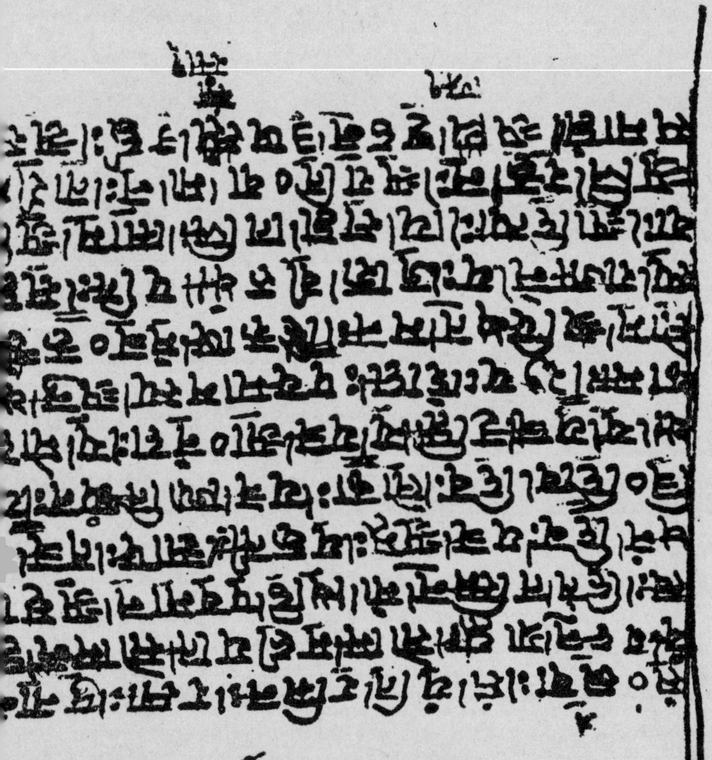

The Ve

The Vedas

HARMONY,
MEDITATION AND
FULFILMENT

Jeanine Miller

RIDER & COMPANY
LONDON

Rider & Company
3 Fitzroy Square, London W1

An imprint of the Hutchinson Publishing Group

London Melbourne Sydney Auckland
Wellington Johannesburg Cape Town
and agencies throughout the world

First published 1974

Photosetting by Thomson Press (India) Limited,
New Delhi
Printed in Great Britain by The Anchor Press Ltd.
and bound by Wm Brendon & Son Ltd.
both of Tiptree, Essex

ISBN 0 09 121060 7 (C)
0 09 121061 5 (P)

To Professor Jan Gonda who opened a way
To S. Ahmad whose encouragement never flagged
To I.T. as ever

Contents

SECTION III

VEDIC ESCHATOLOGY

SECTION IV

SELECTED HYMNS WHICH ILLUSTRATE SUBJECTS DISCUSSED

Foreword

The Ṛgveda is not only a highly important religious and literary document, and as such the object of study for philologists and historians, it is also a work of art and a source of inspiration and edification. The wide and very controversial field of inquiry it offers to scholars does not always discourage them from establishing hazardous and disputable theories, from entering into polemics about trifling problems or balancing themselves on the verge of the unknowable. On the other hand, mystics and philosophers, in India and abroad, contemplating the spiritual elevation of their fellow-men, have, rightly or wrongly, regarded it as a foundation stone of their speculations. Is it surprising that those who, believing that beyond the divisiveness among men there exists a primordial unitive power, and cherishing the hope that the ṛṣis of yore may help modern man a little to find some answers to his own problems, should consider it worthwhile to investigate this ancient collection of inspired poetry from the angle of psychology? Every approach is one-sided. Philologists, attempting to find in the fluid myths and often floating ideas of the Veda complete and well-considered cosmological myths and theological systems, often missed the exalted fulfilment which contemplation could bring their ancient practitioners. Psychologists and seekers after wisdom may easily run the risk of anachronistically or subjectively reading into the texts other things than were intended by the poets, of going too far in considering mythical reality to be only or mainly the product drawn forth out of the subconscious layers of the psyche.

Nevertheless, an attempt at detecting the deeper meaning of the visions of the religious beliefs and conceptions as they stood in the eyes of their protagonists, at finding a psychological key to these products of inspiration—to the images, the relations assumed to exist between this world and the Unseen, between the living and the beyond—is no doubt legitimate. Philologists will often disagree with Miss Miller in the interpretation of texts, censure a certain lack of criticism and the emphasis laid on the element of meditation, many questions raised in her book, many suggestions made and solutions proposed seem interesting and worth considering. Those who are convinced that philology has hitherto not exhausted all possibilities and that there is in principle no objection to reading and studying all religious poetry, including the often highly ambiguous hymns of the Veda, from psychological and meditative points of view, may find in Miss Miller's book if not stimulation into study of the texts, at least material for reflection and contemplation.

J. GONDA

Acknowledgements

Parts of the study on Meditation were published in the *Yoga Quarterly Review*, London 1971 and *Hinduism*, Journal of the Bharat Sevashram Sangha, London Branch. This also applies to certain parts of Vedic Mythology and Eschatology.

Select List of Books

AUROBINDO
On the Veda. Pondicherry, 1964.

BENVENISTE, E., and RENOU, L.
Vṛtra et Vṛẹragna. Étude de mythologie indo-iranienne, *Cahiers de la Société Asiatique* (Paris, 1934).

BERGAIGNE, A.
Études sur le lexique du Rig-Veda (Paris, 1884).
Manuel pour étudier le Sanskrit védique (Paris, 1890).
La religion védique, École des Hautes Études (Paris, 1878–83).

BOSE, A. C.
Hymns from the Vedas (London, 1966).

BHATTACHARJI, S.
The Indian theogony. A comparative study of Indian mythology from the Vedas to the Pūraṇas (Cambridge, 1970).

CAILLIET, E.
'Mysticisme et mentalité mystique'. *Études d'histoire et de philosophie religieuses*, no. 36 (Paris, 1938).

CASAL, J.-M.
La civilisation de l'Indus et ses énigmes (Paris, 1969).

FALK, M.
'Il mito psicologico nell 'india antica'. *Atti della Reale Accademia Nazionale dei Lincei*. Scienzi morali, etc. ser. 6, vol. 8, fasc. 5 (Roma, 1938).

FARQUHAR, J. N.
An outline of the religious literature of India (Delhi, 1967).

GELDNER, K. F.
Vedische Studien. Der Ṛigveda (Cambridge, Mass., 1951).

GLASENAPP. H. von
Religionen Indiens (Stuttgart, 1943).
Immortality and salvation in Indian religions (Calcutta, 1963).

GONDA, J.
Epithets in the Ṛgveda ('S-Gravenhage, 1959).
Ellipsis, brachylogy and other forms of brevity in speech in the Ṛgveda (Amsterdam, 1960).
Concise elementary grammar (Leiden, 1966).
Four studies in the language of the Veda ('S-Gravenhage, 1959).
Loka. World and heaven in the Veda (Amsterdam, 1966).
Notes on brahman (Utrecht, 1950).
'Some notes on the study of ancient-Indian religious terminology'. *History of religions.* vol. 1, no. 2 (Chicago, 1962).
Some observations on the relations between 'Gods' and 'powers' in the Veda ('S-Gravenhage, 1957).
Die Religionen Indiens. 1. *Veda und älterer Hinduismus* (Stuttgart, 1960).

GRISWOLD, H. D.
The Religion of the Rigveda (London, 1923).

HOPKINS, E. W.
The Religions of India (Boston, Mass., 1895).

JUNG, C. G.
Memories, dreams, reflections. Recorded and edited by A. Jaffe. Translated by R. and C. Winston (London, 1963).

JUNG, C. G. and KERÉNYI, C.
Introduction to a science of mythology. Trans. by R. F. C. Hull (London, 1970).

KAEGI, A.
The Rigveda: the oldest literature of the Indians. Trans. by R. Arrowsmith (Boston, Mass., 1886).

KAHLER, E.
Out of the labyrinth. Essays in clarification (New York, 1967).

KEITH, A. B.
The Religion and philosophy of the Veda and Upanishads. H.O.S. (Cambridge, Mass., 1925).

KRISTENSEN, W. B.
The meaning of religion. Lectures in the phenomenology of religion. Trans. by J. B. Carman (The Hague, 1968).

LANMAN, C. R.
A Sanskrit reader (Cambridge, Mass., 1967).

LEVY-BRUHL, L.
Les fonctions mentales dans les sociétés inférieures (Paris, 1910). Trans. by L. A. Clare as *How natives think* (London, 1926).
La mythologie primitive (Paris, 1935).

LEEUW, G. van der.
L'Homme primitif et la religion. Étude anthropologique (Paris, 1940).
Religion in essence and manifestation. A study in phenomenology. Trans. by J. E. Turner (London, 1938).

LINDEN, C. W. J. van der.
The concept of deva in the Vedic age. Utrecht, 1954.

LÜDERS, H.
Varuṇa (Göttingen, 1951).

MACDONELL, A. A.
A Vedic grammar for students (London, 1966).
Vedic mythology. Grundriss der Indo-Arischen Philologie und Altertumskunde. Band III. Heft A. (Strassburg, 1897).

MACDONELL, A. A. and KEITH, A. B.
Vedic index of names and subjects (London, 1912).

MCKENZIE, J.
Hindu ethics. A historical and critical essay. Oxford, 1922 (The religious quest of India).

MALINOWSKI, B.
Myth in primitive psychology (London, 1926).

MARSHALL, SIR J.
Mohenjo-Daro and the Indus civilization (London, 1931).

MASSON-OURSEL, P., WILLMAN-GRABOWSKA, H. de and STERN, P.
Ancient India and Indian Civilization (London, 1934).

MONIER-WILLIAMS, M.
A Sanskrit-English Dictionary (Oxford, 1970).

MUIR, J.
Original Sanskrit texts on the origin and history of the people of India O.S.T. (London, 1868–70).

MULLER, M.
The six systems of Indian philosophy (London, 1899).
Lectures on the origin and growth of religion (London, 1878).

THE NIGHANTU and NIRUKTA
The oldest Indian treatise on etymology, philology and semantics. Critically edited by Lakshman Sarup (Delhi, 1967).

NILAKANTA SASTRI, K. A. A.
Cultural contacts between Aryans and Dravidians (Bombay, 1967).

OGIBENIN, B. L.
Structure d'un mythe védique: le mythe cosmogonique dans le Ṛgvéda. (The Hague, 1973).

OLDENBERG, H.
Die Religion des Veda (Stuttgart, 1923).

PIGGOTT, S.
Prehistoric India to 1000 B.C. (London, 1962).

PRAKASH, B.
Ṛgveda and the Indus Valley Civilization (Hoshiarpur, 1966).

PURANI, A. B.
Śrī Aurobindo's Vedic Glossary (Pondicherry, 1962).

RENOU, L.
'L'ambiguité de vocabulaire du Ṛgveda'. *Journal asiatique*. tome 231 (Paris, 1939).
Grammaire de la langue védique (Lyon, Paris, 1952).
Hymnes spéculatifs de Véda. Traduits du Sanskrit et annotés par L. Renou (Paris, 1956).
Les maîtres de la philologie védique (Annales du Musée Guimet. *Bibliothèque d'Études*. tome 38.) (Paris, 1928).
Religions of Ancient India (London, 1953).

RENOU, L. and SILBURN, L.
Sur la notion de brahman. *Journal asiatique*. tome 237. pp. 7–46 (Paris, 1949).

SASTRI, K. N.
New light on the Indus civilization. (Delhi, 1957).

THIEME, P.
Pāṇini and the Veda. Studies in the early history of linguistic science in India (Allahabad, 1935).
Der Fremdling im Ṛgveda. Eine Studie über die Bedeutung der Worte Ari, Arya, Aryaman und Ārya (Leipzig, 1938).
Studien zur indogermanischen Wortkunde und Religionsgeschichte (Berlin, 1952).

WALLIS, W.
The Cosmology of the Rigveda (London, 1887).

WHEELER, SIR M.
The Indus Civilization. Supplementary volume to the *Cambridge History of India*. 3rd edition (Cambridge, 1968).

WINTERNITZ, M.
History of Indian Literature (Calcutta, 1927).

SANSKRIT TEXTS

ATHARVA-VEDA SAṂHITA
Herausgegeben von R. Roth und W. D. Whitney (Berlin, 1855).
Translation by W. D. Whitney. Revised by C. R. Lanman. H.O.S. vol.7, 8. (Cambridge, Mass.), 1905).

RIG-VEDA-SAṂHITA
The Sacred hymns of the Brahmans. Together with the commentary of

Sāyanākārya. Edited by F. Max Müller, 4 vols. 2nd edition (London, 1890–1892).
Standard translation: GRIFFITH, R.T.H. *The Hymns of the Ṛigveda*. 2nd edition (Benares, 1896). 4th edition (Varanasi, 1963).

YAJURVEDA
Vājasaneyisaṃhitā (v.s.) of the white Yajurveda (Bombay, 1884).
Standard translation: GRIFFITH, R.T.H. *The Texts of the white Yajurveda* (Benares, 1899).

UPANIṢADS
Īśā
Kaṭha
Maitrī
Chandogya
Māṇḍūkya

BRĀHMAṆAS
Śatapatha (Śat. Br.)
Taittirīya (TB Br.)

PERIODICALS

Numen. International review for the history of religion. Leiden.
Indo-Iranian Journal. The Hague.
History of religions. Chicago.

D.M.G.Z.	*Deutschen Morgenländischen Gesellschaft*. Zeitschrift. Leipzig.
H.O.S.	Harvard Oriental Series. Cambridge, Mass.
J.A.F.	*Journal of American Folklore*. Boston.
J.A.O.S.	*Journal of the American Oriental Society*. New York.
O.S.T.	Original Sanskrit Texts. See MUIR, J.
S.B.E.	Sacred Books of the East. Ed. Max Müller. Oxford, 1879–1910.

ABBREVIATIONS

Ṛgv.	Ṛgveda
Ath.v.	Atharvaveda
Yj.v.	Yajurveda
YS	Yoga-sūtra
ff.	following
fn.	footnote

Introduction

The Ṛgveda, the oldest of the four Vedas, is extremely rich in lore of every kind: social, psychological, religious, philosophical, historical, anthropological, mythical; even rudimentary astronomy has been claimed to be found in its verses. It is a relic preserved for us out of the prehistory of the human mind, a mind that reveals itself as by no means undeveloped in its struggle to understand itself and its environment. In so far as Indian civilization is concerned, 'The Vedas are nothing less', to quote Bankim Rachanavali, 'than the basis of our entire religious and social organization. What the roots are to the tree, the Vedas are to our present elaborate religious system, and to our present complex social organization'.[1] They form the foundation of the whole Indian social structure. But their influence extends quite beyond the confines of India, for we find traces of many of our religious ideas, rites and myths in the Ṛgveda, the *wisdom* of the *word* or *logos*. When a deeper study of the hymns will have been completed in the future, we shall then understand and appreciate René Daumal's enigmatic but apposite reference to 'les formidables explosifs que sont les Védas'!

Such a wealth of information as may be gathered from the Ṛgveda certainly warrants specialised investigations into any of its particular branches as revelatory of steps in the history of human knowledge. Only one aspect of Vedic life has been chosen for consideration here, the religious cult which itself is so vast that restrictions had to be imposed upon further research. The latter has been reduced to three main topics: the myth, the meditation and eschatology, leaving out the no less important conception of sacrifice.

Myth is the *substratum* of the Veda in one sense, just as meditation is its basis in another sense. It colours every invocation; it is used as a background of reference to enforce a specific point or recall an original deed, the fruit of which is still being enjoyed by the *ṛṣis* or wise men as they were then called, and through them by mankind, and to perpetuate certain rites left as a legacy by those ancestors who showed men their inherent link with the numinous. An understanding of the Vedic myth yields a key to a better appreciation of the Vedic religion. Without it the Ṛgveda will remain a closed book.

The Ṛgveda gives voice to early Vedic man's wonder at life, at nature and beauty, his concern about his place in the universe and his homage to the regents of that universe. Throughout the ages prayer has distinguished human activity. Temples, shrines and churches that dot the face of this earth are the superb symbols, in concrete forms, of mankind's age-old aspiration—orisons not made with words but stones—of that yearning to worship something beyond self which has ever characterised the human being. In times and places when man did not—to all appearances—erect his sanctuaries in stone, he yet built thought monuments, sacrificial rituals of verbal images and symbolic action rich in profound insights into the meaning, effect, purpose and place of prayer in his life. Such a monument is the Ṛgveda. Every thought, every tale, every myth, every symbol was conceived, developed and expressed through and as a result of meditative absorption, and it is the purpose of this book to demonstrate how far this claim holds good. Every action performed by the *ṛṣis* in so far as their religious rituals were concerned was a meditation. To press the *Soma* plant, to blend it with the milk, to offer it up to the gods, to invoke these, was a rite dependent upon the thought process and the thought force expanded. The hymns themselves are expressions of the *ṛṣis'* meditation. The song, hymn or prayer of the Vedas is a search for light, enlightenment, and an endeavour to win heaven for its successful practitioner (*cf.* Ṛgv. I.61.3; V.45.11, *svarṣa*). The Ṛgveda is a meditation in itself and so is its study. Every attempt to understand, clarify, analyse and interpret it is an attempt at grasping archaic vision. Hence the title of this book.

What is prayer? All too often it implies a petition, a request for well-being for one-self or for others. This is the ordinary man's prayer which remains on the fringe of true prayer. Essentially and foremost, prayer denotes the stilling down of the mind's whirlpool of thoughts, the raising of the ordinary, mundane consciousness—the observing principle—to such a level of pure awareness as transcends the everyday mental state in its quality and depth of tranquillity and harmonization; the opening of an inner window upon a different horizon, a striving to attune man's whole being to the beat of the universal pulse whether that be called God, or Lord, or nature; the awakening of wonder and longing for the transcendent; a communion fruitful of serenity, acceptance, invigoration, upliftment. All these aspects belong to prayer. What is the difference between prayer and meditation? The former accentuates worship and the emotions; it is an outpouring of the heart; the latter puts the stress on methodical thinking; it is a deepening of thought. Both are found in the Ṛgveda not explicitly but always implicitly. Both are evidently stepping stones towards a profounder state of being whence emotions and thoughts recede and finally disappear and the human being reaches beyond himself. This is the true purpose of all aspiration, meditation, prayer.

Any meditation on the meaning of the life process is bound to take the thinker outside the confines of terrestrial existence to a consideration of what lies beyond, and its possible implications both ethically and psychologically. One of the early Vedic scholars, R. Roth, considered that a religion may be judged on its eschatology. If this be so, the Ṛgveda shows us one of the richest of ancient cults. Though, as revealed in the extant fragments from which we may reconstruct it, Vedic eschatology is not as complicated as Egyptian eschatology, it has remarkable similarities in its depth of thought lavished over the problem of life and death and its aftermath, man's part in it and the role played by the gods and man's ancestors. The Ṛgveda confronts us with a wealth of rather complex ideas all too often quite hidden in passing references to which we may not always find a key and which in some cases may remain nebulous for us, but which yet form the philosophical basis of later eschatology.

It may now be apparent that such studies permit of various methods of approach. The early Western scholars were necessarily concerned more with philology, the analysis of words and grammatical structures. But they marred their conclusions by their attempts at proving the then prevalent contention of 'primitive' mentality as typical of prehistoric religion, contentions which are disproved by the Ṛgveda itself, as indeed by any ancient religion. Fortunately, such an unfounded attitude is being superseded through further investigations, although not so completely as to eradicate the false notions thus introduced into Vedic exegesis; wrong statements based upon these early ignorant and prejudiced ideas are still commonly found in the more popular type of survey of early Indian religious culture and history.

Our line of approach to Ṛgvedic interpretation will be mainly psycho-philosophical. Philological analysis[2] will be resorted to when the need arises as with many Vedic words which have no real equivalents in English. Our aim will be to try to understand certain Vedic religious conceptions which have either been misunderstood, as some aspects of prayer, treated superficially as in the case of eschatology, or simply ignored in their deeper implications as the myth for want of serious investigation. The Ṛgveda proceeds by hints only since it is not a philosophical treatise but a collection of hymns based upon ancient traditions, beliefs and teachings. Whatever may be gleaned from its verses assumes the form of allusions, no explanation being given. In order to analyse its contents we have to proceed by inferences from data scattered in the texts. The main text remains the Ṛgveda as the oldest of the four Vedas. The Atharvaveda, considered a later addition to the three main Vedas, has been used only in so far as it throws further light on certain questions, notably eschatology. This applies also to the Yajurveda.

Two approaches might be glanced at here: that of language and that of worship. In spite of all that has already been done, philology[3] has not exhausted its possibilities and might still help in determining more accurately the various epochs to which belong the many myths and their variations as well as the forms of worship. Even a superficial study reveals different layers of thought, and it is not clear whether they belong to different tribes of the one period or to various periods. Books I and X of the Ṛgvedic collection, it is generally agreed, belong to a later time of composition, Book IV to an earlier. But the same kind of difference may hold within each book, some hymns dating further back than others. It may also be that the poems, as extant[4] today, were only the last composed and gathered together out of a far vaster original collection orally handed down and possibly partially lost before such time as the priests decided to commit the remaining to writing. No satisfactory answer has been given to three important questions. For how long were the hymns orally transmitted? How many centuries elapsed between the age of the patriarchs to whom the bards look back and the age of the seers who sing their praises and desire to follow in their footsteps? How long did each last? We should keep in mind the slow tempo of the ancient civilizations with their all-powerful *tradition* which prevented changes from occurring too frequently (unless brought about by great revolutionary personalities such as Zoroaster in Persia and Akhenaton in Egypt). Moreover, Vedic *bhāṣā*, the language of the priests, was developed as such by them and would not alter so much over the ages as would any vernacular. Nevertheless developments in the language are noticeable and point to the duration of time extending over a long period during which the Vedic civilization flourished.

A. B. Keith's very summary and disdainful judgment of

Ṛgvedic language is certainly unfounded and not countenanced by any of the great Hindu scholars. It reveals a complete lack of appreciation of basic Vedic Sanskrit qualities:

> . . . the poets never attain any very great command of their material, whether in language or metre, though in certain cases poetic results are attained by simple means. To the end the structure of the sentences remains naive and simple, and, when the poet seeks to compass more elaborate thought, his power of expression seriously fails him: it can hardly be supposed that in a period of many centuries the Vedic poet's control over his instruments of expression would not have risen superior to the difficulties which faced him.[5]

Anyone familiar with Latin and Greek knows that logical, matter of fact structure is typical of these ancient languages, and this applies to Sanskrit. Keith apparently fails to realise that a highly inflected language such as Sanskrit will necessarily seem simple and somewhat stiff by comparison with such a non-inflected, occasionally sophisticated but always flexible language, as English. We might recall that anyone who tries to render Pushkin's powerful but simple style into English, for example, without falling victim to the charge of naivety which is absent from the original Russian, will certainly be a master of translation. Inflected languages have the advantage—if economy of words be considered an advantage—of using but a few words to evoke a vast panorama or describe a long series of events which our modern tongues (English, French, Italian, etc.) would need to expand into many more words.[6] This gives inflected languages, and Sanskrit in particular, compactness, vigour as well as power. However, some of the verses of the Ṛgveda do lend themselves to a literal translation, and in these cases the power of the original is fully transferred to the English:

> Self-bestower, might-bestower, He, whose command all acknowledge, the gods also; He, whose shadow is immortality, whose shadow is death! (X.121.2)
>
> For he is creative-power, he, the wooer, he, the holy; he, as the Friend has become the vehicle of the Transcendent! (I.77.3)

> They harness their minds, they harness their visions, the seers of the vast seer, the inspired one! (V.81.1)

Furthermore, apart from the question of the grammatical structure of a language, simplicity has always been the hallmark of powerful expression. We have but to turn back to Shakespeare's great monologues and to his sonnets, to convince ourselves as to this truth. Likewise, the profound thoughts of the Ṛgvedic cosmogonic hymns could best be couched in the simplest, unobstrusive language which at times, in the lofty vistas revealed by the underlying thought, rises to the sublime (*cf.* X.129 and X.72). Nothing is more suggestive of great heights scaled in meditation with the resulting depths of conception and understanding. and yet greater heights still to be scaled than the pithy description of the One 'whose shadow is death, whose shadow is immortality' (X.121.2) or the last few words of the well-known creation hymn concerning the Overseer in the highest heaven: 'Even He may not know' (X.129.7) the ultimate mystery of who caused this whole cosmos to be. That supreme knowledge is beyond all manifested, limited minds—even godly minds; only the Absolute 'knows'.

Contrary to Keith's judgment we find that the poets have full command of their language and that simplicity is one of their greatest assets. The hymns addressed to Uṣas (Dawn), Agni, Sūrya and Varuṇa show not merely a fine lyrical gift but also a dramatic power. The destructive might of Agni and Rudra, Indra's martial splendour and intoxicating valour, Parjanya's stormy blessing are painted with vigorous strokes and yet admirable precision. On the whole, the language is that of a vital race, full of joy and wonder at the beauty of the universe and life itself. When we enter the Ṛgvedic field we enter into a world of sunlight both in its thought and its expression. Directness and sincerity are two outstanding qualities which give the whole collection a freshness which later literature lost to a great extent. What can be more poignant through its very directness than this imploration of the human heart: 'May I not live to know my friend or son in need! O bounteous god, turn hither thy gaze!' (VIII.45.36). Finally, we should always keep in mind that the hymns are liturgical in character and that therefore repetition in both words and thought for that type of recitation is inevitable, but on the whole does not detract from the beauty of the song as much as one might suspect.

More difficult, perhaps, in any attempt to date Vedic civilization, but also more revealing than the subtle changes in grammar, might be a study of the changing attitude of Vedic man towards the gods as observed in the varying worship paid to them, in their rise to supremacy and their decline. In this domain of the Vedic gods, as of all ancient gods, we tread on most controversial ground.

What the gods[7] represent has remained a stumbling block to the Western mind and the unsolved question till today. The Vedic pantheon provides a complete picture of the complexity of the human mind and of its attempt at understanding the order of the universe, with rich promises of insights into the human *psyche*—for one aspect of the gods, often overlooked, represents an externalisation of certain features of the *psyche*. The *devas* or 'shining ones', are not a motley group of different entities on whom strange worship is lavished, without any meaning apart from a meteorological basis which indeed does not apply to each and everyone of them. It is doubtful that the *ṛṣis* considered the *devas* as mere personifications of natural phenomena.[8] The divine and the natural, in all ancient cosmologies, are indissolubly linked, the one being the invisible cause of the other, the physical world being rooted in the divine action brought about by means of forces or entities, the informing principles which in due course of time were more and more anthropomorphised. The question: 'Who can here declare what pathway leads on to the gods? Their lower habitations are perceived [but they abide] in remoter, hidden dominions' (Ṛgv. III.54.5) leaves no doubt as to the existence of the gods beyond any physical phenomena.[9] They are the personified agents of the *ṛta*[10] or cosmic order or harmony whose ordinances shine through *ṛta* (X.65.5), that eternal foundation of all that exists as summed up by Max Müller. We ouch here one of the deepest key-concepts of the Vedas. This *ṛta* implies that perfect harmony existing between he essence of being, *sat*, and its activity, i.e. the inner and he outer, the latter being but the effect and in some sense, he mirror of the former. It implies also the spontaneous rightness observable in the majestic movement of the stars, the recurrence of the seasons, the unswerving alternance of day and night, the unerring rhythm of birth, growth, death of each form of life, that rhythm which is he very breath of the divine action.

But there are other aspects to the gods, of equal weight, to be noted. Apart from being deities in their own right, cosmic agents who obey the great law—*ṛta*—of which they are the willing instruments, divinities who won their own immortality long before man came upon the scene of this world, the *devas* are also, through their gifts to men, powers inherent in man through and by means of which man can enter into communion with and participate in the divine process. We catch here a glimpse of the elaborate interlinkedness of the cosmos and its creatures, a typical, if philosophically unformulated, Vedic doctrine which would repay a deeper study.

The dual role, indeed at times the triple role, assigned to the gods is well exemplified in Agni. Agni, the divine force which builds the cosmos, the destructive energy which shatters unwanted forms, is also the great purifying agency hidden in all things and the 'sacrificial priest' and 'invoker', the 'guest' in the human tabernacle, the 'immortal in mortals' which 'makes the gods manifest' (I.77.1: *kṛṇoti devān*). Again and again he is called upon to bring the gods 'to birth' for his torch once kindled reveals in their fullness the divine powers both in man and the universe. Through that flame power hidden in man the latter becomes conscious of the other divine powers. The physical fact—fire—is made use of in the figure of Agni as a tangible token to express the activity and impact of that other, intangible fire which keeps vigil in the darkness of the human awareness and is made perceptible in the illumination of awakened man. The hidden divinity, the profound mystery of which no mind can solve, is beautifully expressed in the Yajurveda:

Vena beholds That Being, hidden in mystery,
in whom all find one single home;
in That all this unites; from That all issues forth.
He, omnipresent, is warp and woof in created things.

Varuṇa is another complex deity with ambivalen aspects. He seems to have ruled supreme among all th gods at a remote time until he was dethroned by the mo human, war-like Indra. There is no indication as to ho long Varuṇa's dominion lasted,[12] and here we migh question whether many old hymns were ever collected c have been lost. The songs addressed to Varuṇa are recog nised as being of a lofty moral character and practicall the only ones of their kind.[13] This should not, howeve make us overlook the fact that moral elevation is als found scattered about in those addressed to Agni wh strikes the sinner (VI.8.5) but whom men nevertheless see as a refuge (I.58.9), and a father (II.1.9) who forgive transgressions (IV.12.4, VII.93.7).

Although the hymns are more or less homogeneous in their totality, it may be that certain tribes had a particula preference for one set of gods and other tribes for anothe In this respect we might compare Agni and Rudra; th latter, in many of his aspects, is similar to Agni, both bein destroying and preserving, fierce and soothing; but Rudr plays no part in the *Soma* ritual as described in the Ṛgved although he does so in the more popular ceremonies o later times (e.g. the *śūlagava*, *āśvayujī* and *pṛṣātaka* rites) Is Rudra[15] an ancient god of non Vedic origin who in th Ṛgvedic period did not win dominion over the tribes as whole, his place being taken by Agni, but who subsequentl assumed precedence under the name of Śiva, a wor already used as an epithet for Rudra in the Ṛgveda?

The question of the predominance of one god or anothe opens up many an avenue of research. We have, fo example, the problem of the Aśvins, the divine horsemen to whom many hymns are dedicated and who are considere to have been the great helpers of mankind in former ages. They may, at a certain time of early Ṛgvedic civilizatio retching back perhaps to the Indo-European period, ave been given priority of worship as supreme deities.[18]

What was the reason for the rise and decline in the apremacy of various gods? Was such turning away from ae god to favour another one (apart from any personal vouritism which is also exhibited in the hymns but with hich we are not concerned) in any way connected with odiacal signs? Many of the great Vedic gods are given the oithet *bull* (Agni, Viṣṇu, Indra, etc.) and only Indra is so called *ram*.[19] Why the choice of such particular oithets for the deities being worshipped?[20] We should not e too dogmatic about these questions and declare that ae Vedic people knew nothing of the zodiac.

A great lesson may be learnt from Keith's chapter on The Rigveda and the Aryans'.[21] Arguing against the ieory that 'The Aryans who invaded India were then ivilized by the Dravidians', he writes in the following orthright way:

he fatal difficulty from the point of view of proof presented by this theory that there is not available any evidence by which it can even be made lausible. If the Sumerians were originally Dravidians, and attained a igh civilization in the Indus valley, it is remarkable that no trace of this igh civilization is to be found in India.

'he Indus valley has since yielded many a surprise, and he buildings, drainage system and planning of Mohenjo-aro and Harappā now excavated belie Keith's statement. Iere is what Sir John Marshall writes in the preface to *Aohenjo-Daro and the Indus Civilization*[22] of which he is he editor:

Never for a moment was it imagined that five thousand years ago ... the 'anjāb and Sind, if not other parts of India as well, were enjoying an dvanced and singularly uniform civilization of their own, closely akin out in some respects even superior to that of contemporary Mesopotamia nd Egypt. Yet this is what the discoveries at Harappā and Mohenjo-daro ave now placed beyond question. They exhibit the Indus peoples of the ourth and third millenia B.C. in possession of a highly developed culture n which no vestige of Indo-Aryan influence is to be found.[23]

n the religion of the Indus peoples there is much, of course, that might e paralleled in other countries ... But, taken as a whole, their religion s so characteristically Indian as hardly to be distinguishable from still iving Hinduism or at least from that aspect of it which is bound up with

> animism and the cults of Śiva and the Mother Goddess—still the tw most potent forces in popular worship. Among the many revelations th Mohenjo-daro and Harappā have had in store for us, none perhaps more remarkable than this discovery that Śaivism has a history going bac to the Chalcolithic Age or perhaps even further still, and that it thus tak place as the most ancient living faith in the world.[24]

Whether or not there is no vestige of Indo-Aryan influenc yet remains to be proved. As was pointed out Rudra ma be considered as the prototype of Śiva.[25]

Opinions vary as to who were the builders of the ancient cities, some identifying them with the Dravidiar who in turn are identified with the Dasyu[26] and *Dāsa* c the Ṛgveda whom the Vedic people conquer and despis The absurdity of turning the *Dāsa* into the highly culture Dravidians warns against any rash identification at thi stage of investigation.[27] It is true that conquering peopl tend to belittle the vanquished. But this can stand as n proof that the Ṛgvedic Dāsa are the ancient Dravidian They may simply be primitive aboriginal races of whic there are still many remnants in India. Further discoverie may in due course alter our present views.

Turning now to the philosophical background of th Ṛgveda we can reconstruct it yet again through an exami nation of the part played by some of the gods. Heaven an Earth are considered to have been already old divinitie when the songs were composed. Hence their apparen subordinate place. But we might also consider the following To the Vedic bards Heaven and Earth, *dyaus* and *pṛthiv* seem to have been the concrete representation of an ultimat abstraction present in the Sanskrit words themselves—th first differentiation, spirit and substance, of the original undifferentiated ONE, the *tad* of X.129. For the philosophi hymns do refer to an original *one* either as *eka* or as *tad* What meaning do the words *dyaus* and *pṛthivī* reveal Dyu (nominative *dyaus*) has as its root *div* to shine. *Dyau* or heaven is the luminous one, the enlightener, the *spirit* hence the *father*. We notice similarly that *deva* can b traced to *div* and that the *devas* or 'shining ones' are th children of *dyaus* and *pṛthivī*. *Pṛthivī* has as its base *pṛth* 'to extend' or *prath* 'to spread, stretch' (*cf. pṛthu* 'broad')

Matter, philosophically, is extension. *Pṛthivī* is the formative womb of matter in which all manifested things are generated, hence the mother-substance which spreads itself out in three dimensions. The conception of spirit and matter, *puruṣa* and *prākṛti* of later *Sāṃkhya* philosophy is rooted in these two old Vedic deities, the original two poles of the cosmic order (*cf.* X.121.1 *prathame ṛtena*) 'born of old in the matrix of law', the parents of all things (X.65.8).[28] Standing at the ultimate foundation of the universe they do not participate so closely in its life as their offsprings, the *devas* who are its direct agents and regents. They are thus left more or less in the background as the basis of manifestation, not as old divinities '. . . little more than conventional figures, mythological fossils, as it were, which possibly bear witness to a time when the conception of Father sky was taken more seriously than it was in the Vedic age', to quote H. D. Griswold.[29] It is nevertheless true that in due time they fade away from the Hindu pantheon.

The Vedic *ṛṣis* were so struck by the duality, or complementary aspects of manifestation, that this is constantly reflected both in their thought and also in their language. Manifestation meant for them the emanation from the ONE of two poles, the positive and the negative, the father and mother, Heaven and Earth, Spirit and Substance, two poles whose interaction produces the active flame (Agni, Kāma) which itself was latent in the ONE as *desire* (X.129.4) and which in turn becomes the propelling force behind creation. That the *ṛṣis* employed the devices of paradox and permutation does not mean in the least that they were hopelessly mixed up. Believing as they did in various levels of life, or rungs in the ladder of manifestation, of which their six earths and six heavens are a symbol and an expression, they used the same image which, taken at different levels, has its own specific meaning. Whatever can be explained in terms of one applies also to the other with slight changes as the former is reflected in the latter. So we have sky and earth 'the two world halves' (I.160.2) and the sun between, or Agni, son of two parents, who at his birth swallows his parents (X.79.4), a graphic image which points to the change that takes place with the emergence of the third factor. Spirit and substance, in their ultimate, original essence, disappear as such, but to reappear under a different garb.[30] Sky and earth objectify the abstract concept of Spirit and Substance which at a different level signify the energy and concrete form, the basis of manifested existence, with as its central dynamic force the creative power, the propeller that links both and by means of which each acts upon the other—that force, the root of all desire, love, action, personified in Agni of which the sun, Sūrya-Savitṛ is an aspect, the solar energy indispensable for growth. The famous creation hymn states clearly 'Desire, primordial seed of mind, in the beginning, arose in That' (X.129.4), the word *kāma* being personified in Agni in the Atharvaveda. Duality emerges, fission occurs; the cell separates into two, the world is born. A cryptic parallel to the above conception is found in the Kaṭha-Upaniṣad (IV.6.7 & 8) from which one may reconstruct exactly the same account of primordial action.

Stepping down the scale of the manifested universe, a second differentiation caused by the interaction of the poles of existence now appears of which Varuṇa, the omniscient and omnipresent God 'in whom all wisdom centres' (VIII.41.8) was at one time the grandiose personification. He too firmly fixes on their props Heaven and Earth (a task assigned to Agni and many other gods) for it is the action of the great gods (expression of the universal intelligence) to separate in order to define. In Indra, who at a later stage supersedes Varuṇa, the defining process is even more marked until he too slowly disappears from the scene.

Death and immortality are two sides of the One 'whose shadow is death, whose shadow is immortality' (X.121.2).[31] Furthermore, divinities such as Varuṇa, Rudra, Agni, have two sides to their nature, the kindly or auspicious, the baneful or malevolent, the loving and the punishing. This is not considered as good and evil as such for as in all things in nature outlines are not rigid but rather each fades into the other and all depends upon the vantage point of the observer. This indirectly points to a tacit acknowledgement on the part of the *ṛṣis* of the relativity of all things. Likewise, some *devas* are also often considered in pairs: Dyāvā-pṛthivi, Mitra-Varuṇa, Indra-Agni, Indra-Viṣṇu, Agni-Soma, the Aśvins.

Similarly the Sanskrit language itself reflects this great preoccupation with the two sides of the one life. Words like *manyu*, *māyā*,[32] *yakṣa*, *asura*, have two sets of meanings.[33] But the most interesting feature is found in substantives such as *aditi*, *advaita*, *amṛta*, where the prefix *a* gives the opposite of the meaning ascribed to the root so that the word contains both aspects: e.g. the concept of boundlessness, monism and immortality is automatically shown as inclusive of constriction, dualism and death. It is true that Indians prefer negative expressions. *Advaita* is stressed as being 'non-duality', *amṛta* as 'non-mortality', instead of continuance of life. The two sides (negative and positive) are inextricably linked and present in each word to remind us that manifestation is a play of the opposites. Monism is the underlying note, dualism is the order of manifestation.

The *ṛṣis* viewed the universe as the divine poem inscribed upon the screen of life in letters of light and sound. So the gods as cosmic agents and the sages, their worshippers and followers, participate in the universal process of creation by their very being and action.[34] Both gods and poets or wise men are the 'inspired ones', the true meaning of 'poet' (*kavi*);[35] they are the enlightened ones to whom one turns for inspiration, for strength (*cf.* III.38.1). Agni himself is the seer-poet, the inspirer of prayer (*brahmaṇas kavi*). The sages are in constant search for an ultimate answer to that ultimate secret of life which only the Absolute knows[36] and the gods themselves 'like-minded and like-visioned'[37] proceed to that one intelligent and creative awareness (*kratu*) which Varuṇa placed in the human heart (V.85.2).

The Ṛgveda, as we see it, is thus not the work of primitive tribes, or the first babblings of infant humanity as described by M. Müller, but the complex song of a highly elaborate civilization of long standing establishment—whether on

Indian soil or not is of no concern to us here. The sceptic will declare, as indeed nineteenth century exegesis tried to prove, that Vedic man was not capable of conceiving complicated doctrines. The Ṛgveda demonstrates the opposite. Vedic thought, especially with regard to meditation and eschatology, reveals an unexampled depth of insight into the intricacies of the human mind, the background philosophy of which was the root of all subsequent speculations.[38] The hymns do not mark the start of the Vedic cult, they rather embody the culmination of a culture whose beginnings were already remote in the eyes of its promoters and to which they constantly looked back. The layers of thought that may be distinguished—mythological and philosophical—are steeped in an age-old tradition going back to a distant past ever present in the *ṛṣis*' mind as the time of their ancestors, the beneficent patriarchs whose heirloom was their treasure and the foundation of their civilization.

The Ṛgveda—like the Bible indeed—lends itself to various interpretations. The one chosen for analysis here is only one, let it be repeated, out of several no less important. As this book is meant as an introductory study of certain aspects of Ṛgvedic belief centred on meditation, supplemented by readings from the Atharvaveda, for the student, it can only give outlines which may serve as a foundation from which deeper investigations could be undertaken. We have used our own translation of the Ṛgveda except where stated, and Whitney's translation of the Atharvaveda except where stated otherwise. The quotations should not be taken as the complete stanzas but as the relevant parts of the verses under discussion. Ṛgvedic stanzas are so packed with different thoughts that one has to eliminate all irrelevant parts, in other words, to dissect them, in order to concentrate upon the particular point considered. The lay out shows when a full quotation is given.

NOTES

1. *Collected Writings*. Edited by J. C. Bagal (Calcutta, 1969) p. 150.

2. See J. Gonda's discussion of the etymological method and its relative value in his 'The Vedic concept of aṃhas', *Indo-Iranian Journal*, **1,** pp. 33 (1957). For a summary of the contribution of philology up to 1928 see L. Renou, *Les Maîtres de la philologie védique* (Paris, 1928).

3. For a summary of what has been undertaken in the field here cursorily reviewed see Keith's *Religion and Philosophy of the Veda and Upanishads*. (Cambridge, Mass., 1925), H.O.S. vol. 31, pp. 2–3. For the controversy concerning the dating of the Ṛgveda see p. 4–6.

4. *cf.* L. Renou, *Religions of Ancient India* (London, 1953). Jordan Lectures 1951, p. 9.

5. *op. cit.* p. 6.

6. The translation of selected hymns will show how succinct the Sanskrit can be.

7. See *The Concept of deva in the Vedic age*, by C. W. J. van der Linden (Utrecht, 1954) for a well-balanced exegesis.

8. For J. N. Farquhar 'All the great, and nearly all the minor gods, are deified natural phenomena, and the interest of the presentation springs from the fact that they are still identified with those glorious things and yet are distinguished from them.' *An outline of the religious literature of India*, p. 12 (Delhi, 1967).

9. *cf.* Ṛgv. III.56.5.

10. See also C. W. J. van der Linden, *The Concept of deva in the Vedic age*, p. 17 (Utrecht, 1954). 'In my opinion *ṛta* and later *Brahman* may be considered as God in sensu stricto, however, we do not leave out Lüder's note: 'Man hat das *ṛta* in Indien niemals personifiziert'!

11. Yaj.v. vs.32.8. Abinash Chandra Bose's translation, *Hymns from the Vedas*, p. 301 (London, 1966).

12. See L. Renou, 'Hymnes à Varuṇa: notes', *Études véd. pān.* VII. fasc. 12, 1960. 'On y sent un personnage qui a subi une longue élaboration et autour duquel on aurait voulu laisser planer une sorte d'ambiguité fondamentale' (p. 4).

13. *cf.* A. Kaegi, *The Rigveda*: *the oldest literature of the Indians*. Tr. by R. Arrowsmith (Boston, Mass., 1886). '... the relatively few hymns to Varuṇa belong to the most exalted portions of the Veda. They recall especially the tone of the Psalms and the language of the Bible in general' (p. 62).

14. *cf.* C. R. Lanman, *A Sanskrit reader* (Cambridge, Mass., 1967). 'That the hymns themselves are of diverse origin, both in respect of place and of time, is probable *a priori* and is shown by internal evidence. Accordingly, if we find, for example, two hymns involving inconsistent conceptions of the same deity or of different deities, this is to be deemed quite natural, inasmuch as they originated among clans dwelling in diverse regions' (p. 354.)

15. On the subject of Rudra as well as the other Vedic gods see J. Gonda, *Die Religionen Indiens*. I. *Veda und alterer Hinduismus* (Stuttgart, 1960) and E. W. Hopkins, *The Religions of India* (Boston, USA, 1895).

16. *cf.* the Greek Dioscuri and the Lettic godsons.

17. *cf.* Ṛgv. VIII.8.6 and I.112.

18. *cf.* Ṛgv. I.112.3.

19. *cf.* Rgv. I.51.1, 52.1, 10.2 where he is addressed as the *ram*.

20. Why the sign 'fish' used by the early Christians whose era starts with the Piscean age? It is interesting to observe how the very strong Jewish element influenced the new Christian religion to such an extent as to eradicate even the new symbol of the *fish* which disappears from Christian iconography leaving the *lamb* as the epithet of the Lord, although the sign itself belongs to a former age,

to that time when the Jewish civilization flourished as a homogeneous whole.

21. *op. cit.* p. 10.

22. London, 1931.

23. p.v. As pointed out by K. N. Sastri, *New light on the Indus Civilization* (Delhi, 1957) the mother element is also present in the Ṛgveda in Pṛthivī and Aditi.

24. p. vii.

25. For a summary of the contrasting features of Vedic and Indus civilization see *Mohenjo-Daro and the Indus Civilization*, edited by Sir John Marshall (London, 1931) pp. 110–111; see also J. M. Casal, *La civilisation de l'Indus et ses énigmes* (Paris. 1969) and Sir M. Wheeler's *The Indus Civilization* (Çambridge, 1968) for recent studies. Indus contacts with Mesopotamia, Hindu religious characteristics which can be traced back to the Indus civilization and the various causes that may have brought about the disappearance of Mohenjo-Daro and Harappā are well discussed.

26. *cf.* Ṛgv. III.29.9 where the gods are said to overcome the Dasyu.

27. *cf.* L. Renou's *Religions of Ancient India*, pp. 3–4 (London, 1953).

28. *pitarā pūrvajāvarī ṛtasya yonā. cf.* I.159.2: *suretasā pitarā bhūma.*

29. *The Religion of the Rigveda*, p. 100 (London, 1923).

30. *cf.* X.82.7: 'That which generated these things you will not find; something else has emerged to being from amongst you.'

31. *cf.* Ath.v. X 7.15 and Ṛgv. X.129.2.

32. For the word *māyā* see 'The original sense and the etymology of Sanskrit māyā by J. Gonda in *Four Studies in the language of the Veda* ('S-Gravenhage, 1959).

33. *cf.* in this connection L. Renou, 'L'ambiguité du vocabulaire du Ṛgveda' in *Journal asiatique*, tome 231, 1939, and his remarks in 'Les Pouvoirs de la parole dans le Ṛgveda' in *Études véd. pān.* I.fasc. 1, 1955. 'L'ambivalence ... est au fond même de la pensée, et partant de la sémantique védique' (p. 6). The same word according to different contexts has one meaning or its opposite. See also P. Thieme, *Der Fremdling im Ṛgveda. Eine Studie über die Bedeutung der Worte Ari, Arya, Aryaman und Ārya* (Leipzig, 1938).

34. *cf.* Ṛgv. X.71.1; 68.11; 56.4–6.

35. *cf.* Ṛgv. V.81.1; III.38.2. See also C. W. J. van der Linden, *The Concept of deva in the Vedic age* (Utrecht, 1954). '*Kavi* and *ṛṣi* both indicate lofty and august personalities. They are human beings, but stand in contemplative contact with the supernatural sphere; and caught by heavenly inspiration they utter god-inspired words' (p. 26).

36. *cf.* X.81, 82, 129.

37. *cf.* VI.9.5: *sa manasaḥ saketāḥ.*

38. *cf.* X.129 with Sāṃkhya and Vedānta and X.136 with Yoga philosophy. See also F. Edgerton's opinion: 'Every idea contained in at least the older Upaniṣads, with almost no exceptions, is not new to the Upaniṣads but can be found set forth, or at least very clearly foreshadowed, in the older Vedic texts.' *Sources of the philosophy of the Upaniṣads.* J.A.O.S. 36, p. 197 (1917). See also E. W. Hopkins. *The Religions of India* (Boston, U.S.A., 1895), pp. 22 and 23. *cf.* also the Vyākaraṇa and the *Agamas* with the doctrine of *Vāc* in the Ṛgveda.

SECTION I
Mythology and the Vedic Myth

PART I

Meaning and Function of Myth

Until the second quarter of this century misconceptions as to the fundamental meaning of myths were prevalent among scholars and militated against any improvement in the interpretation of all the old religions such as the Egyptian, the Vedic, the Scandinavian, the Greek, the roots of which are deeply buried in myths. Furthermore, complete lack of psychological insight and also extreme prejudice as well as confusion between archaic and primitive mentalities both of which are not necessarily equal, inhibited any real development in the study of mythology. However, the investigations since undertaken, more or less free, at least from religious bias, by anthropologists from Malinowski to C. Levi-Strauss and A. Montagu, and the great contribution offered by psychologists of C. Jung's school to our understanding of the human mind have considerably disturbed the pattern of nineteenth-century scholarly thought and have given valuable help in opening up new and wider vistas in so far as prehistoric humanity is concerned. Nevertheless, the whole subject is still widely open to controversy, some favouring one approach, e.g. the psychological, some another, e.g. the structural. Agreement will not be reached for a long time. It may be noted in passing that structural analysis of myth, however brilliant and illuminating, like any attempt at dissecting art or music for purposes of study, if carried to the utmost limit, may kill the very life of myth, the very essence which makes it what it is, a fundamental expression of the human *psyche*,[1] the very core which we want to understand. If we take the life away from myth, we cannot fathom its depth, we are left with mere 'bones'.

A. A. Macdonell's introduction to his *Vedic Mythology*[2] is a classical example of the best of early twentieth century Western scholars' usual approach to Vedic mythological interpretation, following in the tradition of nineteenth century views, but marking a slight step forward—having passed beyond laboured and futile efforts at reducing all Vedic myths to mere meteorological phenomena:

> Such myths have their source in the attempt of the human mind, in a primitive and unscientific age,[3] to explain the various forces and phenomena of nature with which man is confronted. They represent in fact the conjectural science of a primitive mental condition. For statements which to the highly civilised mind would be merely metaphorical, amount in that early stage to explanations of the phenomena observed . . . The basis of these myths is the primitive attitude of mind which regards all nature as an aggregate of animated entities. A myth actually arises when the imagination interprets a natural event as the action of a personified being resembling the human agent. Thus the observation that the moon follows the sun without overtaking it, would have been transformed into a myth by describing the former as a maiden following a man by whom she is rejected.

This explanation is not acceptable. Myth is not at all an attempt to explain natural phenomena. Myth is a view of life no less valid in itself for those who propound it than any rational view for its own adherents. Its roots plunge much deeper in human nature than was ever suspected by the superficial nineteenth century mind. The process, as described in Macdonell's explanation, touches only the fringe, not even the surface, of human consciousness. It fails in two ways: first, it reveals an inability to penetrate into ancient man's mentality—which may have been different, but is not, as further investigations will indicate, *ipso facto* as simple as nineteenth century prejudice would have it—and therefore it fails to give an adequate analysis and assessment of it. Then, it relies upon the meaningless categories of 'highly civilised mind'—which is not defined but taken for granted—as against what is called 'the primitive attitude of mind' which it fails to fathom and indeed to understand. This is the supposed 'highly civilised mind's' attempt at finding the simplest explanation that would fit in with preconceived notions of prehistoric mentality confused with the 'primitive'.[4] Primitive mentality is as prevalent among modern highly sophisticated societies as among so-called primitive societies, the latter of which evidence as many complexities in their outlook, social organisations and languages as so-called advanced nations.[5] What *essentially* characterises prehistoric man as he was and as he may still be found among 'primitive' societies, is that kind of outlook which *perceives* a *divine reality* throbbing with life behind natural phenomena; this may be set against the *dead world* of matter of the 'highly civilised mind', or rational brain, capable of giving a purely rational explanation of nature (in which the primitive is, as a rule, not interested) but incapable of probing beyond the physical and rational, either because of lack of interest or of an ingrained, unconscious fear, and therefore able to take in only two dimensions of existence. For it the psychic and the spiritual are non-existent. How shall we call the type of mind that can take in these two further dimensions?

That which is 'divine' to the 'primitive' mind is generally not grasped as such by the 'civilised' mind except for the mystic and the poet. For the rest there is nothing behind the material or phenomenal, though birth and growth remain a standing miracle. This unbridgeable gap between those two different approaches may account for the perennial misunderstanding evidenced even now among anthropologists.

C. Kerényi[6] makes it clear that 'True mythology has become so completely alien to us' because, as he puts it, 'we have lost our immediate feeling for the great realities of the spirit—and to this world all true mythology belongs'. B. Malinowski[7] corroborated this view in a different way when he wrote: a myth '. . . is not merely a story told but a reality lived'. This constitutes the crux of the problem and one of extreme difficulty for the rational mind to grasp for it no longer lives in that particular *reality* and denies any kind of divine significance to nature and thereby to its human representation of it, namely the myth.

What are these *realities* which appear so unrealistic, which seem like dreams or wonders suitable for children and out of touch with the hard, concrete level of ordinary experience? They may be considered expressions of the archetypal life of the *psyche* which for ancient man underlies empirical experience and which for modern man is best ignored. The difference in approach may be understood by examining the origin of myth in the light of Jung's school of thought, as rooted in the depth of the subconscious and as closely related to the fundamental archetypes of the *psyche*. Jung's contribution to psychology is in this respect of the highest importance for it allows us to consider myth in its essence and true perspective, as a live product of human mental activity and it does not take away from it its essential worth. There is no question of a comparison with a rational element arbitrarily elevated to the supreme rank. Thanks to his profound psychological insight, Jung defined myth thus:

> Myth is the natural and indispensable intermediate stage between unconscious and conscious cognition. True, the unconscious knows more than consciousness does; but it is knowledge of a special sort, knowledge in eternity, usually without reference to the here and now, not couched in the language of the intellect.[8]

Three points of importance emerge here, expressed as 'knowledge of a special sort', 'knowledge in eternity', and 'not couched in the language of the intellect'. These points emphasise the numinous quality which Schelling must have sensed as deeply as Jung when he made his sweeping and far reaching assertion, as quoted by C. Kerényi, that mythology 'in profundity, permanence and universality is comparable only with nature herself'.[9] This certainly runs counter to the usual misconception of myth based upon an evaluation on rational grounds and an irrational lumping together of the supra-rational or wondrous with the irrational. Mythology is not fundamentally irrational. As an expression of the *psyche* and not of the intellect, its field extends beyond the narrow limits of logic. Like nature of which it is the human mirror it embraces all three elements, the rational, irrational, supra-rational, in varying degrees.

Ancient man's outlook allowed him to consider these 'realities of the spirit' far more easily than modern man whose rational mind has more or less shut the door to the other side of his nature and now constitutes that impassable chasm between him and these *realities* and between him and his ancestor. To the latter a mechanical universe or even one with an extra-cosmic deity ruling from above was inconceivable. Sharply defined ideas and contrasts, each in its own pigeon-hole, are alien to prehistoric man but characterise modern man. The former looked to the wholeness of things and not to their mere outer separate aspects. The whole cosmos was alive, from centre to circumference, from height to depth, was pulsating with the great life of myriad forces, intelligent and intelligible, manifesting in different aspects and degrees of matter along the ladder of existence. Herein lies one reason why every modern attempt at understanding and defining mythology fails in one particular respect: the modern mind does not grasp the fact of the different psychomental constitution of early humanity and thereby fails to examine and evaluate the further fact of *seership*. For example, the Vedas are the result of a *seership* which manifested at two levels, psychic and mystical[10] and which only the science of yoga fathomed out.

W. B. Kristensen[11] however, did realise this different nature and approach, and so points out the incontrovertible fact that:

> The Ancient's view of nature ... was directed especially towards the essence of phenomena, and the essence determined all the constituent elements. Thus the Ancients saw in the earth or in the fire in the first instance energies or living beings. The essence of phenomena was divine life. This is the religious view of nature.
>
> That which is characteristic of the Ancient civilizations and religions is the vivid consciousness of the cooperation between, indeed a fusion of, the finite and infinite factors in all phenomena connected with the essentials of life.

The fusion of the finite and the infinite characterise myth which views both sides of nature—the light and dark—as one living whole: this blend of the subjective and the objective, the active and passive, the physical and the spiritual, the constructive and the destructive (*cf.* the ambivalence of the Vedic gods as observed by L. Renou and others); this apparent blurring of the boundary lines between the outer and the inner worlds, is the archaic mind's representation of the living wholeness of a reality perceived or sensed in depth. This is peculiar to mythology and in a sense to dream. It arises, as C. Kerényi explains, out of a 'a kind of immersion in ourselves that leads to the living germ of our wholeness'.[12] Mythology as an expression of the human *psyche* is far closer to the dream consciousness and its set of symbols than to the conceptual consciousness of brain activity. Just as each person has his or her own set of symbols taken from everyday life, images peculiar to the mentality and life of each person and which his dreams reveal, so mythology, like dreams, obeys its own peculiar laws and has its own proper set of images often descriptive of states of consciousness, of observations, views and conceptions perhaps originally unconscious to their progenitors, but finally expressed in a colourful way. This again shows myth as the mental activity resulting from a digging deep within the *psyche* to the very source whence images issue full of life, a going back to the source, that state whence the barriers of the subjective and the objective vanish away.

C. Kerényi rightly points out that the question 'why' is not answered, but 'whence'. Similarly there is no question as to 'why' in dreams. Mythology never explains anything according to the rational sense, hence myth in its popular deformed sense has been denied any authenticity.[13] In so reverting to the origin, to the primordial source, myth establishes a ground of being, and thereby a secure basis for further action always in conformity with the origin. What is structured on such a foundation is *true*. It is the *ground of being*. C. Kerényi explains:

Going back in ourselves in this way and rendering an account of it we experience and proclaim the very foundations of our being; that is to say, we are 'grounding' ourselves. This mythological fundamentalism has its paradox, for the man who retires into himself at the same time lays himself open ... the fact that archaic man is open to all the world drives him back on his own foundations and enables him to discern in his own origins the ... origin.[14]

Similarly Erich Kahler[15] maintains that myth:

... deals with the fundamentals of our existence, it does not explain, but simply relates; ... its assumptions are unquestioned, surrounded by an aura of sanctity and venerability; it bears with it a kind of awesome breath from regions unreachable.

Tracing *mythos* as the 'word' in 'divine revelation or sacred tradition', to *logos* 'the word as rational construction', he makes the most important point:

Yet *mythos* has never been completely obliterated by *logos*; it has persisted through all the ages until today. It can no more be abolished by reason than the deepest, elementary layers of our existence can be completely penetrated by rational thinking.[16]

A *myth* is thus not a miraculous story invented for the sake of entertainment, but a pictograph purporting to image an original (whether human, divine or cosmic) state whence proceeds action which itself results in a different state of being and effects changes of lasting importance; the whole as reflected in the human mirror, the mind, and projected on the screen of cognition in the guise of a highly coloured or dramatic story. Remarkable is the dramatic quality of myth which like dream has an evocative power reaching out to cosmic proportions.[17] It is fundamentally an attempt to express in terms of positive, dynamic representations and therefore concrete deeds what the intuition has grasped of that which normally remains latent in the subconscious. A case in point is the myth of the fall of man described in a particular forthright and anthropomorphic manner in the Old Testament. A myth which finds a philosophical basis and a completely different colouring in the Hindu doctrine of involution and evolution where there is no *fall* in the Biblical sense and yet a gradual immersion in matter from the *satya* to the *kali yuga*, and thus in a certain sense a fall, and a gradual emergence out of this state, or from another point of view, a *redemption*. This is also summed up in the Hindu myth of the churning of the ocean of matter whence the nectar of immortality was quaffed. That which, in the Hindu mind, was conceived as a cosmic process to which man is bound as an inherent part, but out of which he has the capacity to rise (*viz* the doctrine of *mokṣa*), was in the Hebrew mind, described as a human choice of action, a deliberate turning away from a set divine will, a dramatisation of a somewhat similar idea, the dramatic part being completely lacking in the Hindu story. But the essential point here is the living truth behind both representations: the mind's attempt at apprehending and then expressing certain cosmic and human laws. This grandiose kind of myth cannot be dismissed as pure fiction as it has been done in the past. It opens up immense vistas as to human thinking and action and reveals man's eternal search for truth. In this respect myth has its own incontrovertible validity.[18]

The core of myth is an experience intensely lived, either at the physical level and thus involving physical action, or in the depth of the *psyche,* both finding expression in terms of a *wondrous* or *dramatic* tale. Such an experience may stem from an event which happened long ago retold as a marvellous action because of some element in it which belongs to the categories of the great acts of courage and self-forgetfulness of lasting benefit to mankind; it may be an insight or illumination with a consequent transformation of the human being, and his mark left upon subsequent generations; the former, the action, often developed into legend with its many accretions of details, the latter, the experience lived in depth, remained much closer in pattern to its original and so was ever sacred.[19]

We could still further narrow down this definition in so far as the Vedic myth is concerned: it depicts in dramatic terms certain insights realised in deep absorption such as characterises every mystic (the Vedic *ṛṣis* were fundamentally mystics who *saw* the Vedas), realisations whether resulting from *dhī*[20] (visionary perception) or *manīṣā* (wise-thought or intuition) or even *brahman* (the invocative and evocative power of prayer which is the Ṛgvedic meaning of the term), which when first sensed in depth, are devoid of any structure to which the mind can hold in order to grasp the content; such a structure being worked upon and made into a body of knowledge, *veda*, expressed concretely by means of imagery taken from nature. Living so close to the latter, prehistoric man could but translate his subjective life into the rich lore of natural phenomena and use his pastoral or agricultural pursuits as the bricks with which to build the outlines of his mental world.

The Vedas reveal a form of mythology which has not yet crystallised into a set anthropomorphic pattern such as characterises the Greek myths and later Hindu myths. They are indeed the best representation of mythology in the making that has come down to us. Curiously and contrary to expectation, we often find a development from the more abstract to the more concrete anthropomorphic form[21] which finally sweeps away every other presentation. Furthermore, in the earlier portions of the Vedas, each myth varies according to the nature, insight and purpose of the poet.

It might be appropriate to question here the oft used and abused expression *meaningful*. That—whatever that be, a story, an idea, an injunction, a book—which appeals to our whole nature, inner and outer, evoking from us a response of basic satisfaction, revealing something that adds to, or deepens our grasp of, or approach to, life and its problems and mysteries, gives it a reason, a purpose, invigorates, stimulates or exalts as the case may be, is *meaningful*. So Jung claims that myth reveals 'the meaning of human existence in the cosmos, a view which springs from our psychic wholeness, from the cooperation between conscious and unconscious. Meaninglessness inhibits fullness of life and is therefore equivalent to illness'.[22] These are forceful words. Their implications are far-reaching and indirectly denounce the modern demythologised world which is ill because of a lopsided approach to the vital problems of life, its refusal to admit the spiritual dimension of man and the vital necessity of its development. To use David Bidney's own expression, the '. . . deep immediate feeling of the fundamental solidarity of life that underlies the multiplicity of its forms' (*op. cit.*, p. 385) is an integrating factor fully present in archaic and primitive man but not in modern man who in this respect has alienated himself from his natural surrounding through his own choice of artificial life. Furthermore Jung's claims embody remarkable truths concerning the human *psyche* which the *ṛṣis* of old India fathomed. In mythology is mirrored archaic man's psychological wholeness. The Vedas reflect his conception of cosmic and human significance which it is the purpose of this book to examine.

In this connection of wholeness, one factor of supreme importance to the understanding of Vedic mythology, and indeed of all prehistoric mythology, and one which derives from its mystical foundation, is that of *seership*. There is here no question of *credere* as against *scire*, as in Christianity, of belief against knowledge, revelation against reason. There is indeed revelation, belief, but each is grounded in what is perceived and what is seen is the yardstick of what is known. The Ṛgveda emphasises by every means this grounding in seership. Though the significance of such an admission escaped the scrutiny—however detailed—of all the early scholars, it has only now been given proper investigation in J. Gonda's profound study *The Vision of the Vedic Poets*.[23] We should, however, distinguish here two main aspects of seership: that which takes place at the psychic level, which views the multiplicity of *noumena* underlying phenomena and on which is based the ritual life of all prehistoric societies, of which Ṛgv. X.136 gives us glimpses; and that which takes place at the mystical level, i.e. that which goes much further in depth, which pierces through the multiplicities of phenomena and noumena to their one underlying factor giving rise to the vision of oneness, the great characteristic of all the mystics of all races and creeds and ages. The famous Ṛgvedic verse 'to what is essentially one in being poets given many names' (X.114.5) is a typical example.

To the *ṛṣis* of Ṛgvedic India can be traced the roots of Indian philosophy and also the fact that any doctrine, any speculation was based upon the experience of sage after sage and not mere abstract theorising, however rational and brilliant; in the case of the *ṛṣis,* their view of life, of the universe, had its foundation in their *seership,* in their meditation, what they actually experienced in their vision, through the power of *dhī*. This means that the Ṛgveda is not a collection of hymns of purely imaginative purport but the poetic expression of visionary or supersensuous experiences, a mythology lived in actual fact and fashioned into songs as a result; the testimony of what and how the *ṛṣis* found that truth which to them gave significance to life and nature. Every step taken to discover it was a meditation. Hence the whole Vedic cosmogony, indeed religion, and in later times, the philosophy of the Upaniṣads, is the outcome of meditation and seership.

There was then no need for the Vedic bards to pass, as Max Müller was at great pains to prove, thereby evincing nineteenth century inability to grasp the basic elements of psychic vision, 'from the visible to the invisible, from the bright beings, the Devas, that could be touched, like the rivers, that could be heard, like the thunder, that could be seen, like the sun[24] to the devas or gods that could no longer be touched, or heard, or seen.'[25] Rather were the visible objects the outer garb of inner forces or energies considered as entities in the tradition of mystics: they were made use of as tangible epithets to describe what was seen and felt in moments of closer communion with nature when in the silence of absorption or ecstasy, the veil of matter was temporarily removed and the great pulse of nature was felt throbbing and actually 'seen' clothed in the radiance of light.[26]

Religion in Ṛgvedic days, as will be seen in the sections on Vedic meditation and eschatology, was very far from a simple preoccupation with natural events and pastoral activities, with sun, moon, rain, thunder and lightning as nineteenth century scholarship tried to make out at considerable pains. The gods were not personifications of nature's phenomena. The latter were, in the true primitive as well as prehistoric and mythical tradition, expressions of certain forces, unpredictable, mighty and divine, which ruled from behind the veil of material or concrete forms and whose real dwelling place could not be seen. These forces, powers, energies, inconceivable to us, were apprehended as the invisible but intelligent causes or *noumena* behind phenomena, perceptible under certain conditions which, we surmise, were fulfilled in meditation. The Vedic bard plunged into deep absorption before he could actually behold these or could enter into communion with them,[27] and give them a name and a place in his cosmogony. 'Their lowest abodes are visible' (*dadṛśra eṣām avamā sadāṃsi*) 'they [dwell] in realms concealed beyond' (*pareṣu yā guhyeṣu vrateṣu* Ṛgv. III.54.5). Such an admission hints at a dual nature whereby one aspect is manifested on earth, the lowest, but the real or vital essence remains invisible in heaven where the gods abide 'flame-tongued, fosterers of truth, meditating in the abode of law' (Ṛgv. X.65.7).[28] They thus contribute to the universal process, they are the architects of the world and themselves obey the supreme Order (*ṛta*). Thence the *ṛṣis* drew their own conclusions and established rules, rituals, doctrines which themselves are the more or less rationalised results of seership.

The abstract presentation of the gods, their lack of many very specific, anthropomorphic attributes, has been observed by scholars. They are both projections of human characteristics and entities in their own right who may be perceived with the help of Soma (Ṛgv.VIII.48.3) or meditation (III.38.6) and whatever physical traits are ascribed to them such as 'golden hands' or 'ruddy beard and lips', are descriptive epithets of no vital significance to the particular god.[29] The important point is that they are known in a transcendental state and what man can grasp of them on earth is but their shadow, the phenomenal effect of noumena perceived in a state of heightened awareness. Here we come back to Jung's emphasis on mythology being 'knowledge of a special sort. . . knowledge in eternity'. *The ṛṣis* used their visionary gifts, their own method of observation to determine what lies beyond physical appearances. The symbols they used to express their viewpoint are different from those used by our modern scientists for the obvious reason that their attempt was to probe beneath nature's veil, a field which to this day remains a mystery to us.[30]

Upon the ground of mysticism, primitive, prehistoric and religious lore find their common meeting-place.

L.Lévy-Bruhl makes the following important assertion:

La mentalité primitive, orientée autrement que la nôtre, est avant tout, intensément mystique. En mettant à l'origine des mythes un 'postulat logique', on faisait fausse route.[31]

We could here compare C. Lévi-Strauss' no less important claim that structural analysis:

enables us to perceive some basic logical processes which are at the root of mythical thought.[32]

Since myth is the product of the *psyche* expressed by means of the mind, it cannot altogether discard the logic of the mind!

L. Lévy-Bruhl uses the word 'mystic' as implying 'belief in forces and influences and actions which though imperceptible to sense, are nevertheless real'.[33] The primitive '...feels himself surrounded by an infinity of imperceptible entities, nearly always invisible to sight,[34] and always redoubtable'.[35] The fundamental difference between the mystic and the primitive is that to the latter the multiple phenomena are underlined by an equally multiple set of powers, usually forbidding; to the former, beyond all these multiplicities, there is but one, all sustaining, all enfolding, beneficent power.[36]

A great scare and shock overtook certain minds on realising that the mystical element characteristic of so-called 'inferior societies' was the same as that of 'highly civilized' religion. The latter was thereby threatened with being regarded as 'retarded' and primitive, an inferior activity of the human brain, an opinion doubtless held nowadays in certain quarters of our society. 'Would religion be more particularly linked to primitive mentality?' asked E. Cailliet in his *Mysticisme et Mentalité mystique*.[37] L. Lévy-Bruhl tried to smooth away the unpalatable difficulty with the following remark: 'Toute proportion gardée, les mythes sont l'histoire sainte des sociétés de type inférieur.'[38] The obvious implication contained in 'toute proportion gardée', namely that myths expressed in the Bible are superior to those expressed anywhere else, is a typical example of that ingrained prejudice under which some of the early scholars laboured. No particular set of myths is inferior to any other set. They simply appeal to us more or less according to our education and therefore conditioning. Likewise mythical presentation of aspects of human life, longing and striving, is no more inferior than rational surmises, theories, hypotheses or imaginative speculations, none of which gives the ultimate key or the whole truth; only the intellect makes the one set superior to the other.[39]

As pointed out by W. B. Kristensen, religious data, whether couched in myth, symbol, hieroglyphic or any other language, viewed historically, must be assessed in their own essence and not in the light of a personal conception of their merit. Investigations must bear upon

'... what religious value the believers (Greeks, Babylonians, Egyptians, etc.) attached to their faith, what religion meant for them. It is *their* religion that we want to understand, and not our own ... No believer considers his own faith to be somewhat primitive, and the moment we begin so to think of it, we have actually lost touch with it. We are then dealing only with our own ideas of religion.'[40]

We would draw a line between purely primitive myths on the one hand, and, on the other, prehistoric myths already (as evidenced in the Vedas) well developed into a system with its points of reference and specific themes as far removed from primitive lore as are any of the great religions with their sacred myths—e.g. the myths on which Christianity is based, the garden of Eden, the fall of man, the death and resurrection of the Saviour,[41] the redemption—the main difference being usually found in the symbolical and aetiological[42] aspects which Malinowski denies in the primitive myth. According to his own experience among Trobriand Islanders:

Studied alive, myth ... is not symbolic, but a direct expression of its subject-matter; it is not an explanation in satisfaction of a scientific interest, but a narrative resurrection of a primeval reality, told in satisfaction of deep religious wants, moral cravings, social submissions, assertions, even practical requirements.[43] Myth fulfils in primitive culture an indispensable function: it expresses, enhances, and codifies belief; it vouches for the efficiency of ritual and contains practical rules for the guidance of man. Myth is thus a vital ingredient of human civilization ... it is not an intellectual explanation or an artistic imagery, but a pragmatic charter of primitive faith and moral wisdom.[44]

On this pragmatic charter embodied in myth all religions, without exception, were established and everything stated above applies to the first phases of religion. But as soon as certain images are used again and again for particular experiences or particular ideas and expressions we witness the second phase of religion. They have become symbols. This is evident in the Ṛgveda.

Why use symbols at all? The *psyche* works in terms of images as both the dream and the thought process show. A thought is first a picture, then a word. Upon the screen of consciousness images are constantly being thrown up indicating the state of consciousness, the level of the mental outlook, ideas, qualities. Hence the use of an image to represent a string of ideas resulting in action is a natural outcome. Until recently the theory was that early man supposedly equated the image with the thing.[45] As Keidar Christiansen sums it up:

. . . primitive man was assumed to ignore the distance between his direct impression of facts and the expressions he found for them. His expressions, his images, were to him actual realities, and the connection between fact and image was to him, it was maintained, so real that image or symbol was equated with the object itself . . . What does no longer seem to be tenable is the idea that at any time man, illogically or 'prelogically', did actually *believe* in the identity of an object and the metaphor he used to denote it . . . The disinterested intellectual function of the mind of primitive man was, by such general theories, given a part far too prominent, and was even carried to the length that myths proper, i.e., the legends about gods and heroes, originally arose from the misunderstanding of a metaphor: witness the catchphrase that myths were nothing else than the result of 'a disease of language'.[46]

Certain experiences in depth cannot be expressed in the rational language of the intellect but lend themselves far better to a language of images on which the mind automatically falls back: e.g. enlightenment can find its fit expression in terms of the sun and dynamic power released at such time in terms of lightning or fire. The purifying waters as a symbol of spiritual life and regeneration date back to the Ṛgveda. To the Vedic bards the kine—perhaps the main prop and the greatest wealth provider in that pastoral age—were the rays of light released at dawn and by the same token those released through the action of prayer at the dawn of illuminated consciousness, as well as the divine powers seated in man as cows in a cowstall. Hence the many myths of the cows set free from the caves by means of chants, prayers and meditations, and the sun equally found in darkest mountain rocks and set up in the sky, and the conquest of heaven by means of chants,[47] myths which may appear naive to the superficial brain but which surely do not need interpretation. We have here the dramatic tale recounting a feat performed by god or ancestor full of action and suspense but also a symbol deeply expressive of psychological action and discovery capable of changing human life and outlook. The wonder of the sun being made manifest in the heaven through godly or human agency is a fiction to the brain, but to him who will look at the core of the myth there will emerge the common factor which here is the inner experience of enlightenment, described in Ṛgv. V.40.6 as occurring in the fourth degree of prayer, and in Ṛgv.VIII.6.10 in terms of the birth of the poet as a sun—the theme of all religions.[48] What the Vedic bards secretly knew as the sun beyond the darkness (Ṛgv. I.50.10) is spiritual illumination.

In the Ṛgveda itself many are the reminders that what is named has a far deeper significance than appears on the surface and that the Vedic bards are the recipients of a hidden knowledge. In other words, they confess to a purposeful use of terms with a meaning stretching far beyond that ascribed to their literal reading. Such an admission removes the Ṛgveda away from a purely primitive mythology such as experienced by Malinowski and sets it in its right place as a long established cult with its own laws and specific terms of reference:

> Soma is thought to have been drunk when they press the plant.
> The Soma whom the brahmāṇas know, of that no one tastes.[49]

In other words, what the brahmāṇas know as Soma is the

quintessence of spiritual ecstasy since Soma is known as the beverage of immortality. Verse 4 adds: 'No earthly born can taste of thee'.[50] In Ṛgv.I.105.16 we find an indirect confession as to a secret meaning to the sun: 'That pathway of the sun in heaven, made to be highly glorified, is not to be transgressed O gods. O mortals ye behold it not'.[51] The same kind of secret knowledge is referred to in both Ṛgv.X.85.16 and IV.5.3. In the first, only the sages deeply versed in wisdom know the hidden second wheel of Sūrya; in the other, Agni the knower, proclaims or reveals to his devotee that which is concealed in the station of the cow.[52] Such language is not merely symbolic, but recondite or esoteric. It implies an audience comprising those who know, or wise ones who are initiated into the hidden wisdom, as well as those who are learning.

As myth is rooted in the great visions of the *psyche* and constantly reverts to a primordial source, it establishes a secure ground of being, a basis for further action in conformity with the *origin*. Hence the importance and sacredness of myth. To it may be traced rites and ceremonies, customs and beliefs. A perfect example is provided in the Ṛgveda. There is evoked in V.45.3[53] a mythic primordial event, the opening out of the mountain (*vi parvato jihīta*) at the sounding of the word (*asmā ukthāya*) resulting in the generation of the 'great ones' (*mahīnāṃ janeṣu pūrvyāya*)—the waters of life or, as some would explain, the dawns. An invitation is then extended to the bards to commemorate this ancient birth whereby 'the great mother opened out the cowpen' by re-enacting it through the power of visioning, through *dhī*; a reminder is given that this original meditative vision was the cause of victory to mankind's ancestor, Manu (V.45.6). In such visionary thought the ancient sages discovered the original sacrificial formula (X.181.3).[54] Such formulas which later formed part of rituals were therefore sanctified as rooted in truth. Indeed each vision had to be so filled up with truth as to mirror the cosmic order (*ṛta*) before it could be accounted truth. Hence the Vedic patriarchs 'established the law of truth and made its realisation possible' (Ṛgv. I.71.3)[55] Here is J. Gonda's clear explanation:

. . . they are related to have established a special manifestation of ṛta, of the regular, normal, true, harmonious and fundamental structure and nature of the universe, underlying and determining the cosmic, mundane and ritual events and to have started its *dhīṭiḥ* 'vision'.

They made of its '. . . intuitive-and-visionary "sight"' an *institution*.[56] In other words, these ancestors, by their realisation of truth established an outer rite which translates into human terms of orderly action what they sensed or *divined* in the 'ground of being'. This visionary insight was expressed both in terms of myth and of rite. J. Gonda's explanation takes us back to C. Kerényi's (and others') views on the origin of mythology, the return to a primordial state or performance, the significance of which is valid for all times and establishes a ground of security.

The patriarchs play a most important part in the securing of light and order for mankind, two basic factors in the civilizing process, light implying knowledge, education, enlightenment and power, order implying organisation, government, society. Within themselves, Ṛgv.I.83.4&5[57] emphasises, they first established that power which is brought to birth through good deeds, sacrifice, and the kindling of the fires. Here we have hints as to a moral discipline of a higher order. Then they discovered the hidden treasure rich in *horses* and *cattle*. Vedic myths are full of treasures to be dug out of caverns by god (Indra) or man (ancestor). Ṛgv.VII.76 gives a typical example of the *ṛṣis*' method: turning first to the cosmic order, the unfailing pattern of ever recurring dawn in accordance with the eternal law, the poet visualises that original action whereby his ancestors, in harmony with the divine law which brings the light, themselves discovered light. What kind of light is here in question? The stanza itself holds the key to its deeper understanding:

They were rejoicing together with the gods, the sages of old, the followers of truth. The patriarchs did find the hidden light and with effective words of truth produced the dawn.[58] (VII.76.4)

This should be compared to IV.1.13: 'Here' (in the abode of the mighty one which in the same hymn is shown to be the 'womb of law' *ṛtasyayonā* IV.1.12) our human forefathers took up their seats that they might fulfil the law.[59]

No literal generating of dawn is meant in VII.76.4, as scholars at first believed, but a bringing to birth of that spiritual light which enlightens the mind and is the sure guidance to *heaven*. The element of marvel, typical of mythology, should warn us that some mystical action is referred to, if the expression 'hidden' (*gūḷhaṃ jyotiḥ*) light had not already hinted at it. Working together from the abode of harmony (IV.1.13) the patriarchs burst open the firmly fixed fortresses where the cows were imprisoned (*aśmavrajāh*) by means of sacred song—another aspect of the efficacious uttering of the word—and thereby they made for us (*asme*) human beings, a path to heaven[60] and found the light.[61] With mind intent upon the light they discovered the truth.

Ṛgv. III.31 recounts a similar story to that of VII.76 in even more obscure terms, using natural imagery concerning the discovery of a treasure hidden away, with as usual, a key to a deeper understanding of the implications:

The seven inspired ones mentally drove them [the kine] out; they discovered the whole pathway of truth.

Myth thus provides an outer husk in which the miraculous or wondrous element plays an external part yet one fully descriptive of an inner or psychological experience, the latter itself being so out of the ordinary as to border on the miraculous. There is no real breaking of mountains or fortresses holding imprisoned cows by means of chants, but rather the rending of the rock-like subconscious which hides treasures and in its compact darkness prevents man from seeing or contacting the light. The mountain, the cavern, or *tamas*, conceals but at the same time nurtures the rays of light which once released are poured into human consciousness and grant spiritual perception, the generating of the dawn. So the patriarchs 'awaken' (*bubudhānā*) to a 'heaven allotted treasure' (*ratnaṃ*. . .*dyubhaktim*) and then realise that the gods abide in every human habitation (*viśve viśvāsu duryāsu devā* IV.1.18). Divinity has taken up its dwelling in humanity. Does this merely mean that Agni, the flame (the hymn is addressed to Agni) is being kept on the altar of human houses or that the divine spark or potentiality abides in every human being? Man, in other and more familiar words, is the tabernacle of the holy spirit, that spirit which grants the baptism of fire. So by their incantations, by their sustained meditation, opening their minds to the light of which dawn is the herald and the kine the symbolic rays, the patriarchs were able to take up their seats in the home of cosmic order (IV.1.13) in the company of and rejoicing with the gods (VII.76.4). The very element of marvel expressed as the generating of dawn points to the birth of a spiritual dawn qualified as 'hidden light'. Just as the dawn bursts forth out of the darkness heralding the sun, so the sun of illumination, the flash of spiritual insight, bursts through the darkness, illumining the mind; and those ancestors who discovered that sun beyond the darkness (I.50.10) by their own exertion brought forth the dawn for their descendants. This was their legacy to mankind, for thanks to them the way was open to heaven for men. Hence the ritual institution as a commemoration of ancestral deeds.

NOTES

1. Jung writes: 'We can perhaps summon up courage to consider the possibility of a "psychology *with* the psyche"—that is, a theory of the psyche ultimately based on the postulate of an autonomous, spiritual principle'.

'To primitive man the psyche is not, as it is with us, the epitome of all that is subjective and subject to the will; on the contrary, it is something objective, self-subsistent, and living its own life.'

The Structure and Dynamics of the Psyche (London, 1960). Collected Works, pp. 344 and 346.

2. In *Grundriss der Indo-Arischen Philologie und Altertumskunde* (Strassburg, 1897). III Band, 1. Heft A, p. 1.

3. *cf.* L. Renou's description of the Vedic age as 'prescientific' and his assessment of Vedic mythology with its philosophical implications in *Religions of Ancient India*, p. 13 ff. (London, 1953).

4. *cf.* the modern attitude: 'In fact, the very dichotomy of "primitive" versus "civilized" is to be questioned.' *Kinship and Culture*. Edited by F. L. K. Hsu, p. 3 (Chicago, 1971).

5. *See* A. Montagu, *The Concept of the Primitive* (New York, 1968).

6. 'Prolegomena' to *Introduction to a Science of Mythology* by C. G. Jung and C. Kerényi. Translated by R. F. C. Hull, pp. 1–2 (London, 1970).

7. *Myth in Primitive Psychology*, p. 21 (London, 1926).

8. *Memories, Dreams, Reflections*'. Recorded and edited by Aniela Jaffe.

Translated by R. and C. Winston, p. 343 (London, 1963).

9. *op. cit.* p. 1.

10. The difference between these two will be considered in due course.

11. *The Meaning of Religion.* Lectures in the phenomenology of religion. Translated by J. B. Carman. pp. 36 and 20 (The Hague, 1960).

12. *op. cit.* p. 11. *cf.* C. Levi-Strauss '... mythical thought always works from the awareness of oppositions towards their progressive mediation'. 'The Structural Study of Myth. J. A. F. **68,** p. 440 (Oct. Dec. 1955).

13. The word in popular speech has been reduced to mean a lie or fiction.

14. *op. cit.* p. 12.

15. *Out of the Labyrinth. Essays in Clarification,* p. 42 (New York, 1967).

16. *op. cit.* p. 42.

17. The Australian aborigines called prehistoric times 'in the dreamtime.' During that time they learnt everything that was necessary for their earthly needs. For the meaning of aboriginal rituals, the aborigines, power of visualization and the link between their psycho-religious views and those of the Orient see A. P. Elkin, *Aboriginal Men of High Degree* (Sydney, 1944).

18. For an assessment of myth and truth in the light of the theories promulgated by modern thinkers from Vico, Schelling to Cassirer and Bergson, see D. Bidney's 'Myth, Symbolism and Truth' in J. A. F. **68,** pp. 379–92 (Oct. Dec. 1955).

19. Such intensely felt experience arouses wonder and finds its best expression in terms of the miraculous. The kernel of myth is thus not pure invention but a sensing of deeper dimensions extending from the human unit to the cosmic whole. Only the husk is fiction and that was all that could be seen in myth until recent studies. Its core, however, projects for us the intensive life of the *psyche.*

20. For a deeper understanding of this word we are fully indebted to J. Gonda's *The Vision of the Vedic Poets* (The Hague, 1963).

21. *cf.* S. Bhattacharji's *The Indian Theogony,* p. 39 (Cambridge, 1970).

22. *op. cit.* p. 373.

23. *op. cit.* (The Hague, 1963).

24. Max Müller here reduces the origin of the devas to mere physical phenomena, a conception quite alien to Vedic seership, the phenomenon being but the ultimate concrete expression of the shining force behind it.

25. *Lectures on the Origin and Growth of Religion,* p. 214 (London, Oxford, 1878). Hibbert Lectures.

26. That there was a communion between man and supernatural powers is borne evidence to in the Ṛgveda. (*cf.* X.139.5 & 6) and the Atharvaveda (*cf.* II.1.2)

27. *cf.* Ṛgv. VII.88.2; VIII.69.7; III.38.6; I.164.1; VIII.48.3.

28. *divakṣaso agnijihvā ṛtāvṛdha ṛtasya yoniṃ vimṛśanta āsate.* Natural phenomena play a minor, external and often metaphoric part in an otherwise majestic harmony where the interblending of all things moving in accordance with one supreme law is the essential characteristic.

29. For J. Mckenzie (*Hindu Ethics,* Oxford, 1922): 'In the character of the Vedic gods the moral features are far less prominent than the physical' (p. 3); this is debatable. Some consider the physical traits as not at all prominent and all agree that the gods are all generally moral. Frequent epithets ascribed to the gods are *adruḥ* 'free from malice' and *adabha* 'without falsity', hence true. See also A. A. Macdonell, *Vedic mythology,* p. 18 (Strassburg, 1896). 'All the gods are "true" ... being throughout the friends and guardians of honesty and righteousness'.

30 *cf.* Sir Arthur Eddington's words in *Science and the Unseen World,* p. 20 (London, 1929). 'If today you ask a physicist what he has finally made out the

aether or the electron to be . . . he will point to a number of symbols and a set of mathematical equations which they satisfy. What do the symbols stand for? The mysterious reply is given that physics is indifferent to that; it has no means of probing beneath the symbolism.'

31. 'Primitive mentality differently orientated from ours, is above all intensely mystical. By placing at the origin of myth a logical postulate we were going the wrong way.' *La Mythologie primitive*, p. 80 (Paris, 1935). This quotation trans by J. M.

32. 'The Structural Study of Myth,' J.A.F. **68**, p. 440 (Oct. Dec. 1955).

33. *How Natives think*. Trans. by L. A. Clare. p. 38 (London, 1926).

34. 'invisible to "our" sight' might be more appropriate.

35. *op. cit.* p. 65.

36. *cf.* Ṛgv. X.114.5. Also X.129.4 and I.164.4.

37. In *Études d'histoire et de philosophie religieuses*, no. 36, p. 10 (Paris, 1938

38. *Les Fonctions mentales dans les sociétés inférieures*, p. 436 (Paris, 1910

39. With regard to the intellect the following is interesting to note: 'During the sixties of this century both in anthropology and in linguistics increasing attention has been given to the implications of the fact that man's intellect may be no more than the tip of an iceberg of unknown dimensions, and that new techniques must be elaborated to establish the relations between the conscious and the unconscious levels of social and linguistic activity. This awareness is as evident say, in the abstractions of the French school of structural mythology as it is in the deep structures posited by the American school of transformational grammar.' *The Quartered Shield*: *Outline of a semantic taxonomy* by G. B. Milner In *Social Anthropology and Language*. Edited by Edwin Ardener, p. 253 (London 1971).

40. *op. cit.* p. 13.

41. The myth of the Saviour is found in the Indian Kṛṣṇa, in the Chinese Tien, in the Persian Mithra, in the Egyptian Osiris, in the Phrygian Attis, in the Greek Prometheus and the Mexican Quetzalcoạtl.

42. L. Lévy-Bruhl offered this explanation: 'Si les primitifs ne songent pas á rechercher les liaisons causales, si, quand ils les aperçoivent ou quand on les leur fait remarquer, ils les considèrent comme de peu d'importance, c'est la conséquence naturelle de ce fait bien établi que leurs représentations collectives évoquent immédiatement l'action de puissances mystiques'. *La Mentalité primitive*, p. 19 (Paris, 1922).

43. Where does the Roman Catholic belief in the transubstantiation of the bread and wine into the body and blood of the saviour fall in this category? To the believer it is not a symbol but an actual identification and an unarguable fact.

44. *op. cit.* p. 23.

45. Among many so-called civilized people there is often an unconscious confusion between the idea of a thing, especially an abstract quality, and the thing or quality itself.

46. 'Myth, Metaphor and Simile,' J.A.F. **68**, pp. 418–19 (Oct. Dec. 1955).

47. *cf.* Ṛgv. III.31.9; also I.62 and II.23 and Roth's commentary as quoted by Griffith: 'It is therefore brahma, prayer, with which the god breaks open the hiding place of the enemy'. *The Hymns of the Ṛgveda*, p. 85, vol. I (Varanasi, 1963) Also Ṛgv. IV.16.4, 'When by hymns of illumination heaven was discovered.'

48. *cf.* the twice born of Brahmanism. cf. Ṛgv. X.61.19 and the 'second birth of Christianity.

49. Ṛgv. X.85.3

somaṃ manyate papivān yat saṃpinṣanty oṣadhim
somaṃ yaṃ brahmāṇo vidur na tasya aśnāti kaś cana.

50. *na te aśnāti pārthivaḥ.*
51. Griffith's translation.
52. *cf.* also Ṛgv. X.71.4.
'One man hath ne'er seen Vāk and yet he seeth; one man hath hearing but hath ne'er heard her'.
riffith's translation.
53. *cf.* A. Bergaigne's *La Religion védique*. Bibliothèque de l'École des Hautes tudes, tome II, p. 316 (Paris, 1878): 'La montagne a été fendue par les hymnes .. La prière reproduite par les prètres actuels ... y est appelée 'la mère qui a uvert l'étable de la vache'.'
54. The following is J. Gonda's translation of this verse: 'They, receiving isionary illumination with their "thought" (*manasā dīdhyānāḥ*) found the first ajus (sacrificial formula) which had fallen along the path of the gods'. *op. cit.* . 206.
55. *dadhann ṛtaṃ dhanayann asya dhītim.*
56. *op. cit.* p. 174.
57. The first part of I.83.4 runs thus:
ād aṅgirāḥ prathamaṃ dadhire vāya iddha agnayaḥ śamyā ye sukṛtyayā.
58. *te id dhevānaṃ sadhamāda āsam ṛtāvānaḥ kavayaḥ pūrvyāsaḥ gūlḥaṃ otiḥ pitaro anv avindan satya mantrā ajanayam uṣasam.*
59. *asmākam atra pitaro manuṣyā abhi pra sedur ṛtam āśuṣāṇāḥ.* IV.1.13.
60. *viḷu cid dṛḷā pitaro na ukthair adriṃ rujann aṅgirasā raveṇa cakrur divo hato gātum asme.* I.71.2.
61. *ahaḥ svar vividuḥ ketum usrāḥ.* I.71.2. *vidanta jyotiḥ* IV.1.14.

PART II
The Vedic Myth

The recurring mythical theme central to the Ṛgveda takes the form of a primeval feat performed either by certain gods, or by mankind's ancestors, the sons of heaven (*aṅgirasaḥ*), and described either as the slaying of a primeval monster, Vṛtra, which prevented the waters from flowing, or as the breaking asunder of the rocky cavern by means of *mantras*; the result in both is the same: the setting up of the sun till then hidden, in the sky, the release of the waters of life, the giving of light as a permanent boon to mankind, the finding of the path to heaven.

Indra is the great hero who originally slew the monster of the deep. Although the central theme of the tale remains unchanged, the accounts vary as to details even in the Ṛgveda itself, with regard to the description of Vṛtra, the actual fighting, the participants and witnesses, so that the transformations themselves trace the history of the human mind and reveal mythology in the making.

What does Vṛtra mean? The word contains the root √vṛ to cover, constrict, obstruct, keep back. In Book IV, considered one of the earliest, he is described as 'undivided' (*aparvan*) or without joints, 'unawakened' (*abudhyam*), indeed far more since the next rather redundant epithets mark him out as 'sunk in deepest sleep' (*abudhyamānaṃ susupānam*) IV.19.3)[1]. Such adjectives picture Vṛtra as elemental, rock-like, primeval chaos, inertia and darkness. Out of this he emerges as the personified[2] power of obstruction and constriction[3], as the enemy which has to be overcome, as the mountain cavern which holds all things and has to be burst open before the orderly, well defined universe can be established, before the waters of life can flow unimpeded, before the rays of light can be let out. The obstructing power of Vṛtra is brought out in VIII.100.7:

na iha yo vo avāvarīt ni ṣiṃ vṛtrasya marmaṇi vajram indro apīpatat	he who obstructed you is not here for Indra has plunged his bolt in Vṛtra's mortal spot.[4]

The implied, resulting freedom is expressed at the beginning of that same stanza: 'now you can run [or flow down], each in your own separate way' (*pra nūnaṃ dhāvatā pṛthak*).

The dragon and the mountain seem to have held a similar significance, at least in one of their aspects, both representing that which by its very nature prevents *expansion,* hence *liberation*; the latter is described as the release of the kine[5] or as the downward rushing of the rivers[6] and the setting up of the sun on high[7]. Vṛtra lies upon the mountain as though covering it up[8]. Both the mountain and the dragon are juxtaposed in IV.19.3 & 4. In stanza 3 Indra comes upon the shapeless mass of Vṛtra and in the next stanza he cleaves the mountain peaks (*abhinat kakubhaḥ parvatānām*). The mountain which may also mean the rocky thunderbolt[9] is said to lie in Vṛtra's entrails[10].

Modifications of the Vṛtra myth change it from one concerned with the slaying of a dragon (I.80.10) to one merely relating the bursting open of the mountain or the rending of the strongholds (*dṛḷhāni dardra* VI.17.5. *cf.*X. 139.6) in which the participants change, e.g. the patriarchs are brought in, or to the stealing of cows imprisoned in caves (the Vala myth). In time the myths clustering around the central theme become more and more anthropomorphised. From the shapeless undivided monster of Book IV to the serpent with attributes such as snort (VIII.96.7), virility or lack of it (I.32.7)[11], there is quite a distance and quite a difference in presentation, a definite development from the abstract, almost philosophical idea, to the concrete, anthropomorphic crystallisation of that idea.

The element of exaggeration also sets in and can be studied through the various narratives. Thus Indra in I.84.13 strikes 'nine and ninety Vṛtras' or ten thousand Vṛtras for the singer (I.53.6)[12] or pierces 'thrice seven close pressed ridges of mountains'[13]. All the gods fly away from Vṛtra's hissing (*śvasathād īṣamāṇā* VIII.96.7) and Heaven itself reels at the mightiness of Indra's feat (I.52.10 and VI.17.9).

A variation which throws further light on the Vṛtra myth is its counterpart, the Vala myth, the word itself being considered as coming from the same root and meaning 'enclosure' or 'cave'. Here again Indra split open Vala (*abhinad valam* VIII.14.7), the guardian of the kine (*rakṣitāraṃ dhughānām* X.67.6). A faint suspicion at personification is found in the tale that Indra hurled Vala downwards (VIII.14.8) whereas in VIII.14.7 the latter is simply a cave rent open.[14]

Both Vṛtra and Vala are linked in the one hymn I.52.4 & 5: 'Indra, the Vṛtra-killer' (*vṛtrahatye* I.52.4) 'broke through Vala's enclosure (*bhinad valasya paridhīn* I.52.5). The idea is the same: the breaking open of some obstruction which holds treasures.[15] But the Vala myth has a significant variation (out of several). In II.24.3 it is not Indra, but Bṛhaspati, the Lord of Prayer who pierces through Vala by means of *prayer*, driving the cattle out.[16] The result here too is the same: darkness dispelled, heaven's splendour discovered. Like Indra, Bṛhaspati 'cleft the rock, found the cattle.[17] After dispelling the darkness (*vibādhya . . . tamānsi*), he mounts the refulgent chariot of truth,[18] that terrifying demon-slaying car which takes the sacrifice to the gods, opens out the cowpen (*gotrabhid*) bestowing divine light (*svarvid*). Commenting upon the whole account Roth remarks:

> It is therefore brahma, prayer, with which the god breaks open the hiding place of the enemy. Prayer pierces through to the object of its desire and attains it.[19]

This yields a psychological key to the myth and all its variations. Prayer is Bṛhaspati's instrument but it is also used by Indra, though the lightning flash or thunderbolt is his tool par excellence and the means of his victories; the latter, being an aspect of Agni—the finder of light (*svarvid* III.26.1)—shows the close connection existing between the two gods.[20] Prayer, however, also plays a role with Indra, the thought bestirrer (*codayanmati* VIII 46.19),[21] who is called the meditating or mindful god (*dhiyasāna* X.32.1), who is stimulated by prayer and waxes strong thereby.[22] Thus, exalting the *brahman*[23] in the ecstasy of Soma (*cf.* II.17.2) which was brought to him by the heavenly falcon, Agni (I.80.2 & VII.15.14), Indra with his thunderbolt forcefully expelled the dragon out of the earth (I.80.1).[24] Here are combined the three elements which give the tale not a mere meteorological but a cosmic as well as a psychological intent. Through prayer and intoxicated by *Soma*, the elixir of immortality, Indra is able to perform his deed to wield the weapon of destruction which is also the weapon of construction. This is confirmed in II.17.3 where his heroic feat is ascribed to prayer.[25] A further obscure verse shows us that through Indra's loosening of the rock (*aśrathāyo adrim*) he made it easier for the *brahman* to find the cattle.[26] In other more explicit terms, Indra's action of shattering obstacles made it possible for man (the ancestors, *aṅgirasaḥ*) to find the treasure—the rays of light hidden in darkness—through the power of prayer.[27]

A link between Agni in his lightning aspect and Indra's bolt[28] is found in III.34.3: 'he who fiercely burns (*uśadhag vaneṣu*) amidst the forests killed Vyaṁsa', the demon of draught.[29] In I.103.2 Indra 'strikes the serpent' and 'slays Vyaṁsa'. Whether the two are identical and whether both refer to Vṛtra, the idea is the same. As Agni—as well as being 'Vṛtra's slayer' (VI.16.14 & 48: *vṛtrahan*)—is also the breaker of strongholds[30] which is really Indra's prerogative, the question comes up whether the Indra-Vṛtra myth was not grafted upon an earlier tale of the fire which gives release by disintegrating that which constricts and thereby grants liberation.

That Agni and Soma are also credited with the feat of recovering cows, killing demons' offsprings as a result of which they 'found the one light for the many' (I.93.4 *avindataṃ jyotir ekaṃ bahubhyaḥ*) is evidence enough of the close connection of all these myths and their use of different approaches, different participants in the action, for the one end, the one intent. The finding of the one light for the many confirms the psychological significance and the religious purport underlying the prowess which as a quest of light now becomes a sacred action performed for the benefit of all men.[31] Myth here reveals the full quality of *holiness* which has always been associated with it.

The very thunderbolt which Indra hurled into Vṛtra's vital spot (VIII.100.7) severing his head (I.52.10), that thunderbolt which smashes chaos, separating off heaven from earth, 'lies within the ocean' (*samudre antaḥ śayata*) and to it (*asmai*) the waters in their everlasting rolling out stream forth their tribute (*prasravaṇā balim* VIII.100.9). The myth here opens up a further horizon. That bolt which VII.104.19 describes both as 'mountainous' (*parvata cf.* I.54.10) and as 'rocky' (*aśmāna*), hurled down 'soma sharpened' (*somaśita*) from heaven into the dragon of primeval chaos, that bolt is now the flame spirit, Agni's lightning aspect, the builder and the destroyer, the root of creation, pervading the waters of space, bringing the cosmos into being by its creative separation of heaven and earth.[32]

Another pictograph evokes the downfalling or vertical lightning flash crossing the horizontal line of the waters, forming a cross, the cross of manifestation:

apāṃ napād ā hi asthād upasthaṃ jihmānām ūrdhvo vidyutaṃ vasā-nah. (II.35.9)	The Son of waters, lightning-clothed, has descended upright into the lap of the reclining ones.

The whole picture is strangely evocative of the spirit's descent into matter, the waters of space.

Furthermore, this illuminating bolt combines Agni's fiery, dynamic power and Indra's intelligent discrimination (*kratu*). This is borne out in VIII.15.7 where *kratu*, intelligent power, and *śuṣma*, vigour, courage, energy, are juxtaposed with *vajra*, bolt, and spiritual insight (*dhiṣaṇā*) is said to sharpen that bolt which is *kratu* and *śuṣma*: 'Wise insight sharpens that excellent bolt of thine, O Indra, which is might and courage and ability'.[33] It was needed to accomplish the division of the world (*cf.* II.17.5) symbolised in Vṛtra's death (*cf.* X.113.5) for the gods themselves had tried their strength with Vṛtra but had not prevailed: 'the gods gave up as though worn out'.[34] In some accounts the gods are witnesses but fly away (VIII. 96.7: *īṣamānā*). In one narrative Indra appears to have to fight the gods themselves (IV.30.5)[35] who are certainly not called demons. Yet in III.34.7 he, 'lord of truth' (*satpati*) gave the gods freedom (*varivaś cakāra devebhyaḥ*).[36] There seems to be a kind of reciprocal giving out for, according to VI.20.2, the gods did entrust Indra with *asura* lordship when he slew Vṛtra.

Whether alone (VII.21.6) or with assistants (I.52.4, III.34.3), or calling on the gods (IV.18.11), whether wounded (IV.18.9 *viddha*) or intoxicated[37] and emboldened (I.52.5 *dhṛṣamāṇaḥ*), Indra gains the victory, it seems, once and for all (I.32.13). Yet there are curious signs (*cf.* VI.18.9) that this particular victory is being repeated in time in so far as human beings are concerned.[38] Thus the poet invites Indra: 'let us both slay Vṛtra' (X.124.6). Is this really a desire to re-enact the primordial deed? Other similar invitations are found in I.80.3: 'go forward . . . slay Vṛtra', in VI.44.15 and VI.18.9: 'Indra, ascend thy car to smite down Vṛtra'.[39] Yet I.80.4 had declared that this slaying occurred in the past. With no psychological key the contradictions are meaningless. The first part of X.124.6 throws further light:

idaṃ svar idam id āsa vāmam	This is heaven; this is lovely
ayaṃ prakāśa uru antarikṣam	this wide middle region is bright with light
hanāva vṛtraṃ.	let us both slay Vṛtra.

Paraphrased, this verse runs thus: the constrictor blocks the way; let us do away with it, for beyond is heaven, is ight's wide region. Another verse informs us that human beings, the ancestors, slaying the constrictor, have crossed beyond both earth and heaven and made the wide world their dwelling place (I.36.8).[40] Again, a clue is found in VI.24.6 where the primeval deed of releasing the waters from the mountain is aligned with the human action of prayer: 'From thee, Indra, as from a mountain's height, by means of chants and worship they brought the waters down'.[41]

This implied continuity in time applies not to the deed itself but to its intrinsic significance; each man must slay the constrictor before he may conquer heaven, or light or immortality (*cf.* VI.60.1), each one must make the effort, go through the action or experience, something quite in line with the myth of the Garden of Eden wherein the implication is that each one must taste of the fruit of the tree of knowledge, that is must go through experience, before he may know or 'become as one of us'[42] (i.e. one of the Elohim).

Many meanings[43] may be attributed to the Indra-Vṛtra epic battle. This kind of fluidity is characteristic of myth in general. No myth has one specific meaning and none other. Each holds in its narrative certain keys as to its various levels of interpretation. In its general significance this battle refers back to an original state of confusion, cosmic and earthly, and thus also human, a disorder or chaos which was transformed into order by a special action. Philosophically, only by the domination of the obstructing forces in nature could an orderly universe emerge. In 'encompassing the encompasser' Vṛtra (III.34.3)[44] Indra fashioned the existent (*sat*) out of the non-existent (*asat*)[45] and throughout the darkness he made pathways with the sun's help (VI.21.3).[46] The philosophical idea implied in the myth is given full expression in Book X where *sat* or existence is said to evolve from *asat*, non-existence or the unmanifest (X.129), that which holds all in potentia.[47] In Norse cosmogony, when life awakens in the waters of space the giant Ymir, or seething clay, is formed. This is the Vedic Vṛtra. Originally Vṛtra does not seem to have been considered a demon.

He became so in men's minds in course of time as his anthropomorphic presentation tended more and more to exaggeration and to obscure his original meaning,[48] though that meaning was preserved in the philosophical portion of the Ṛgveda.

But in primordial chaos, or the 'waters', as the Ṛgveda itself tells us, 'was immortality, was healing balm' (I. 23.19).[49] The waters are qualified as celestial (V.2.11 *svarvatīḥ*). This elixir was to be dug up or released by Indra's lightning—a somewhat similar story as was to be told in the Pūraṇas concerning the churning of the primeval ocean of matter which yielded the elixir of immortality, an allusion to which is also found in the Ṛgveda as the churning and the pounding of the unbendable and the drinking from the poison cup (X.136.7). The thunderbolt, combining as it does dynamic power and dynamic insight, brought about the mastery of the waters and freed that which they held concealed, the sun, fire or immortality. For the gaining of the sun, Indra's mighty victory (II.12.7, I.51.4) resulted in his claiming the Soma.[50]

Between Vṛtra, chaos, and *asat*, non-existence, between the mythic concrete version (with its later accretions and exaggerations) and the abstract philosophical idea, stands a third conception implied in both: this is the divine man, *puruṣa,* the Vedic demiurge, originally sacrificed that from his remains the world might be fashioned. In the Vṛtra myth the element of sacrifice is found in the killing of the dragon, similar to the killing and dismemberment of *puruṣa*, the difference being mainly in the divine quality of *puruṣa* as against the chaotic Vṛtra. Puruṣa was divided by the gods (X.90.11): 'Puruṣa is all this world, Puruṣa is far beyond this' says verse 2 and 3.[51]

These three ideas gravitate around one fundamental theme: from darkness emerges light, from chaos order, from the unknown the known, from the unconscious, the conscious. Therefore darkness must be dispelled, the sun must be set up. So Indra, the conqueror of Vṛtra and the sun, becomes the great hero of the song of the Vedas. The sun becomes the symbol, the trophy of victory.

Throughout the Ṛgveda Sūrya (like Agni in similar

myths) appears the great treasure to be won and its hiding and its seeking form part of a recurring theme closely connected with the mastery of the waters and the rending open of the mountain. As with the dragon, the mountain and the cavern myths, so with the sun myth, Indra is the main hero, but so are also mankind's ancestors, the Aṅgirasaḥ. To Sūrya Indra gives birth (II.19.3 and II.12.7)[52] for the worshipper (*sunvate*), for the mortal (*martyāya* II.19.5) he speeds forth the sun (IV.30.6) and conquers it as a gambler (X.43.5), this being a gain rather than a vanquishing of an opponent—as interpreted by Macdonell.[53]

The quest, however, is a very difficult one, for the sun is hidden doubly, triply hidden, as the accumulation of epithets with similar meaning emphasises: 'that which lay hidden, kept secretly concealed in the waters' (III.39.6)[54] is that treasure which, once found, Indra holds in his right hand. On his knee (*abhijñu*) he first looks out for the cattle (III.39.5) whose release will eventually lead to the sun. Again and again he finds the sun dwelling in darkness.[55] Like Agni who is son of the waters (II.35.1, etc.) Savitṛ, the stimulating aspect of the sun, is also offspring of the waters.[56] Knowingly, from the darkness, Indra selects the light.[57]

All this involves effort, the moving of the immovable,[58] the forcing open of strongholds (VI.17.3) and of mountains, the epic struggle with Vṛtra, feats similar to Agni's boast of having broken through 100 iron fortresses and flown forth therefrom a falcon (IV.27.1), and the releasing of rivers from their 'curse' (I.93.5 *sindhūn abhiśaster avadyād . . . amuncatam*).

A summary of the main steps in this great endeavour is given in I.51.4:[59]

tvam apām apidhānā avṛṇor apa	thou hast uncovered the coverings of the waters
adhārayaḥ parvate dānumad vasu	thou hast let loose from the mountain the fluidic beneficent gift

vṛtraṃ yad indra śavasā avadhīr ahim	when thou didst slay with might the serpent Vṛtra, O Indra,
ād it sūryaṃ divy ā arohayo dṛśe.	then didst thou set up on high in heaven the sun [for all] to see.

The same idea is repeated in I.52.8 as in many other allusions, here with the additional information that after smiting Vṛtra Indra 'caused the waters to flow for man' (*manuṣe gātuyann apaḥ*), the 'most maternal waters (*matṛt-amaḥ*) in which the sun is dwelling (X.72.7). It is thus not surprising to find the Atharvaveda (IV.10.5) describing the sun as *divākara* 'born from the ocean, born from Vṛtra'. If the waters are primeval chaos holding all things in potentia then they may be identified with Vṛtra which originally (IV.19.3) was not conceived as a malignant serpent but personified elemental chaotic forces. For A. B. Keith this is '. . . a late and absurd legend of the Atharvaveda [which] makes the sun as divākara born from the demon Vṛtra',[60] a perfect example of misunderstanding of the complexities of these ancient myths.

Whether cows are released, or the waters, whether Vṛtra is slain or the mountain rent, the result is the same: the sun is made to shine on high. In one verse Savitṛ is directly responsible for 'opening out as it were a cowpen' (IX.110.6) so that the sun itself actively participates in the opening out of treasures for man.

This development of the solar myth takes us right to the core of its inner significance. In its light, Indra's constant fights and his establishment of the sun in the sky are expressive of that never slackening effort towards enlightenment and that love of freedom from all shackles which characterise the human mind, and the sun is revealed as the fruit of all quest (and all meditation).[61] Man invokes him in the 'light-bestowing conflict'[62] for through 'conflict' (*yudhā*) Indra found for man the way to fulfilment (*iṣṭaye* X.49.9).[63]

What exactly is that sun which Indra seeks, wins and establishes? He finds, says III.39.5 'the true sun' (*satyaṃ sūryam*). The sun of truth as this may be interpreted, that state of being which the cosmic order (*ṛta*) mirrors, from which issue the divine ordinances which the gods themselves obey, truth from whose mansion visionary thought (*dhī* or *dhīti*) itself emerges (X.111.2), immediately lifts the word sun beyond the literal meaning and points to a significance out of relation to the mere physical orb, the blazing forth of truth underlying the image of the sun. What is that truth so difficult to discover? It is far-reaching insight, *sucetasa* (VII.3.10), flawless understanding (*medhām ariṣṭam* II.34.7), that creative resourcefulness (*kratu*) which enables the gods to see by the light of heaven (*svardṛśaḥ*), to be 'sun-eyed' (*sūracakṣuḥ*). From that realm of truth (*ṛtasya hi sadaso* X.111.2) shine thought-visions which are rooted in truth; they glow with the light of the sun, 'truth outspread as the sun' (I.105.12: *satyaṃ tatāna sūrya*).

In all the myths the recurring theme is the same: a religious quest; the actions converge on one central focus, the release of waters with subsequent manifestation of light, setting up of sun or bringing about of enlightenment or heaven. The words kine, rock, mountain, stronghold, rivers, waters, serpent, sun, heavenly light (*svar*) are evidently part of a mythological inheritance with a peculiar significance of its own but with the keys to their meaning in the very verses where they appear. The protagonists or agents may differ, but here again each has his own proper place and meaning. The action differs superficially only. It always implies effort, even a degree of violence when required. The Vedas express action; like the Bhagavad-Gītā, they enjoin action and thereby are relevant to our time. The means of effecting the various feats also differ: the thunderbolt, clamour, mantra, meditation in the heart, and *māyā*. Each has its own peculiar significance and each subserves the one supreme end: enlightenment, the finding of the sun, the truth, in other words, the *ātman*, for the *ātman* is the sun of what moves and moves not (Ṛgv. I.115.1).

Dramatic and marvellous elements are skilfully woven around the central nucleus to enhance it. Myth provides and links the outer or *wonder* element, as though, e.g.

dawn was literally generated, or the rock was rent by prayer or the sun established in the sky, and the inner achievement which under cover of a search for a hidden treasure that will change men's lives, takes us back to a vision rooted in our ground of being, takes us back to illumination born from truth, an inner apprehension from which the seer emerges as a wise knower (*ṛṣi*). The outer marvel is also a way of revealing the inner wonder—to find the light or way to heaven is no mean achievement—as well as of masking it from the profane. But the very mixture of the marvellous and the factual with, as time elapsed, the tendency to exaggerate the former, militated against the credibility of myth as truth and brought about the final degradation of what once meant a sacred truth to a mere fiction!

The Vedic myth shows a continuity of apprehension: from chaos to cosmos, macrocosmically; from cosmos to man, microcosmically, to man's place as a potential god, to his enlightenment and hence his link between heaven and earth. This is material enough for an epic poem. The Ṛgveda is not such a poem, it was not intended as such. Like its later development commonly called Hinduism it is profuse, prolific, rich. It is the early, exuberant, vibrant song of conquering Vedic man, full of trust, faith, hope, of boundless vigour and dauntless courage, full of wonder and sunshine.

NOTES

1. In X.67.12 Indra slays *Arbuda* the watery monster whose name implies a shapeless form.

2. *cf.* 'Vṛtra et Vreragna. Étude de mythologie indo-iranienne, Par E. Benveniste et L. Renou. *Cahiers de la Société Asiatique*, **3,** p. 95 (Paris, 1934). Arguing from the etymological standpoint, the authors make this comment: 'Ainsi le Vṛtra- nom propre résulterait d'une personnification comparable a celle que M. Meillet a posée pour *mitra* ... et en tout cas philologiquement mieux établie ... La personnification d'abstraits conçus comme des forces est un procédé assez courant dans le Véda.'

3. *cf.* W. N. Brown's interpretation in 'The creation myth of the Rig Veda', J.A.O.S. **62,** p. 95. *cf.* IX.61.20 where *Soma* itself is said to put down hostile resistance (*vṛtram amitriyam*) and to gain energy.

4. *cf.* Benveniste and Renou's interesting remark: '... le mot *vṛtra* ne figure jamais au nominatif dans le RV., sauf dans deux hymnes du livre I qui marquent à bien des égards les tendances extrèmes de la légende ... Vṛtra- est une force

qui subit une action, mais qui ne la commande pas.' *op. cit.* p. 97. We would have here an example of an original abstract conception only later on duly anthropomorphised and personified. Again: 'Tout se passe comme si l'on partait d'un emploi appellatif neutre ... soit comme l'étymologie y invite "obstruction, résistance, défense, d'où un masculin correspondant "obstructeur".' *op. cit.* pp. 94–5.

5. *cf.* IV.17.3; X.139.6: the rocky cowpen contains the elixir of immortality.

6. *cf.* IV.19.2; I.32.2; I.80.5.

7. *cf.* II.19.3; I.52.8; I.51.4; II.12.7; VI.17.5.

8. I.32.2 *ahiṃ parvate śiśriyāṇam.*

9. *cf.* VII.104.19 *asmāna.*

10. I.54.10: *antar vṛtrasya jaṭhareṣu parvataḥ.* A similar idea under a slightly different garb is found in the Vala myth. Vala is a rocky cavern holding cows imprisoned. Indra pierces it through and hurls it down (VIII.14.7 & 8).

11. In 1.32.7 Indra strikes Vṛtra with his bolt on the back (*adhi sānau jaghāna*). Elsewhere he crushes the head (I.52.10 *śavasā abhinac śiraḥ*) or jaw (*hanu* IV.18.9) or back (*sānu* I.80.6) of Vṛtra. The epithets *apad* and *ahasta* (I.32.7) may be used for an anthropomorphic effect but the poet may also have the image of a serpent in mind.

12. *cf.* IV.18.9; 42.7; VI.26.5. These thousand vṛtras may just mean 'barriers'.

13. VIII.96.2. Griffith's translation.

14. *cf.* Griffith's translation: 'When he cleft Vala limb from limb' and the text: *indro yad abhinad valam.*

15. *cf.* IV.14, 15 & 18 where the rending of the mountain and the driving out of the cattle result in men's awakening to a 'heaven-allotted treasure'.

16. *ud gā ājad abhinad brahmaṇā valam*
agūhat tamo vi acakṣayat svaḥ

17. I.62.3: *bhiṇad adriṃ vidad gāḥ.*

18. *jyotiṣmantaṃ ratham ṛtasya.* II.23.3.

19. Quoted in R. T. H. Griffith's *Hymns of the Ṛgveda.* vol. 1, p. 85 (Varanasi, 1963).

20. This connection is also brought out in VI.59.2 a hymn addressed to Indra-Agni.

21. This epithet is also applied to Agni: V.8.6.

22. *cf.* Ṛgv. VII.19.11 *brahmajūtas tanvā vāvṛdhasva* and Ṛgv. III.34.1 and Ath.v. X.37.11.

23. I.80.1: *brahmā cakāra vardhanam*—he made the brahman increase.

24. I.80.1: *vajrinn ojasā pṛthivyā niḥ śaśā ahim.*

25. *adha akṛṇoḥ prathamaṃ vīryaṃ mahad yad asya agre brahmaṇā śuṣmam āirayaḥ.*

26. X.112.8: *suvedanām akṛṇor brahmaṇe gām.*

27. *cf.* I.71.2, after bursting open the rock the Aṅgirasaḥ find for man the way to heaven, and IV.1.14–18. A curious verse reveals that Indra also pierced the *gandharva* who is no demon of the deep but a celestial entity, after which action the *brahman* thrived (VIII.77.5).

28. It is interesting to note J. Gonda's commentary on this instrument of both light or enlightenment and destruction: 'Being a manifestation of celestial light it could ... have been credited also with a role in the process of the manifestation of "visions"'. *op. cit.* p. 85. By it Vṛtra's head is broken and chaos or *tamas* is mastered, order and light are made out of these.

29. *cf.* VI.18.10.

30. *puraṃdara* VI.16.14. *cf.* IV.27.1. *cf.* also VI.59.2; 18.9–11; VIII.60.16.

31. *cf.* again I.71.2.

32. *cf.* VI.8.4: *apām upasthe mahiṣā agṛbhṇata.* 'The mighty ones [the gods] grasped him [Agni] in the lap of the waters.'

33. *tava tyad indriyaṃ bṛhat tava śuṣmam uta*
kratuṃ vajraṃ śiśāti dhiṣaṇā vareṇyam.

For *dhiṣaṇa* see Renou: *Études Védiques et Pāṇinéennes* (Paris, 1955–.) I. p. 4 ff. IV p. 54, 60; VII p. 50

34. IV.17.2: *ava asṛjanta jivrayo na devā.*

35. *yatra devān ṛghāyato viśvān ayudhya eka it tvam indra vanūn ahan.*

36. *cf.* X.104.10 and see J. Gonda's *Loka. World and Heaven in the Veda* (Amsterdam, 1966) for elucidations of the idea of space and freedom in the Veda. On p. 23 he writes: '. . . it is room, and hence freedom of action and movement that is asked for men'. See p. 89 of the present study for *uruṃ lokam.*

37. *cf.* VIII.14.7: *made somasya.*

38. This lends weight to the thesis that the name Vṛtra may not always of necessity refer to the mythic serpent but may simply mean obstruction.

39. The poet may strive after rhetorical effects, nevertheless the invitations are too numerous to be disregarded.

40. *ghnanto vṛtram ataran rodasī apa uru kṣayāya cakrire.*

41. *vi tvad āpo na parvatasya pṛṣṭhād ukthebhir indra anayanta yajñaiḥ.*

42. The word *Elohim* has a plural ending inclusive of masculine and feminine genders.

43. For W. Wilson it 'is merely an allegorical narrative of the production of rain'. Quoted in Griffith. *op. cit.* vol. I, p. 43. *cf.* M. Bloomfield's interpretation of the theft of the divine fire which he too reduces to a mere meteorological phenomenon. 'Contributions to the Interpretation of the Veda. 1. The Legend of Soma and the eagle'. J.A.O.S. **XVI,** pp. 23–4 (1896).

44. *asac ca san muhur ācakrir indraḥ.*

45. VI.24.5.

46. *cf.* also II.17.4.

47. For a summary of the Vedic creation myths see W. N. Brown's 'The Creation myth of the Rig Veda'. A.O.S.J. **62,** pp. 85–98, and the same author's 'The Rigvedic equivalent for Hell', A.O.S.J. **61,** pp. 76–80. Philosophically *asat* means non-existence not in the sense of destruction but in that of what holds in itself the potentiality of manifestation. It may have come to mean destruction, the place of evil, of untruth, as against true being, *sat,* in course of time, but it cannot be identified with such a meaning in every instance.

48. The dragon may personify matter (the waters of space) or chaos which has to be conquered but matter is not a demon except as an idea developed through excessive personification. It is first the nurturing principle which, once its task has been accomplished, just has to be by-passed.

49. *apsu antar amṛtam apsu bheṣajam apām uta.* For a discussion of *amṛta* as meaning 'vitality' see P. Thieme, *Studien zur Indogerm. Wortkunde und Religions-gesch,* p. 52 (Berlin, 1952).

50. III.36.8. *cf.* I.32.12 and VI.20.2 & 3.

51. *cf.* the Norse cosmogony where the giant Ymir also is dismembered.

52. *yaḥ sūryam . . . jajāna.*

53. See *Vedic Mythology.* In *Grundriss der Indo-Arischen Philologie und Altertumskunde.* III. Bank, 1. Heft A. (Strassburg, 1897), p. 31. A. Bergaigne (*La Religion Védique*) makes the pertinent remark: 'Sometimes the sun is no longer considered as the fruit of the victory but as the very weapon by means of which the latter is won.' (See Ṛgv. II.11.4 and VIII.12.9). *op. cit.* tome II, fasc. 53.54, p. 188 (1883).

54. *guhā hitaṃ guhyaṃ gūḷham apsu.*

55. III.39.5: *sūryaṃ viveda tamasi kṣiyantam. cf.* X.72.7; X.46.2, 51.1 where the hiding place for sun or fire is the waters, and III.39.5, V.40.6, I.50.10 where the hiding place is darkness.

56. I.22.6 *apāṃ napat. cf.* X.149.2.

57. III.39.7: *a jyotir vṛṇīta tamaso vijānam.*

58. II.12.9: *yo acyutacyut.*

59. *cf.* also VI.17.

60. *The Religion and Philosophy of the Veda and Upanishads.* H.O.S., vol. 31, p. 104 (Cambridge, Mass. 1925).

61. *cf.* IV.16.9; VI.33.4; IX.88.2; VI.17.8; I.131.6.

62. I.63.3: *svarmīdhe nara ājā havante. cf.* I.130.8.

63. *cf.* the Christian idea that the kingdom of heaven suffereth violence.

SECTION II

Vedic Meditation

PART I

I. THE PROBLEM

The practice of meditative absorption (*dhyāna*) as the crux of yoga goes back to Ṛgvedic times when the *ṛṣis* had already achieved mastery in the wielding of thought as an instrument of power and consequently of the *word* as a means of creative activity. The Vedic bards were *seers* who *saw* the *Veda* and sang what they saw. With them vision and sound, seership and singing are intimately connected and this linking of the two sense functions forms the basis of Vedic prayer. We have chosen to use the word meditation as inclusive of prayer, ritual and orison, for every such act is indeed basically a meditation. Prayer and meditation may be thought different but they have a common basis: concentration of thought upon a given subject. The emphasis in prayer is usually on asking (e.g. 'give us this day our daily bread and forgive us our trespasses', etc.) or on glorifying a deity, for which purpose it relies upon the repetition of words (the rosary) or beliefs (the credo). This is not found so much in meditation which is the individual's own peculiar tuning of the mind according to his own choice of thought and method of thinking. But the word *meditation* is not a translation of *brahman* which in the Ṛgveda has a very specific significance and which is one of the keywords that may unlock the mysteries of Vedic religion. Explained in Monier Williams' dictionary as 'religious devotion, prayer or any pious expression in the worship of the gods, a hymn of praise', its essential meaning reaches out far beyond these expressions which nowadays have acquired a somewhat superficial connotation.

Prior to recent Western investigations such as those carried out by J. Gonda in his *The Vision of the Vedic Poets*[1] and L. Renou in his article 'Sur la notion de brahman',[2] the deeper aspects of Vedic meditative absorption, as exemplified in the two words *brahman* and *dhī* as well as in all derivatives of √*man*[3] had not been recognised, let alone properly investigated. These two words have no real equivalents in modern European languages. The shade of meaning and the idea of power inherent in both are lost in any translation. The same applies to the derivatives of √*man* as well as of *dhī*, e.g. *dhīti*, *dhyāna*, etc. *Brahman* is far more than prayer; *dhī* is more than mere thought. These are examples among many that flatly contradict A. E. Gough's unfounded and supercilious assumption that 'in treating of Indian philosophy a writer has to deal with thoughts of a lower order than the thoughts of the everyday life of Europe',[4] a fine example of that absurd nineteenth century European superiority complex which only blinded scholars to the depths of Vedic insights. Further studies into the whole problem prove the opposite.

II. THE BRAHMAN

Brahman as used in the Ṛgveda was defined by Max Müller as follows:

> That Brahman means prayer is certain, and that the root Bṛh meant to grow, to break forth, is equally certain and admitted by all. What is uncertain are the intermediate links connecting the two.[5]

A. Hillebrandt admitted to the difficulty of grasping the original sense:

> . . . for as early as the Rigveda it appears endowed with various meanings, and cannot be identified precisely with any of our conceptions. The Indian thought is hardly adequately expressed either in the definition of Roth,

'the devotion which manifests itself as longing and satisfaction of the soul, and reaches forth to the gods or in general, every pious utterance in the service of God' or in that of Deussen, 'aspirations and cravings after the Divine'. It is Haug's merit to have made it clear that everything which recalls the Christian ideas of 'devotion' or 'prayer' is wholly foreign to the Indian *brahman*, and that the entire sacrificial act was no more than a kind of magic, which compelled the gods to gratify the wishes of their worshippers ... research inclines now to the view that the fundamental meaning of the word is neither 'devotion' nor 'prayer' but 'magic'; and that its origin is to be sought in a primitive and rude stratum of human thought, from which it was gradually developed into an expression for the loftiest conception formulated by Hinduism.[6]

The word,[7] however, cannot be dismissed as a mere sacrificial act which is 'no more than a kind of magic, which compelled the gods to gratify the wishes of their worshippers'. It is indeed a kind of magic, one of the meanings attributed to it by fourteenth century Sāyaṇa, but in a peculiar sense of which the European critics had no idea. If its origin can be sought in a primitive stratum of human thought it had already completely passed this phase in Ṛgvedic times.

L. Renou also wondered at the precise meaning of *brahman* and its development:

Between the significance of universal principle acquired in the Brāhmaṇas and already solidly established in the Atharvaveda and the significance of hymn or formula shown in the Ṛgveda as a whole there is a gap difficult to cross.[8]

He gives further elucidations in his lectures on the religions of ancient India:

The aim was to compose on a given theme ... not introducing direct accounts of the lives of the gods so much as veiled allusions, occult correspondences between the sacred and the profane ... These correspondences, and the magic power they emanate, are called *brahman*: this is the oldest sense of the term. They are not intellectual conceptions but experiences which have been lived through at the culmination of a state of mystic exaltation conceived as revelation. The *soma* is the catalyst of these latent forces.[9]

This definition comes as close to the fundamental meaning of *brahman* as was possible for twentieth century European scholarship. Nevertheless one important aspect has been left untouched. This is what Śrī Aurobindo, obscurely, for his style is certainly far from clear, defines as the soul that emerges out of the subconscient in man and rises towards the superconscient. The point at issue here is what does he mean by 'soul'? On the same page he explains:

. . . the soul or soul consciousness emerging from the secret heart of things, but more often, the thought, inspired, creative . . . which emerges from that consciousness and becomes thought of the mind '*manma*'.[10]

This is what the Hindu would call the buddhi consciousness which for lack of a more suitable term and following Bergson, we would translate as intuition or spiritual insight. Śrī Aurobindo has a further and more concise definition in *On the Veda*:

Brahman in the Veda signifies ordinarily the Vedic Word or Mantra in its profoundest aspect as the expression of the intuition arising out of the depths of the soul or being.[11]

In order to have a basic understanding of the Ṛgvedic *brahman*[12] before considering the whole question of meditation of which it is the cornerstone we would attempt the following definition:

The ancient *brahman* of the Ṛgveda is a drawing forth out of the subconscious layers of the *psyche* of that power,[13] creative in the widest sense and dynamic, which lies latent in each human being, and which is directly related to the spirit, or *ātman*. The plunge into the depths of consciousness—a subjective action which is the essence of absorption (*dhyāna*) and marks a step further than thinking—with mind completely stilled and in a poised, receptive state of awareness, results in *revelation*. Such revelation or inner seeing may take the form of vision, of sudden flashes and realisations of great truths otherwise left unconceived, or of communion with denizens of another dimension of life, or their manifestation; it expresses itself finally, at the mental level, through what is poorly translated as magic formula, rather a cryptic or shorthand transcript, or equation as Renou terms it, by means of the right combination of sound, rhythm and image values, expressive of cosmic mysteries.

This is the essence of the Vedic *brahman*—the Vedic magic: an invocation and an evocation, an active participation, by means of mental energy and spiritual insight, in the divine process, rather than a mere passive reception of external influences; a deliberate drawing forth out of a probing deep within the *psyche*, and the appropriate formulation thereof; the words themselves into which the orison, now mentally conceived, is finally couched, being but the form in which is clothed the *inspiration-vision-action*. Far more than prayer, far more than petition, far more than magic formula, the generating of the *brahman* which is nevertheless god-given, as the universal divine creative act heralds the conception of the universal principle of the Upaniṣads for *brahman* already in the Ṛgveda is the power of the unborn, *aja*, or *ātman*.

These two facets—the act of creative apprehension and its translation into appropriate verbal forms—evidence a conception in which the power of thought and its application in so far as both vision and communion are concerned, have a major part to play. The constant use of the word *dhī* which—prior to J. Gonda's illuminating study[14]—was poorly translated as thought or even devotion or hymn, with its strong connotation of enlightened knowledge and visionary insight, quite lacking in the English word, and its derivations—*dhīra*, *dhīti*, and later *dhyai* and *dhyāna*—points to a seldom noticed fact, that in Vedic times, at least among the *ṛṣis*, *thought* was not the amorphous and uncontrolled activity of the mind it has generally become, but a recognised force used with a purpose, implying visualisation leading to actual vision, an opening up of the mind, an entering into contact with other fields of consciousness ordinarily hidden from intellectual insight and comprehension.

Such an understanding with its wide implications, is a preliminary step to grasping the fundamental characteristics of *brahman*. This whole Vedic idea should first be explored in the context of thought-vision-wisdom. *Brahman* and *dhī* are different and yet closely linked together as comes out in the following plea:

Invigorate our prayer, invigorate our thoughts.
brahma jinvatam uta jinvataṃ dhiyaḥ. VIII.35.16.

III. THE POWER AND USE OF THOUGHT

It is not quite accurate to assume, as H. D. Velankar does, that what one could designate as Vedic Yoga:

> had not yet been transferred from the external environments to the internal sphere and equipment of a man as in later days.
>
> In the days of the Ṛgveda, Sacrifice consisting of hymns and offerings constituted the Yoga or the means of reaching the goal, while in the times of the Upaniṣads and after, it was the mind and the senses which became the Yoga or the means of reaching the goal, i.e. the realisation of the Self.[15]

This distinction, as it stands, appears to be arbitrary as is clearly borne out by Ṛgveda V.81.1 a–b (which Velankar himself quotes):

Yuñjate mana uta yuñjate dhiyo viprā
viprasya bṛhato vipaścitaḥ.

'The learned poets employ their mind and also their hymns of (i.e. addressed to) the great poet (Savitṛ)'. (Velankar's own translation). Here Savitṛ may inspire the singers, nevertheless the verse states clearly the seers of the lofty seer, the inspired one, harness their mind, harness their illumined thoughts (*dhiyaḥ*). The emphasis upon the yoking of the mind is quite significant and is also borne out in III.38.1 where the poet admits to 'straining after an inspired thought like a spirited, well-yoked horse'. Vedic yoga as later yoga is primarily internal practice. Chanting of hymns or the controlled preparation and execution of the sacrifice only served as aids to this process of internalisation, a process which was characterised by the production of inner and physiological heat or *tapas*.

Dhī[16] is with the Vedic *ṛṣis* more than a mere 'modification of the thinking principle' (*citta-vṛtti-nirodhaḥ*)[17] which must be controlled. It is not to be suspended but used in specific ways. It pertains to the image-making faculty of the mind and is to be harnessed like a steed. As established by J. Gonda[18] it is a thought-provoking-vision; in other words, the power of thought is developed into vision and used to reach out beyond the senses and the mind. It may be regarded as a lens focussed on the would-be object of meditation and thus used to cross over to the other shore, to contact supersensuous realms (I.46.8), to stir the gods and enter into communion with them. This is the first step on the way to the *brahman*; it is no ordinary thinking, but a definite exercise in mental activity which in Ṛgv. X.67.1 is described as having *seven* aspects to it, *sapta-śīrṣṇīm* (seven-headed) and originates in *ṛta*, the realm of truth whence the cosmic harmony. So Ṛgv. X.67.1 clearly states: 'This lofty seven-headed thought-provoking-vision, born of reality, our ancestor discovered'.[19] Rooted in truth, this *dhī* or vision through truth, is prized as a heirloom from the *pitṛs*, the *ṛṣis*' ancestors, as an opening up to deeper knowledge, for it brings aspects of truth into human consciousness. It is that which enabled the *pitṛs* to reach heaven to find the light, and therefore that which will enable the *ṛṣis* to do the same. Verse 2 elaborates: 'Praising truth and thinking aright'.[20] Right thought rooted in truth alone can bear the required fruit which is spiritual knowledge and takes the seeker one step further towards achieving his quest. What is truth? Expressed again and again as *ṛta*,[21] it is the cosmic order whence issue all things, whence the divine statutes or laws can be traced which even the gods follow, and the right following of which, or the right reflecting of which in any action, brings well-being. Therefore, any aspect of truth on earth must be a mirror of the harmony in heaven and a thought vision born of that harmony is truth.[22] So the poet's wish is 'let prayer spring forth from the abode of truth' (Ṛgv. VII.36.1)[23] for Sūrya has unloosed the cattle, goes on the verse, thereby plunging straight into Vedic imagery. Prayer is here a power issuing from that which represents harmony, heralding the light which is Sūrya, spreading forth its rays which are the kine. Shining therefrom the thought-vision is reflected in human consciousness as a facet of that truth from which it issued. Glowing spontaneously, it fills the singer with the streams of truth (VIII.6.8). We notice here three basic and typically Vedic elements: the visionary; the illuminating; the truth. Welling forth from deep within the consciousness, the vision illuminates the seer as brightly as the lightning flash that reveals the hitherto darkly hidden.

IV. THE CHARIOT OR BOAT, THE HORSE, AND THE BRAHMAN

The chariot plays a considerable part in Vedic, as in all ancient, lore and various meanings may be attributed to it in different contexts.[24] More often than not it is no physical vehicle at all. Thus the Ṛbhus 'wrought an effective' or 'suitable car' (*sukhaṃ ratham*) for the Aśvins (I.20.3), that car not made for horses or for reins (IV.36.1: *anaśvo jāto anabhīśur ratha*) or as A. Coomaraswami translates the verse, 'drawn by steeds not born of horses',[25] because the Ṛbhus 'made the easily running chariot out of their mind entirely by thought' or 'mental power' (IV.36.2: *manasas pari dhyayā*). This vehicle could be a way of describing that which helps to find, perform or frame the *brahman* for in the same order of thought we find the *ṛṣis* themselves 'fashion, even as chariots, those prayers (*brahmāṇi*) that yield fulfilment' (*vardhanā*) (V.73.10: *imā brahmāṇi vardhanā...yā takṣāma rathān iva*) just as the Ṛbhus 'fashioned prayer for Agni' (X.80.7: *agnaye brahma ṛbhavas tatakṣuḥ*). Similarly praise is magnified by means of thought as though a chariot (I.94.1: *imaṃ stoman... ratham iva saṃ mahemā manīṣayā* 'this praise even like a chariot shall we magnify with our wise insight'). Panegyric seems to be an essential step in the process of attuning the mind to subtler realms of experience.

Thought is the chariot, or boat, sent forth to stir the gods (*cf.* VIII.96.11)[26] and the means whereby to travel to the other shore, i.e. to super-sensuous realms (*pārāya*);[27] there the *ṛṣi* becomes the recipient of visions and therefore a seer. The chariot is described in various ways. One particular epithet, 'three-seated' or 'having three poles' (*trivandhura* VII.71.4 and I.183.1) or three wheeled (*tri-*

cakraḥ IV.36.1) may be a reminder that the vehicle was capable of taking man or god into the three realms of Vedic cosmogony. On the one hand, in certain cases, it may mean some sort of subtle vehicle which man fashions during his life as a result of his deeds and thoughts and which, after death, he automatically uses to reach the abode of the 'fathers';[28] on the other hand, in other cases it may symbolise a one-pointed concentration of the mind raising thought beyond the realm of the physical senses to a visionary awareness not stimulated by terrestrial phenomena, and in this sense would be the peculiar instrument of the gods and of the *ṛṣis*. Indeed that whole process was likened to the building of a chariot[29] which enabled the worshipper to reach to the gods and facilitated the gods' drawing nearer to the human being. In other words, the chariot (*ratha*) was the symbol of the means of communication and communion. The clearest and most striking comparison between the seer's activity and that of a carpenter or builder (*taṣṭṛ*) is made in Ṛgv. III.38.1.[30] The strong expression *abhi dīdhayā manīṣām* 'I have been absorbed in meditation' emphasises the factor of inner collectedness, and the subsequent simile throws light upon the process of this meditation: 'proceeding like a carpenter or like some well-yoked spirited steed' (*taṣṭā iva. . .atyo na vājī sudhuro jihānaḥ*). There is method, implying stages, demanding a metaphoric building of an instrument which is nothing more than a focussing of the consciousness. It is a specialised process, just as is the building of a chariot, or any carpenter's work. Here we have the first hint as to a technique of meditation which the *ṛṣis* may have employed but which they do not explain.

Both the patriarchs and the gods share the use of this chariot (X.15.10) which in X.63.4 and I.140.1 bears the epithet of 'light' or 'luminous' (*jyotīrathā*), and facilitates the 'crossing' to the other shore (*pārāya gantave* I.46.7); 'in the crossing of the oceans your chariot is heaven's broad-oared-boat' (I.46.8).[31] The ocean meant is not the sea but the intermediate region of Vedic cosmogony which stands between earth and heaven. In due course the word *ratha* embodied the idea of sacrifice, the ritual being a reflection of the cosmic process. So Agni is 'the unflagging charioteer of the vast order' (III.2.8)[32] and Bṛhaspati, the Lord of Prayer, mounts 'the luminous chariot of order,[33] the fearful chariot that fells foes, slaying demons, that opens up heaven's cowpen, finding heaven's light' (*svarvidam* II.23.3). Ṛgv. X.101.2 gives a summary of the process of thought-sacrifice-ritual: here those who come together for worship or 'friends' (*sakhāyaḥ*) are enjoined to make their thoughts (*dhiyaḥ*) harmonious (*mandrāḥ*), to fashion them into an armed boat[34] that will be their means of removing obstacles and to forward the sacrifice.[35]

Prayers ascend to the gods and descend back to men (*cf.* I.46.7) like, or on, chariots loaded with wealth or nourishment,[36] i.e. mental or spiritual food.[37] The chariot (or ship) expresses the idea of swift communication, the words 'thought' and 'refulgent' showing the kind of vehicle meant.[38] The gods receive these prayer-laden vessels with pleasure[39] and in their turn, as in the case of Indra, make the *brahman* most powerful for the bards (VI.35.3).[40] Indra is asked 'when may our prayers find rest in thy chariot' (VI.35.1).[41] He, the knower (*vidvān*) is invoked to let his steeds be yoked (*harayaḥ santu yuktāḥ*) and 'to come to our prayers' (VII.28.1)[42] for in his might lies the power to respond to the worshipper's call and to protect the sages' *brahma*,[43] in other words, to foster divine communion.[44] So also is he asked to make the bard's thoughts (*dhiyaḥ karaṣi*) full of that 'treasured vigour' (*vājaratnaḥ*) or might of spirit—not booty as translated by Griffith.[45] Heroic power or courage (*suvīrya*) is in VIII.3.9 identified with *brahman* (*tad brahma*).

The question may arise whether the word 'horse' when used in connection with the *ratha* has not also a symbolic meaning as claimed by Śrī Aurobindo, in harmony with that of *ratha*. A strong hint is given in I.20.2:

> They [the Ṛbhus] who for Indra's sake, with their mind did fashion horses word-yoked [harnessed by a word] obtained the worship [the fruit of the worship] through sacrificial rites.[46]

The figurative sense here is unequivocal. Again, 'those who are yoked by prayer' (*te brahmayujā*) 'by prayer I harness' (*brahmaṇā . . . yunajmi*) exclaims the *ṛṣi* and then proceeds to compare them to two 'fleet friendly bays (*harī sakhāyā . . . āśū*) who rejoice together' (*sadhamāda* III.35.4). These are Indra's steeds which the poet (in verse 2) harnesses 'to the pole' (*dhūrṣu ā yunajmi*) that they may bring the god hither.[47] Agni is also compared to a 'courser not born of horses' (I.152.5).[48]

In a strange petition addressed to Agni the *brahman* is placed in a position of equation, at least as to value, with the steed or charioteer, thus: 'With steed or with prayer, O Agni (*arvatā vā . . . brahmaṇā vā*), may we show forth our heroism' (II.2.10).[49] Is the steed in its figurative sense just another means of reaching the gods, identical to the *ratha*, there being a play upon the physical sense of speedy transportation, and a figurative allusion to swiftness of thought? The comparison of prayer to a horse brings out its effectiveness in quickly taking the worshipper to his goal. Along similar lines, the mortal whom Indra and the Ṛbhus favour must show his prowess with his thought-visions (*dhībhiḥ*) and with the horse (*arvatā*) at the ritual sacrifice (IV.37.6).[50] Taking the latter literally, it would mean he must succeed as a horseman, but the juxtaposition of visionary thought with the horseman makes it a figurative instrument of travelling through purely mental realms.[51] Harnessing and swiftness of thought are two sides of the one idea, the steed emphasising motion, depicting the thought as it journeys from the human being to the god and vice versa.

But there is more to this conception of thought than what appears at first glance. The celestial vehicle which in I.183.1 the Aśvins are enjoined to 'harness' (*yunjathām*) 'passes mind in speed' (*manaso yo javīyān*), has three poles (*trivandhuro*) and three wheels (*tricakraḥ*), and is to all appearances capable of granting various degrees of insight. By its means the Aśvins, 'flying like winged birds' (*patatho vir na parṇaiḥ*) seek 'the abode of the holy' (*sukṛto duroṇam* I.183.1). The point at issue, 'swifter than mind', clearly expressed in this verse denotes that this chariot is more than thought. From the later literature we know that what 'is swifter than mind' is the *ātman*: 'Unmovable, one, yet swifter than mind', says the Īśā Upaniṣad, 'the spirit speeds ahead.'[52] It outstrips all the devas, yet stands utterly poised.

The word *ātman* was not in such common use in Ṛgvedic times. We might conclude that this chariot is a vehicle framed by means of thought but reaching out to beyond the mind to a state of consciousness capable of expressing itself in threefold manner, i.e. acting upon three different levels of being at one and the same time; that this moulding of thought aroused a power, all dynamic and all creative, which came to be identified with the act of prayer and finally with its verbal expression and its purely sacerdotal use and possession, the outward framing of which was symbolised in the chariot, the swiftness and effectiveness of which was compared to the horse; the inner arousing of that secret which remained beyond human grasp being in the hands of the gods: although capable of being 'fashioned' or brought to birth (VII.22.9 *brahmāṇi janayanta*)[53] like a car or 'generated' for purposes of specific human activity, the *brahman* is fundamentally a 'god given' (*devattam*) power. To these two basic assumptions can be traced the roots of the traditional teachings on liberation or self-realisation. 'Making' or 'generating' the *brahman*, i.e. preparing the vehicle or framing the 'chariot' or the 'praise'—a covert metaphor for practising meditation and one-pointed absorption (*cf.* III.38.1 & I.88.4) is the human preparation; the end-product is god-granted, in later terminology, it is ultimately the gift of the ātman, the divine grace (*prasāda*).

Although expressed in verbal formula, the *brahman* remains inconceivable (*acittam brahma* I.152.5). Words merely limit or condition its essence. Nevertheless, the *brahman* that can be expressed in words outweighs the silent *brahman*.[54] So worshippers are enjoined to 'sing the god-given orison',[55] to give voice to that *brahman* to which Agni found the path.[56] Alone the godly in man can be touched by the god-granted. The *brahman* is the gods' handiwork and of this particular creation Indra is the king[57] and in this godly activity men may share. So the singer wishes that the mighty divine praise-song should accompany Indra (*śloko mahi daivyaḥ* VII.97.3). Song and praise are closely linked to the *brahman* and form one way of helping in its generation. Many *ṛṣis*, old and new, have themselves 'created orisons'[58] in their quality of exalted seers or singers (*vipraḥ*) which Śrī Aurobindo translates as 'illumined singers'. *Brahman*, the god-bestowed orison, is revealed as also an activity capable of digging deep into consciousness to reach out to the godly realm of *svar* or heavenly light, to supreme enlightenment.

Is there a summary of the Vedic prayer? We may take the following as such:

śrudhi brahma	heed the brahman
vāvṛdhasva uta gīrbhiḥ	be invigorated by the songs
āviḥ sūryaṃ kṛṇuhi	make the sun manifest. (VI.17.3)

The purely internal or psychological process here inferred may be outlined thus: the listening intently with mind and senses poised implied in the words 'heed' *śrudhi* and 'be invigorated' *vāvṛdhasva*; the 'expansion' resulting therefrom involving a deepening awareness and an act of creative apprehension, the fruit of which is the manifestion of the sun, a feat ascribed to Indra but also to the patriarchs and by inference to the sage in general. This is the Vedic *brahman*, prayer or magic: to evoke, from deep within, the solar splendour, the flame divine, to radiate it, to be it; *tat tvam asi*, 'that art thou' as was later summed up.

So 'the wise bards, keeping watch in their hearts, take the unaging one to his abode. Longingly they gaze out towards the ocean. By these was the sun made manifest for men' (I.146.4).[59] The implied meaning is thus the realisation of the hidden glory which the Upaniṣads were in due time to express as 'the face of truth veiled by the effulgent chalice' (Īśā Up.15), and as 'he who is in the fire and he who is here in the heart and he who is yonder in the sun, he is one' (Maitrī. Up. 6.17) and the Yajurveda as 'the mighty *puruṣa* refulgent as the sun beyond darkness' (31.18).[60] The core of Vedic prayer is expressed in the Atharvaveda: 'Those who know the most exalted brahman thereafter fully know the axis mundi'.[61]

NOTES

1. *op. cit.* (The Hague, 1963).
2. Written with the collaboration of L. Silburn. *Journal Asiatique* (Paris, 1949), tome 237, pp. 7–46.
3. *matis, manman, manas, manīṣā, mantra.*
4. *The Philosophy of the Upanishads*, p. 4 (London, 1882). The words *samādhi, ātman* and *buddhi* are other cases in point. They have no real equivalents in most European languages and in European concept. Only recently was the word *enstasis* coined to translate *samādhi* a state of being unknown to the West. Intuition is a very poor translation of *buddhi* which is also rendered by reason, understanding, spiritual perception for want of a suitable word.
5. *The Six Systems of Indian Philosophy*, p. 71 (London, 1899).
6. J. Hastings, *Encyclopaedia of Religion and Ethics.* Article on Brahman, p. 796–7 (Edinburgh, 1909).
7. Hillebrandt explains the word philologically thus: 'Accented on the first syllable (*bráhman*), it is neuter; oxytone, i.e. with an accented ultima (*brahmán*), it is masculine. The neuter denotes the object or the thing; the masculine the person who is endowed with or possesses the *bráhman*.' *op. cit.* p. 797. We are concerned with the neuter noun, the power possessed by the priest. Furthermore, Hillebrandt points out how the etymology of *brahman* is obscure. Besides the uncertain possibility of a derivation from the rare root *bṛh*, 'to speak', earlier writers referred to the root bṛh, 'to grow'. *op. cit.* p. 797.
8. *op. cit.* p. 9. As the article is in French all quotations are translated by J. M.
9. *Religions of Ancient India* (London, 1953), p. 10 (Jordan Lectures, 1951).
10. *Ṣrī Aurobindo's Vedic Glossary.* Compiled by A. B. Purani, p. 67 (Pondicherry, 1962).
11. *op. cit.* p. 331 (Pondicherry, 1964).
12. For a comprehensive survey of the etymology and meanings of the word throughout its development see J. Gonda. *Notes on brahman* (Utrecht, 1950) and also his 'Some notes on the study of ancient-Indian religious terminology' in *History of religions* **1,** 2, pp. 267–73 (1962). 'There can be no doubt whatever that for the Indians *brahman,* which already in the Ṛgveda repeatedly appears as a *vardhanam,* that is 'something that causes to increase, strengthens, animates and grants prosperity' was to be connected with *bṛh,* notwithstanding the possibility that this association was an 'a posteriori etymology' and that this 'popular etymology' may have contributed to a change in the meaning of the word.' (p. 269).
13. *cf.* E. W. Hopkins, *The Religions of India* (Boston, Mass. 1895), '*brahma,* power, prayer', p. 136 and J. Gonda, 'Some notes on the study of ancient-Indian religious terminology in *History of religions,* **1,** 2, pp. 270–1 (1962). 'The most ancient 'sense' . . . of *brahman* is, as far as we are able to know, the power immanent in the words, verses, and formulas of the Veda.' (p. 270).
14. *The Vision of the Vedic Poets* (The Hague, 1963).
15. H. D. Velankar, *Yoga in the Vedas*, in *Yoga in Modern Life*, ed. by Śrī Yogendra, pp. 23, 24–5 (Santa Cruz, Yoga Institute, 1966).
16. For a comprehensive study of *dhī* see J. Gonda's *Vision of the Vedic Poets* (The Hague, 1963).
17. Patañjali's definition, *Yoga-Sūtra*, 1.2.
18. *op. cit.*
19. *imāṃ dhiyaṃ saptasirṣṇīṃ pitā na ṛta prajātāṃ bṛhatīm avindat.*
20. *ṛtaṃ śaṃsanta ṛju dīdhyānā.*
21. *Sat* means what exists, *being*, and *satya* what is in accordance with *sat* hence truth. But the action which takes place in accordance with truth and is

thus also truth itself is *ṛta*. *Satya* is knowledge of truth, *ṛta* action according to such knowledge.

22. In his article on the brahman (*op. cit*) L. Renou argues that 'one might have in the brahman a power which could be the "realisation" or the "revelation" of ṛta, i.e. of the cosmico-ritual disposition' (*agencement*) (p. 10) or fitting together, what we would express as cosmic interlinkedness.

23. *pra brahma etu sadanād ṛtasya. cf.* also *ṛtasya hi sadaso dhītir adyaut* X.111.2.

24. When it appears to be a war chariot it may also symbolise the battle between good and evil in man as in nature.

25. *The Ṛgveda as Land-Nama-Bók* p. 4 (London, 1935).

26. *cf.* also VII.64.4.

27. I.46.7: *ā no nāvā matīnāṃ yātaṃ pārāya gantave*.

28. In X.135 which will be discussed in the section on Vedic eschatology, the child unconsciously mounts his chariot after death, a chariot he 'made in the mind' (*manasā akṛṇoḥ*) during life.

29. *cf.* VII.64.6 where the word used is *garta* given as throne, seat of a war-chariot or chariot. We have in this verse an invocation to Mitra-Varuṇa that they might anoint the bard who has fashioned by means of his mind a chariot for them (*gartaṃ manasā takṣat*) and who makes the thought-vision rise upwards (*ūrdhvāṃ dhītiṃ kṛṇavad*). That vehicle is no war-chariot but prayer as a vehicle through which the gods' blessing may be poured.

30. *cf.* I.130.6.

31. *aritraṃ vāṃ divas pṛthu tīrthe sindhūnāṃ rathaḥ*.

32. *rathīr ṛtasya bṛhato vicarṣaṇir agniḥ*.

33. *jyotiṣmantaṃ ratham ṛtasya*.

34. the image of boat or chariot is interchangeable. *cf.* the Aśvins' ship of thought *nāvā matīnām*, I.46.7.

35. *mandrā kṛṇudhvaṃ dhiya ā tanudhvaṃ nāvam aritraparaṇīṃ kṛṇudhvaṃ iṣkṛṇudhvam āyudhāraṃ kṛṇudhvaṃ prāñcaṃ yajñaṃ pra ṇayatā sakhāyaḥ. cf.* also X.110.2.

36. *cf.* II.18.1; VII.71.2; VI.35.1; I.30.16.

37. A. Bergaigne observed that 'the assimilation of prayers to harnessing [attelages] is one of the most familiar ideas of Vedic poets'. See *La Religion Védique* tome I p. vii (Paris, 1878). fn. 3. Bibliothèque de l'École des Hautes Études. fasc. 36.

38. *cf.* I.46.7: *nāvā matīnām. cf.* also VII.64.4.

39. *cf.* VII.91.1; II.20.5.

40. *karhi . . . yaj jaritre viśvapsu brahma kṛṇavaḥ śaviṣṭha. cf.* also VI.35.1.

41. *kadā bhuvan rathakṣayāṇi brahma*.

42. *brahmā na indra upa yāhi*.

43. VII.28.1 & 2. 1. *viśve ciddhi tvā vihavanta marta*. 2. *havaṃ ta indra mahimā vi ānat*.

44. *cf.* VI.35.3.

45. *cf.* also I.30.16.

46. *ya indrāya vaco yujā tatakṣur manasā harī śamībhir yajñam āśata*.

47. It may be remarked that to achieve one-pointed concentration both the breath (or Vāyu master of the life-breath) and the thought (Indra master of the mind) must be brought under control, or suitably harnessed by the will of the practitioner.

48. *anaśvo jāto . . . arvā*.

49. *cf.* also VI.45.12. *dhībhir arvadbhir arvato vājān indra śravāyyān tvayā jeṣma hitaṃ dhanam*.

50. *sa id ṛbhavo yam avatha yūyam indraś ca martyaṃ sa dhībhir astu sanitā medhasātā so arvatā.*

51. As the cow is used as the symbol of light, so according to Śrī Aurobindo, the horse symbolises vital force. *On the Veda* p. 99 (Pondicherry 1964). That force carries the seeker through to the other shore beyond the darkness (*tamas tiraḥ* I.46.6).

52. Trans. J. M. Stanza 4.

53. *cf.* I.62.13 *navyam atakṣad brahma.* Nodhas (the son of the *ṛṣi* Gotama) has fasioned the new *brahma* as a result of which he hopes that Indra, now abounding in thought-vision (*dhiyāvasuḥ*) will favour him with his company.

54. *vadan brahmā avadato vanīyān*, X.117.7. The whole stanza is a fine specimen of Vedic imagery:

kṛṣann it phāla āśitaṃ kṛṇoti yann adhvānam apa vṛṇkteṃ caritraiḥ vadan brahmā avadato vanīyān pṛṇan āpir apṛṇantam abhi ṣyāt. 'The ploughing plough which completes its orbit with its legs produces food. More auspicious is the speaking brahman than the speechless. The generous friend stands above the ungenerous.'

55. *devattaṃ brahma gāyata*, I.37.4 and VIII.32.27.

56. *brahmaṇe vinda gātum*, VII.13.3.

57. *brahmaṇo devakṛtasya rājā*, VII.97.3.

58. *brahmāṇi janayanta viprāḥ*, VII.22.9. *cf.* VII.31.11: *suvṛktim indrāya brahma janayanta viprāḥ.*

59. *dhīrāsaḥ padaṃ kavayo nayanti nānā hṛdā rakṣamāṇā ajuryaṃ śiṣāsantaḥ pari apaśyanta sindhum āvir ebhyo abhavat sūryo nṛn.*

60. This interpretation runs counter to Bergaigne's own interpretation which sees in the longing for solar conquest mainly longing for long life and the glory contemplated that of war victory. *op. cit.* tome II pp. 187 ff. But *svar* is the light of heaven and the conflict is *life* and the conquest celestial realms.

61. Ath.v. X.7.17: *jyeṣṭhaṃ ye brāhmaṇaṃ vidus te skambham anu saṃviduḥ.* Trans. J. M.

PART II

To narrow down our study we could divide our approach to Vedic meditation under three points of focus which may serve as landmarks in our investigation remembering that there is really no clear cut separation but that all aspects overlap and even blend·

I. *Mantric Meditation*: absorption in sound and its effects on the psyche. Through the special combination of sound properties that in specific ways act on the human organism a science of sound was developed, the keyword being *mantra*.

II. *Visual Meditation*: the deliberate forging of thought into visionary insight yielding spiritual perception; the keyword being *dhī* which later on gave *dhyāna* used in Hindu philosophy. Here the bard chooses a particular god as the object of his meditation.

III. *Absorption in Mind and Heart*: the deepening of the power of vision i.e. the use of a seed-thought conceived during the contemplation of the god leading to explorations into the mysteries of the world process or the withdrawal and absorption into the heart, with the consequent clarifying and purifying of the vision and the apprehension of great truths. The speculative hymns were thus composed. This led to the deepest insights possible for man.

Each of these three aspects constitutes a complete study in itself. Only when they are blended and fully understood can they yield the essence of the Vedic prayer which is the ancient meaning of *brahman*, the Vedic magic. Vision and speech are the end products of the *brahman*.

I. MANTRIC MEDITATION

For the *ṛṣis* the power of the word, the *logos*, was equal to the power of visionary insight, both stemming from the same source, the heart of man and the universal heart. Like the 'wise gods', those fosterers of truth, to whom they owed their inspiration, whom they described as 'sun-eyed' and 'flame-tongued', (VII.66.10) they too could touch the sunny heights of dazzling vision and with their tongue aflame could sing forth the glory they beheld.

Songs and homage are facets of prayer. They help to lift up the mind[1] open up the insight. They enhance the power of the word for the rhythm of the prayer-song and the repetition of praise affect the *citta* or mental activity and bring about a harmonisation of the whole person. The sages yoke with homage the ancient *brahman* of the sons of immortality (X.13.1)[2] and by means of song send to his own home of truth Agni, sovereign lord of riches (I.143.4), Agni, inspirer of *brahman* (*brahmaṇas kaviḥ*).

In attempting to understand Vedic recitation and orison we should consider three peculiarly Vedic ideas:

(1) The sounding of certain words of power capable of affecting the human constitution in certain ways.

(2) Their originating as a flash of light in the innermost centre, whether that be the heart of the human being, the organ of spiritual insight (*buddhi* of later thought) or the 'seat of truth' *ṛtasya sadas*—hence their quality of truth and their dynamism, their capacity to *affect*.

(3) Resulting from the above two points, the shining quality of the sound, its visibility: to sound is to

> shine, to sing; to praise is to illumine. Hence the Vedic song is an illumination and that is Vedic worship.

The whole problem converges upon the fundamental significance of, and the philosophical doctrines summed up in, five major words:[3]

vāc; *akṣara*; *ṛc*, *arka* and *mantra* ($\sqrt{\textit{man}}$ yielding *matis*, *manma*, *manīṣā*).[4]

Typical of the Vedic ritual is the sounding of certain words and phrases credited with specific evocative power. We should recall in this connection the different psycho-mental constitution of ancient man which allowed him to respond to a far greater degree than modern man to the finer shades of tones.[5] The *ṛṣis* developed a subtle science of sound, but not merely sound by itself but sound and light and their fusion in the orison.

We may gather from the scattered references that the very sound of words inspired from deep within the heart in moments of worship quickened both in men and in the celestial entities being invoked a response to loftier thought and influences which in turn brought the worshipper in harmony with the Cosmic Order, the fountain-spring of truth (*ṛta*). The whole aim of prayer, and this kind of recitation which could be considered as an introduction to it, is to create those harmonious conditions wherein the worshipper may contact the highest within himself, and through that highest that which corresponds to it in the Cosmic Order. Hence every sound-vision of which man is capable, every word made visible is man's expression of the divine harmony of which he is an inherent part. Sound and visionary insight are, in the Vedas, closely interlinked. The *ṛṣis* considered the power of the *word*[6] as equal to their power of visionary insight, both sound and light proceeding almost simultaneously in the act of worship. This doctrine, as revealed in the various hints, is their peculiar contribution to one aspect of prayer.

The idea of creative sound, hence of creative song in prayer, which runs through the Ṛgveda, recalls the New

Testaments famous statement: 'In the beginning was th Word, and the Word was with God, and the Word wa God'.[7] The *verbum* is expressed in the Ṛgveda by the wor *vāc*. This is the creative power[8] which dwells in the 'highe heaven' (I.164.34 *paramaṃ vyoma*) moulded with 'wis insight' (X.71.2: *dhīra manasā vācam akrata*). It is a for mative, feminine force or energy, called the queen (*rāṣṭrī* the collector of blessings, the experienced one (*cikituṣī* the first born of the holy ones (X.125.3), holding all world together (X.125.8 *ā rabhamānā bhuvanāni viśvā*). *Vā* generates the Father, we are told in X.125.7 (*ahaṃ suv pitaram*)—in other words, through the power of the word the creative agent, the Father, is brought into manifesta tion. We shall see that the same idea is expressed with th word *akṣara*. The flying bird (*pataṅga*) or divine spiri holds this *Vāc* in mind (*manasā*) before the celestial ministe or *gandharva* pronounces it in the womb (X.177.2). W have here the formative potency of the word held in abey ance in the divine mind and pronounced or emitted whe conception is to take place.

It would seem that *Vāc*, the verbum, and *Agni*, th flame, are two sides of the one power, perhaps the masculin and the feminine, the positive and the negative sides o that impersonal One in whom *flame-power* originall emerged whence all was kindled to manifestation (X.129.3) Agni pervades all the worlds and he is born in the waters (*cf.* II.1, III.26.7, I.72.7, etc.). *Vāc* extends over all and he home is in the waters (X.125.7 & 8). *Vāc* is the formativ sound hidden behind or within all manifested lives, Agn the propelling flame at work in all things.

Vāc, says the *ṛṣi* Dirghātamas, has been meted out in four *pada* (I.164.45).[9] It is interesting to note that the wor *pada* besides meaning step, foot, section, portion, station division, also denotes a ray of light. Are the four section of *Vāc* four different rays of light? We ask this question because as we shall soon see, to the *ṛṣi* the sound emitted by man shines forth. These four measures of *Vāc*, the wis Brāhmaṇas know. Three of them are hidden away beyon human ken, the fourth only belongs to man's speech (man speaks the fourth division of Vāc I.164.45), this being the utermost or manifest aspect of *Vāc* in which is hidden all he others. We learn from X.71.3 that the *ṛṣis* through heir act of worship understood the mystery of *Vāc*—they tracked down the path of *Vāc* by means of sacrificial ite'. The sinner cannot really master it though he appears o know something of it, yet he 'spins out his web inexpertly' X.71.9) for those who truly know *Vāc* and gather together or common prayer voiced from the heart stand far ahead f others who merely claim to be Brāhmaṇas but speak vithout knowledge (X.71.8). Knowledge is the essential ower, an intuitive knowledge without which *Vāc* is neaningless: 'He who has never seen *Vāc* yet has seen; ne who has hearing yet has never heard her' (X.71.4). The mere repetition of words, without understanding, without that knowledge of hidden truths of which the rāhmaṇas are the custodians, will yield no results. He who has not heard *Vāc* listens with his ears but is incapable of hearing the voice of the silence, that voice which harbours within the *ṛṣi* (X.71.3) whose utterances are inspired because they stem from absorption into divinity.

The *ṛṣi* Dirghātamas yet again makes a strange remark which calls to mind the Greek idea of *theophanos*. Only when visited by the 'first-born of truth' (*prathamajā ṛtasya*) or divine inspiration, does man gain insight into *Vāc*, does he obtain a share of it (I.164.37 *aśnuve bhāgam asyāḥ*); that is to say, only in ecstasy does man become aware of certain potencies of the creative word and how to use them and does he become the bearer of divine eloquence. These powers are referred to in the injunction of VII.101.1: 'Proclaim three words (*tisro vācaḥ*) that are pre-eminent in light' or 'light projecting' (*jyotir agrāḥ*) which 'milk that honey yielding udder' (*duḥre madhu dagham ūdhaḥ*). Here we find the 'word' as emitting 'light' or the word as light. This illuminating power draws down or milks the nectar of heaven. In X.101.9 the divine vision of the gods (*dhiyam . . . devīṃ yajatām*) which the bard wields is compared to a mighty cow pouring out milk in a thousand streams (*sahasra dhārā*). The gods, says VIII.100.11, generated the cow as the divine speech (*devīṃ vācam ajanayanta*). This cow's speech is pleasant, its gift is strengthening food and drink. The hymn addressed t the cows plainly refers to them as auspiciously-voice (*bhadra vacaḥ*) VI.28.6.

The *cow* as *Vāc* the creative *verbum* leads us to anothe word used with similar intent and denoting syllable o letter, but also imperishable: *akṣara*.[10] It does not seen to be used as a synonym of *Vāc* but it certainly bears th same connotation and may have been in vogue at an earlie period of the composition of the hymns.

'In the beginning, when the first of dawns shone forth'– of those countless dawns that recur in their serried orde (*cf*. I.113.15)—'manifested the mighty word' (*mahad v jagñe akṣaram*) in the 'station' or 'seat' of the cow (*pad goh* III.55.1). The latter is none other than the celestial boundless light Aditi. Aditi, the nurturing cow, is furthe described as the thousand-syllabled (*sahasrākṣarā*) 'in th highest heaven' (*parame vyoman* I.164.41). Boundles (*a* + *diti* = unbound) light and all powerful sound are th attributes of Aditi whom men compare to a prolific cow for both are creative. She thus contains in herself al formative powers, hence she is the thousand-syllabled.[1] In the 'everlasting matrix of the mother' (*garbhe mātuḥ* . . . *akṣare*) or in the 'word' dwelling in the light, 'shines' th father's father (*pituṣpitā vididyutānaḥ*) says VI.16.35. I seems clear that the father's father is the ultimately origina creative agent which was propelled into activity—into th shining forth of life—within the matrix of the verbum whe that verbum sounded forth. Through the emitting of th word the father or creator shines. This is the cosmic side o *akṣara* reminiscent of *Vāc* (*cf*. X.125.7 & 8). By means o this syllable the poet measures out his invocation which he purifies in the hub of truth (X.13.3).[12]

Ṛc as the sacred verse recited by the priest has a mor specific reference to the human ritualistic aspect of th verbum. It includes not merely the connotation of chant but also of lustre and thus of light. The root √*ṛc*[13] means both to shine and to sing praise which is a way of paying homage or worshipping. A revealing verse asks the question:

ṛco akṣare parame vyoman yasmin devā adhi viśve niṣeduḥ yas tan na veda kim ṛcā kariṣyati (I.164.39).	Who knows not this in which syllable of the sacred-verse wherein all the gods abide in highest heaven what will he do with the word?

Here is an admission that there is more to the word and verse than what appears superficially. The everlasting power of the *akṣara* is in the *ṛc*. In the syllable of the *ṛc*, we are told, is the highest heaven where abide the gods. The verses are not just a mere repetition of ritualistic formulas but hold a divine potency not easily detectable which, if ignored by the singer, remains latent and without effect, but which, when known and rightly used, charges the word with propelling or creative power. This knowledge which the *ṛṣis* have kept securely hidden may concern the blend of the *svāra* (also *svara* and *svarita*[14]) or right intonation in enunciating the words, and the colour or lustre thereby emitted and seen, the result affecting both the practitioner and the object of his invocation. Here again we have the reminder that mere repetition will avail nothing without knowledge: 'who knows not this (the secret of the syllable in the *ṛc*) what will he do with the word?'

The close connection between the idea of shining and singing, between light and sound, so typical of Vedic doctrine, is well brought out in the Sanskrit word for 'shine forth' and 'sing forth' which is one and the same: $\sqrt{}$*arc*[15]. This verbal root yields many substantives, among which *arcana* celebrating with praise, *arcis* ray of light, flame, *arka* ray, flash of lightning as well as hymn, praise. Its connection with *ṛc* is obvious. 'Who will now attempt to distinguish', writes A. Bergaigne 'those passages where the meaning of 'hymn' should be replaced by that of 'lightning' or 'ray'.[16] 'Sing forth' or 'shine forth' a prayer (*arca . . . brahma* V.85.1) urges the poet 'vast, abysmal' (*bṛhad . . . gabhīram*) 'for supreme Varuna'.

The power of sound and light as an effective instrument, whether for moulding or destructive purposes, is well exemplified in the word *arka*. Brahmaṇaspati 'the Father of prayer' (II.23.2) is said to have rent the cowpen and found the light (II.23.3). In II.24.3 he broke through the cave of the mythical Vala by means of prayer (*abhinad brahmaṇā valam*), after which he dispelled the darkness and revealed the solar splendour (*agūhat tamo vi acakṣayat svaḥ*). The same deed is related to have been performed (X.68.6) by means of *agnitapobhir arkaiḥ*, that is, fire-hot songs! It would be doing injustice to the whole tenor of Vedic prayer to translate these words by 'fiery lightnings' (as done by Griffith), when the lord of prayer himself is the doer. Yet the word *arka* does mean both flashing song and lightning. This typical Vedic image implies that the hymns or songs glow with the force of fire; they are indeed like lightning flashes, hence the dual meaning of song, hymn and ray of light or lightning flash (*arka*). We see here not the confusion but a deliberate merging of two senses; the lightning flash of illumination which dispels the mental darkness and results from the successful chanting, and the meteorological phenomenon of the lightning which rends the darkness or rock as the case may be. The blending of a psychological and a physical aspect is characteristic of the Vedic image. Furthermore, the hymns are red hot and therefore destroy the fortress of the confiner—Vala;[17] they are so strong because the Lord of prayer himself fashioned them. The word *tapas* emphasises the spiritual side of the song which glows through the force of the concentration. *Tapas* is physiological heat provoked through spiritual energy, the latter being the moving and all powerful cause, the former, *tapas*, in the physical sense, resulting from the concentration.

To understand the idea of the flashing song being a ray of light we should go a little deeper into the arcana of Vedic thought. We are told that the ancient patriarchal insight or vision[18] (*sanajā pitryā dhīḥ*) had its origin in heaven and was kept alive ever since, being sung in sacred gatherings (*vidathe śasyamānā*) clothed in bright or radiant vesture (*vastrāṇy arjunā vasānā*, III.39.2). The word *arjuna*, white or clear, is also used as an epithet to describe the dawns (*cf.* I.49.3 and III.34.5). One aspect of this original *dhī* or visionary insight brought over from heaven by the patriarchs (elsewhere described as seven-headed and born of truth X.67.1: *imāṃ dhiyaṃ saptaśīrṣṇīm . . . ṛtaprajātām*) is *matis*[19] thought, that which flowers into *dhī*. *Matis* is offered to Varuṇa as the bright precious possession of the repentant worshipper (VII.88.1). It takes its birth within the heart as light (*hṛdā matiṃ jvotir anu prajānan*, III.26.8) which the bard then clarifies into a flashing song (*arka*) by means of three filters (*tribhiḥ pavitraiḥ*). It is fashioned into a praise within the heart (*stomataṣṭa matir hṛdā*, III.39.1). Its projector in III.26.8 is Agni, but not necessarily always Agni. Together with Soma,[20] the fire personifies the great inspirer, he who awakens the poet to his gift of eloquence (IV.11.3: *tvad . . . kāvyā . . . manīṣāḥ*). His is that power safely hidden away (*guhā niṣīdan* I.67.2) whence all other powers derive (*haste dadhāno nṛmnā viśvāni*) and which meditating men discover (*naro dhiyamdhāḥ*) when they chant mantras shaped in their heart (*hṛdā yat taṣṭān mantrān aśamsan*, I.67.2). His is the flame centred in the human being, flashing out the song, rousing man's insight (X.45.5: *manīṣāṇāṃ prārpanaḥ*), arousing the sun (VII.9.2), bringing it to birth. He proclaims as intuitive perception (*pra id u vocat manīsām*) that which lies concealed—in mythological language—in the station of the cow (IV.5.3), the hidden, closed up cave whence light issues forth.

Matis has now become *manīṣā*, that intuition cherished by the sages which as perception longing to be made manifest is aroused by Soma (VI.47.3 *manīṣām uśatīm ajīgaḥ*), whose matrix is truth (*ṛtasya pade*); whose appearance is refulgent and luminous (X.177.2: *dyotamānāṃ svaryam*); whose concrete effect is speech, the creative *logos*, which the *gandharva* pronounces in the womb as the *Vāc* (X.177.2[21]) for formative purposes. But it has to be brought into the focus of the brain's clear yet limited consciousness. Agni is asked to release it as from a cave (IV.11.2): *vi ṣāhy agne gṛṇate manīṣāṃ khaṃ vepasā tuvijāta stavānaḥ*.

During the action of praising (*stavānaḥ*) the inner flame Agni sparks off the inspiration. The word *kha* is juxtaposed with *manīṣā*, both being in the accusative case and thus equated. What is the meaning of *kha* and why its juxtaposition with *manīṣā*? 'Kha denotes in the Ṛgveda and later the hole in the nave of the wheel in which the axle is inserted.'[22] Upon the hole at the centre depends the good working of the wheel. Both hole and wheel[23] are typical Vedic imagery but the great inner significance of the hole is perhaps better brought out in this verse of the Tao Teh King: 'You fashion clay to make a bowl, the usefulness of the bowl is always in the empty innermost'.

The empty innermost in the human being constitutes a fulcrum of dynamic action. It is the hole in the nave. Ṛgv. IV.11.2 surely implies a deep knowledge of the process of meditation for it is during those moments of perfect emptiness but nonetheless poised awareness that inspirations spring from the depths of the so-called sub-conscious unto the surface of the conscious. Hence the verse's identification of the cave or space or void with the inspiration which in reality emerges out of it from some unknown and invisible source.[24]

It is then stated that the *arka* or flashed out song issuing from the depth of the heart when thought is born as light (III.26.8) is clarified by three filters (*tribhiḥ pavitraiḥ*). What are these? Apart from any ritualistic connotation they may refer to three aspects of consciousness through which the *matis-arka* has to pass to become understandable, hence be cleansed, purified or clarified: the spiritual wherein the essence is apprehended and thus the inspiration born; the mental where it takes shape as a thought and the brain where it is expressed as words.[25] It is interesting to note that the *arka* like the *dhī* (X.67.1) is seven-headed (*arkaṃ sapta-śīrṣāṇām*) and threefold (*tridhātum*) and is sung in the highest station (*uttame pade* VIII.51.4). The poet in VII.85.1 proceeds by cleansing or clarifying or making bright (*punīṣe*) the intuitive insight *manīṣā*, in other words, by illumining his understanding through meditation he is able to offer its product, the bright *manīṣā* which he compares to the divine dawns, to the gods.

As inspired vision *manīṣā* is *dhīti*, again shining from the seat of truth (X.111.2: *ṛtasya hi sadaso dhītir adyaut*).

Truth, we may conclude, is centred in the human heart or innermost point of the human constitution which forms the link between heaven and earth or man.

There is no doubt that for the *ṛṣis* thought shines and is made perceptible through its lustre and audible as it is voiced, it is colourful[26] and vibrates as sound. The *ṛṣis* *heard* as they *saw* the *Veda*.

To the Vedic mind to praise is to sound the right word as well as to illuminate. The whole process of worshipping or praising meant to set up an inner light, hence to illumine. The *ṛṣis'* ancestors by their praises were aiming at resplendent inspirations (IV.2.16 *śuci id ayan dīdhitim*[27] *uktha-śāsaḥ*). The epithets *citra* brilliant, *śundhyu* or *śukra*[28] bright, resplendent, are repeatedly used to qualify the *arka* (hymn or flashing song) or the *dhī* (visionary thought), or the *manīṣā* (intuitive perception). Sing forth a bright hymn is a common injunction (*citram arkam*) (*cf.* VI.66.9 & X.112.9).[29] The priest (*hotā*) by his power (*māyayā*) establishes the resplendent vision (*śucipeśasaṃ dhiyam*, I.144.1). This is part of his *vrata* or function as priest. 'May our refulgent, celestial insight' (*śukrā* ... *devī manīṣā*: VII.34.1), wishes another bard, travel forth like a well-fashioned speedy chariot. The praise (*stoma*) travels on the sun's refulgent path (*dyutadyāmānam* X.93.12). The intuition (*manīṣā*) as earlier quoted is made bright by the poet as though oiled with ghee (*ghṛta pratīka*) like celestial dawn (*uṣasaṃ na devīm*—I cleanse or clarify *puniṣe* VII. 85.1). There is here an undertone of enlightenment. Because prayers shine like the dawns so the dawns in their turn are honey-tongued like prayers (*suvācaḥ* III.7.10. *cf.* III.34.5). From VIII.6.8 we gather that by the current of truth (*ṛtasya dhārayā*) the bards and their thoughts (*dhītayaḥ*) which are concealed (*guhā*) glow (*śocanta*). Light-winning or heaven-possessing (*svarṣa*) is a characteristic of the thought or song or eulogy (*stoma*). Prayer as *brahma* of yore (*prajāva*) has shone in heaven (*dīdayad divi*, VI.16.36). As seen in X.93.12 the praise finds heaven following the path of the sun or light, the aim of all prayers being the sun of truth (*satyaṃ sūryam*), i.e. illumination, understanding, insight. Upon the waters of space the *ṛṣis* place their light-bestowing visions that these might act as signs to the divine entities to beseech their protection.[30]

The resultant hymn or flashing ray of eloquence (*arka*) is a gift of the gods (VII.97.5), the gods themselves in striving for the milk of heaven found the *arka* and the *sāman*.[31]

The gods, we are told, are anointed by those praises and thrive on those illuminations. They become manifest through the power of the word or vision.[32] Thus, when enriched with the bards' devoted vision, Indra is thought to make himself visible or to come to the sacrificial rite.[33] As already quoted the understanding ones (*manīṣiṇas*), the *brāhmaṇa*, impel Agni with thoughts (*cittibhiḥ*) and exalt him with their songs.[34] By means of rays of inspired thought and hymns (*aktubhir matīnām ... ukthaiḥ*) eulogies are uttered to anoint the gods.[35] Shining and singing (*arcantaḥ*) the bards invoke Agni for help[36] and kindle him as though with food which is man's thought sent to the god (III.27.11). What word (*gīḥ*) divinely acceptable (*devajuṣṭā*), asks the bard, should he utter for the refulgent Agni (I.77.1)? It must be a lofty, heart-born praise[37] in order to please the god. Agni is begged to bring to men the prayer (*brahma*) which has 'shone' in heaven (*yad dīdayad divi*, VI.16.36). As the poet sings his praises he brings the light out both from within himself and from the deity; through that manifested light he enters into communion with the latter and is aware of the effectiveness of his prayer by the quality of its resulting colour and sound.

Thus poets offer up their hymns (*suvṛktiḥ*) as refreshment (*iṣaṃ na*) for the gods (VII.36.2). Prayers magnify the Aśvins (V.73.10. *cf.* VIII.44.2 & 19 with reference to Agni). They increase Indra's might (VIII.87.8 *vardhanti śūra brahmāṇi cf.* VIII.6.1). Impelled by prayer Indra grows in stature (III.34.1 and X.50.4).[38] Indeed he finds in prayer his exaltation (I.52.7 *brahmāṇi indra tava yāni vardhanā*).[39] So the worshippers stir him with their thoughts as they do Agni (*te indra matibhir viviṣmaḥ* VI.23.6) and consider him the best *mantra* (*jyeṣṭhaś ca mantraḥ* X.50.4).

There is of course another side to this offer of song to exalt the gods and enhance their well being. Song yokes the god being worshipped (V.17.3: *asya vai asau u arciṣā ya ayukta tujā girā*), or binds to the chariot the two steeds of Indra yoked by the word (*vacoyujā* VIII.98.9). Worshipping mortals seek to win over by their visionary thoughts (IV.11.5 *vivāsanti dhībhiḥ*) the sweet-tongued Agni (*mandrajihvam*). They, in like manner, found a way of access to Indra, sending their visions (*dhiyaḥ*) seeking help (*avasyavaḥ*), winning all manner of wealth (II.21.5).[40] As this is a typically human characteristic and throws no further light on Vedic invocation we shall leave it to the early scholars' exegesis and to the missionaries who pounced upon it and emphasised the spirit of asking for gain, which is not purely Vedic, but universal to the exclusion of every other aspect of Vedic prayer.[41]

The *mantra*[42] is thus that which wells up from the heart as inspiration taking form through sound and lustre and becoming objective as the word or combination of words—the word made concrete and effective.[43] From the heart where it is well fashioned (*hṛda ā sutaṣṭam*) the incomparable *mantra* (*mantram anehasam*) which the bards sing together in their gatherings (I.40.6) is addressed to the god (II.35.2). In that eulogic recitation uttered by the Lord of prayer himself the gods have made their abodes (I.40.5).[44] This reminds us of I.164.9 earlier quoted where heaven and the sacred word are practically identical.[45] A meeting point between gods and men is found through the *mantra* or *verbum*, and the communion and exaltation resulting are expressions of that heaven which to the gods are a permanent state of being.

We are told that those humans who have carefully fashioned their *mantra* surpass all others in their glorious achievements.[46] Through their listening and setting their mind upon the divine law they elevate the people. It is interesting to observe the word *ṛta* always coming up in connection with the *mantra*. Concentration is on the truth (*asya dīdhayan ṛtasya*) or reality of which the ritual sacrifice is a reflection. The result is then assured. The right words will be found, the people's good will be furthered, and the seers themselves will be without peers.

Through the song sprung of truth the sun shines forth

(*śuśoca sūrya ṛtajātayā girā* X.138.2). The 'gleaming' (*śucamānaḥ*) chant of truth (*ṛtasya śloka*) opens the ears even of the deaf (IV.23.8).

Of this bright word (*śukrasya vacasaḥ* II.9.4) evoked from the heart Agni is called the inventor (*manotā* II.9.4), hence his quality of inspirer of poets (IV.11.3). He is the eye that stirs the thought (V.8.6: *cakṣur dadhire codayanmati*).

So we meet with those mythological references which appeared so strange and meaningless to the early Western scholars that they dismissed them as pertaining to the miraculous, incredible and nonsensical. In the light of such a background as has been outlined they lose their apparent nonsense. They become part of a mythological lore with an underlying wealth of meaning. The main theme emerges as the power of vision enhanced through the hymn or song and capable of acting in specific ways. Thus by means of the *arka*, the flashing song—which Śrī Aurobindo translates as 'hymn of illumination' thereby combining the two senses of song and light contained in the word—heaven's splendour (*svar*) was revealed in all its beauty (*sudṛṣīkam* IV.16.4). By their praises (*ukthaiḥ*) the patriarchs performed certain deeds similar to those of Indra, breaking through firm strongholds (*vīḷu cid dṛḷhā*) cleaving the rock (*adrim*) with their clamour (I.71.2) rending the 'treasure-holding mountain' (IV.2.15 *adrim . . . dhaninam*).[47] With 'celestial speech' (*vacasā daivyena*) they opened up the solid rock (*adriṃ dṛḷham . . . vivavruḥ* IV.1.15). In like manner, working with the power of illumined thought (*cakṛpanta dībhiḥ*) 'they freed the cattle and found the light' (*vidanta jyotiḥ* IV.1.14). They found the hidden light (*gūḷhaṃ jyotiḥ*) and with the mantra of truth (*satya mantrāḥ*) they brought forth the dawn (VII.76.4), or by the song born of truth they made the sun to shine forth (X.138.2). Thereby they made for us human beings (*asme*) a way to wide heaven (*cakrur divo bṛhato gātum asme*, I.71.2). With minds yearning for light (*gavyatā manasā*—not booty as translated by Griffith) the patriarchs sat making with their songs (*arkaiḥ*) a way to immortality (III.31.9: *kṛṇvānāso amṛtatvāya gātum*). They established truth (*dadhann ṛtam*) as well as its human realisation or vision, i.e. the possibility of apprehending it (*dhanayann asya dhītim*, I.71.3. *cf.* IV.1.14). Such mythological feats are repeatedly extolled. To the Vedic mind the underlying meaning was a revelation of divine illumination and its legacy to them from the patriarchs.

The perfect blend of lofty aspiration and willed assertion with the choice and music power of each word is best exemplified in the famous *gāyatrī* prayer (III.62.10), the supreme Vedic invocation to the spirit of illumination, the solar splendour, which constitutes the essence of the Veda. It reveals a knowledge of the force of invocation, the calling forth to action of the hidden power latent in the human being, and of evocation, the response to, and the result of, that call on the part of the unseen forces, a knowledge which was buried with the *ṛṣis*. It embodies the essence of that longing for illumined exaltation which glows like Agni the flame divine throughout the Vedas. No translation can render its meaning or do it justice:

Let us meditate[48] upon that celestial splendour the Solar Lord; so may he inspire [so may he pierce through] our thoughts that they may become illumined visions of truth.

tat savitur vareṇyaṃ bhargo devasya dhīmahi dhiyo yo naḥ pracodayāt.

This longing for the transcendent also finds its reflection in the invocation to Soma:

O purifier, place me in that deathless, undecaying state wherein the light of heaven is set and everlasting lustre shines. Make me immortal in that realm where dwells the king ... where is the secret shrine of heaven, where joys and felicities combine. (IX.113–7–11. Griffith's translation).

These two prayers sum up the great song of the Veda, the yearning of the human heart for the sun of illumination and the everlasting bliss of immortality.

II. VISUAL MEDITATION

The method of inducing visualisation whereby the vision was objectified into the clear light of the mind, if it was already formulated, is not of course defined in the Ṛgveda. Yet it is possible from the many hints thrown out and the images used to reconstruct it somewhat and to conclude that by the time the *Brāhmaṇas* were compiled it had reached a high degree of excellence. In the course of this investigation we shall bring together whatever evidence may be found in the Ṛgveda as to the use of a technique.

However, certain details which are certainly all too rare, could be mentioned at the outset. We have already observed the striking comparison made between the seer's activity and that of a builder (III.38.1). This absorption in meditation (*abhi dīdhyā manīṣām*) implies stages in concentration demanding a metaphoric building of an instrument, a chariot symbolic of the focussing of consciousness (*cf.* I.130.6 'as a skilful craftsman builds up a car'). The poet then reflects upon the loftiest, most desirable things (*abhi priyāṇi marmṛśat parāṇi*) (III.38.1), longing to be filled with wisdom that he may contact the wise ones for the sake of knowledge (I.164.6).[49]

A different, very graphic image is used in I.88.4, describing the Vedic meditation. There the Gotama *ṛṣis* are compared to 'vultures' or covetous creatures (*gṛdhrāḥ*) that for days circle or wind round their prey; but the latter is no animal but *imaṃ dhiyam*, that vision-inspired-thought which favours the making of the *brahman*. So the Gotamas 'framing their prayer with chants' (*brahma kṛṇvanto . . . arkaiḥ*) 'have pushed open the well' (*utsadhim*) to drink therefrom. The mixture of images is typically Vedic. The vulture, intent upon its prey, serves as a pictograph to paint the intensive action of those concentrating upon a particular thought which they pursue as vultures do their prey; the image then changes to a well or fountain-spring, the boon that awaits the successful brooding. The act of thinking prepares for the *brahman* which is responsible for opening up the 'fountain'. A description of the latter is given in II.24.4. Its top is of stone and only the Lord of prayer, Brahmaṇaspati, can push it open through his might. It is filled to the very brim with honey and is thus readily outpoured; and 'all those who behold the light' (*viśve svardṛśaḥ*) or who are 'sun-eyed' 'have drunk their fill therefrom', for they made the fountain pour out. This is the spring of living waters or spiritual nourishment from which only the enlightened ones can drink for they know the way to it and the means of opening it.

Two important points which might be left unnoticed in I.88.4 and II.24.4 are the factor of time and the reference to the exertion. 'For days' the seeker strains after his vision or goal, and finally has to 'push upright' that which covers the fountain, i.e. use force. The goal is not reached immediately. There are stages and each step seems to have been marked out though very little is given out in the Ṛgveda itself. Yet the hints speak for themselves and are sufficient to show the existence of a secret knowledge, a knowledge in which *sound* and *light* play a most important role.

Light is both the great purifying agent[50] (*cf.* the purifying Agni VI.6.2) and the goal of the search for truth and of the meditative process. As the patriarchs in days of old sought with their chanting the glowing inspiration (*śuci. . . dīdhitim ukthaśāsaḥ*), rending the ground, finding the dawn (IV.2.16), so the *ṛṣis* follow in their footsteps. First the claim is made that the mind, swiftest among flying creatures, (*mano javiṣṭhaṃ patayatsu antaḥ*) is firmly established as light [for us] to see (*dhruvaṃ jyotir nihitaṃ dṛśaye kam* VI.9.5). This is mental insight and it is interesting to note that this light is not subject to eclipses, it is firmly fixed and perceptible to everyone. The mind is the outward turned lens whereby we perceive the world. By means of it what we thus observe becomes intelligible. But it can be turned inwards also. This light is in VI.9.4 identified with Agni as the immortal light among mortals (*idaṃ jyotir amṛtaṃ martyeṣu*), the high-priest Agni, the foremost, the lord of thought (IV.6.1.: *viśvam abhi asi manma pra*) whom all are invited to 'behold' (*paśyata*), which the wise ones (*manīṣiṇaḥ*) kindle by their thought power (*hinvanti cittibhiḥ* VIII.44.19).[51]

Whatever is perceived inwardly by the *psyche* is automatically projected outwardly into the cosmos. Thus sages (*sūrayah*), behold (*paśyanti*) 'the highest step in the seat of Viṣṇu' as an eye fixed in heaven (*divīva cakṣur ātatam*, I.22.20).[52] So again the *ṛṣi* 'sees' (*apaśyam*) the unfaltering herdsman (*gopām apadyamanam*) approaching and withdrawing by the pathways (X.177.3 = I.164.31). In this shepherd or keeper of immortality[53] some (like Griffith) have seen the sun and others may see Agni or the ātman. He is described as ceaselessly revolving (*ā varīvarti* the intensive form of $\sqrt{vṛt}$ being used) within the worlds (*bhuvaneṣu antaḥ*), assuming (*vasāna*) or invested with *sadhrīcīḥ* and *visūsīḥ*—two adjectives here used in the feminine plural qualifying an omitted noun; each means respectively *converging on* or as we might interpret it centripetal, directed to the centre, and *all-pervading*, or perhaps centrifugal. If the word 'forces' be understood as the implied substantive we may have a vision of the *ātman*, the ceaselessly travelling herdsman or flame pervading these forces which diverge away from it and converge back to it.[54] This aspect of Vedic insight gave rise to the assertion made in X.114.5 'the fair winged one, whose being is one, inspired bards, by their incantations, shape in many ways',[55] a perfect description of the human mind's discriminating, categorising, finding differences with and in so doing forgetting the basic unity of all things.

Because the gods further the course of prayer, because they are past masters in the finding of truth,[56] and open the way to the *brahman*,[57] they are the great inspirers and constitute the main objects of meditation. At each rising of the sun the sages offer up their thoughts with praises to the gods.[58] They beg these to restore fresh vigour (*vāja*) to their visions. They may choose the fire of the ritual (I.164.1), Agni, mediator of heaven and earth, head of heaven (*murdha divaḥ*), lord of earth (*patiḥ pṛthivya* VIII.44.16), whom thoughts of the wise ones stir up (VIII.44.19);[59] they may concentrate on the sun, the great vivifier of all things, the home of every sage; or the dawn, herald of light and illumination which sets all life forward on its never ending course; or Varuṇa, the majestic king of cosmic order, of righteousness, who is always present where two are gathered together (Ath.v. IV.16.2). Hence the apparent extravertive element which is rather but a means to an end—communion with the various aspects of the one godhood (*mahad devānām asuratvam ekam* III.55.1).

Agni being one of the great objects of adoration is meditated on and then beheld, not really in a physical sense but as something quite beyond his normal appearance. Thus pondering upon the three divine brothers or aspects of Agni, fire, sun, lightning, there in the fire whereon he is brooding, the poet suddenly realises that he is gazing upon the seven-rayed lord of beings (*atra apaśyaṃ viś-patiṃ sapta putram* I.164.1). The poet's thoughts are as robes for Agni (I.140.1) whose outer flame he sees but whose inner being he wonders at. A question asked by the bard in IV.7.2 implies that the flame appearance of Agni is not necessarily the whole of the god, his true self lying beyond that flame: *agne kadā ta ānuṣag bhuvad devasya cetanam*. *Cetana* has several meanings but here the question is really when will the god be uninterruptedly conspicuous?[60] We may think that this concerns the keeping alive of the flame but verse 6 in its similar ambiguity lends itself to our first interpretation: though glowing (*citraṃ santam*) he is yet fast hidden away (*guhā hitam*). Agni is indeed hidden in the wood but surely when his flames are brightly shining he cannot at the same time be concealed, unless the poet has in mind the godly nature beyond the fiery appearance.

We find a perfect example of visual communion in the *ṛṣi*'s experience of Varuṇa. 'When shall I be in communion with Varuṇa' asks the poet (VII.86.2: *kadā nu antar varuṇe bhuvāni*), what oblation would be acceptable to the god since he feels that he has fallen in disgrace with Varuṇa. After longing for the wide-sighted one (*urucak-ṣasam*) the poet concentrates his thoughts upon Varuṇa, literally moves his thoughts unto him as cows unto their pastures,[61] and finally beholds the god (*darśaṃ nu viśva-darśatam* I.25.18) and this seeing is a sign to him that his song of praise has been received favourably (*etā juṣata me giraḥ*). Again, 'going into the presence' of Varuṇa (*asya samdṛśaṃ jaganvān* VII.88.2) he beholds the god's form coming into focus, but to his surprise it appears not as he had imagined it, but as the vision of Agni, the face of fire (*agner anīkam*). Such communion which plunges the poet into vision which cannot be preconceived since it turns out to be different from that expected, evidences great depth of absorption. Then do both seer and god embark together moving their boat unto the middle of the ocean (*nāvaṃ pra yat samudram īrayāva madhyam*)—a fine figure of speech expressive of a deepening communion referring to a voyage upon the ocean of the sub-conscious, or shall we say supra-conscious (VII.88.2). The yearning of the poet, as revealed in VII.88.1 is to behold the beauty of heaven (*svar . . . vapur dṛśaye*).

Similar excursions into the world beyond by means of seership are found in X.124.9 where bards have perceived Indra through their mental insight (*indraṃ ni cikyuḥ kavayo manīṣā*) and in III.38.6 where going thither [to the gods' synod] in the mind—*manasā*—the poet beholds (I saw—*apaśyam*) celestial entities (*gandharvaḥ*). In like manner, in X.130.6 he thinks (*man*) he beholds with mental insight (*paśyan manye manasā cakṣasā*) those who of old performed the sacrificial ritual. 'Brooding in their mind' (*manasā dīdhyānā*) they found the original *yajus* (or sacrificial formula important for the ritual) as though it had dropped out of the godly pathway (X.181.3).

The mind must be in harmony with reality, hence must reflect it faithfully (*cf.* X.67.8 *satyena manasā*). 'Meditating in depth' they found the wide light (VII.90.4: *uru jyotir vividur dīdhyānāḥ*) and then uncovered the stall of kine. This stall is also that of heaven which Agni opens up for men with his bright shining eyes (*śukrebhir akṣabhiḥ* IX.102.8). Ṛgv. VII.90.5 emphasises the quality of mind bent on truth or purified by truth as one could interpret *satyena manasā* and goes on to state that the poets journey onwards yoking to themselves their own intelligent penetration (*kratunā*). However, there seems to have been no necessity for high intellectual powers for great insights are referred to as received by 'simple minds' (*pākena manasā* X.114.4 and I.164.21 and IV.5.2). The wise deity is contrasted with the simple mortal who yet received the deity's boon.[62]

III. ABSORPTION

Such mental visioning leads us to our second [somewhat arbitrary] division which is but a deepening of this mental approach leading to meditation in the heart. Having developed his visionary insight into an instrument of perception capable of taking him far beyond the senses and thus of entering into communion with supersensuous realities, the Vedic seer was now able to plunge into that kind of deeper abstract absorption wherein he beheld and participated in divine action and whence he emerged with knowledge of cosmic processes, gaining insight into transcendental states. Seeing with the mind's eyes, not as in modern creative writing, but in actual seership such as characterised the prophets of biblical and the *ṛṣis* of Vedic times, or with the spiritual insight that transcends mental visioning, are two approaches alluded to in the Ṛgveda. They are the result of brooding upon the given object and a decisive step in the meditation leading to direct involvement in the divine process and apprehension of truth—a 'return to the origin' and a fundamental 'grounding'.

Here we should note that there is expressly mentioned two kinds of meditation, in the mind, *manas*, and in the heart, *hṛd*,[63] both being considered organs acting as filters for the thought or inspiration which arises from deep within the consciousness and is then translated into vision and then into a hymn, i.e. a chant. The *dhiyas* or thought-visions are refined by means of the mind, *manas*; the heart, *hṛd*; and the *manīṣā* which L. Renou considers to mean 'inspiration poétique'. The word connotes inspired and thus wise—because divinely grounded—insight. Thus: 'they polish their thoughts with heart, mind, understanding, for Indra the ancient Lord'.[64]

No reason is given as to why concentration occurs, now in the mind, now in the heart, or in both as seems to be the case in I.171.2 where praise and obeisance given shape within the mind and heart are offered to the Maruts who promote worship (*hṛdā taṣṭo manasā dhāyi*).

Meditation on seed thoughts combines cogitative and

visual insights. No reference is made to the heart in this example:

> I saw you deeply brooding in your mind upon what came into being from spiritual energy and from the latter developed.
>
> *apaśyaṃ tvā manasā cekitānaṃ tapaso jātaṃ tapaso vibhūtam.* (X.183.1. *cf.* also X.130.6).

Here is meditation on the origin of life and the cosmic process reaching a great depth of absorption indicated by the intensive form of the verb *cit* (*manasā cekitānam*) and actually witnessed by another person who thus must have been able to tune into the mental processes of the former. This first stanza is answered, presumably, by the husband who says in his turn 'I saw you pondering in your mind (*manasā dīdhyānāṃ svāyām*) and asking (*nādhamānām*) that at the appointed time (*ṛtvye*) you may become the bearer of desirable new life.'

As seen from VI.9.5, the organ of cogitation which is swifter than any winged thing, is firmly established as light within the human being. But the poet soon realises that it is placed in his own heart and his eyes open out to it.[65] We have here the bringing together of heart and mind forming a secure foundation for human intelligence and insight. Is there a clear differentiation in this poet's mind, between this light or insight placed within the heart, and that mental light swifter than wings? He describes his mind as wandering afar (VI.9.6), his ears listening, his eyes beholding; with all his senses he is trying to catch something of its essence which yet remains ungraspable. How to express it? 'What shall I say, what shall I think?'[66]

But there is in the human being a deeper understanding, a wiser insight than mere intellectual knowing and that is *kratu*[67] which was placed in the human heart by the great god Varuṇa: (V.85.2: *hṛtsu kratuṃ varuṇo . . . adadhāt*). Significantly enough Varuṇa reveals his thought by means of the heart (I.105.15 *vi ūrṇoti hṛda matim*). The word heart[68] is a technical term which in Ṛgvedic times seems to have comprised the meaning of understanding-intuition-wisdom. It denotes the innermost centre in the human constitution whence come revelation, spiritual insight. *Kratu* set in the heart combines intelligent awareness and intuitive perception which yields the higher wisdom: 'my thinking powers exert themselves as such within my heart' (X.64.2: *kratūyanti kratayo hṛtṣu*) may seem repetitive in so far as the Sanskrit is concerned, but the phrase does describe the mental exercise going on behind the scenes so to speak, to yield finally an insight into truth which cannot be dismissed. This is depth meditation. The devotee plunges in full consciousness into his inmost centre to touch truth (*ṛta*) or reach out to the heart of the god (*hṛdispṛg* I.16.7).[69] Furthermore it is not enough to think or to frame praise with the mind, but the heart itself must cooperate and be made a sieve which transmutes the visions into appropriate verbal forms. Incidentally we find here the origin of the mantra. Inspired words flow out made clear by heart and mind (IV.58.6).[70]

The importance of the heart or central focus of the human being in the process of prayer or meditation is necessarily related to the *sincerity* of the bard's thinking and worship. What is done with the heart must be effective because sincere. This is a human truth valid for all time. When the heart is touched the interest is aroused, the attention secured and the concentration perfect. Thus the result is assured. The *ṛṣis* with their depth of insight knew this. We find a hint as to the above in X.71.8: the congregation of priests performs the sacrificial rites absorbed in mental impulses formed within the heart (*hṛdā taṣṭeṣu manaso javeṣu*). These are the real *brāhmaṇa* for those who cannot reach that stage do not count as such.[71] The blend of heart and mind is the condition on which depends the deeper seership and the function of the priest. By insights gained in secret within the heart (*niṇyam hṛdayasya praketaiḥ*) the Vasiṣṭha priests approached the thousand-branched [tree of knowledge?] (*sahasra valśam* VII.33.9). Then, as implied in the second part of the stanza, they enter a supersensuous realm donning the garment provided for them by Yama, the king of the dead.

So to Indra is offered the Soma with praises from the

heart (VIII.76.8 *hṛdā hūyanta ukthinaḥ*),[72] and to Agni is brought the oblation which the poet conceives within his heart together with the word or song as the supreme gift of the worshipper (a te *Agna ṛcā havirhṛdā taṣṭaṃ bharāmasi* VI.16.47).[73] This kind of creation is ascribed to Agni, himself the inspirer of poets.[74] As shown in the section on mantric meditation it is in the heart that a thought is brought to birth as light[75] so that heart and mind are blended in the creative act, whilst Agni purifies the flashing song (*apupod hi arkam*). Thought emerges here from the depths—from the heart—as light but the reverse could also be considered: a light hidden in the heart comes to birth, i.e. to the consciousness, as a thought, as a result of which the 'flashing song' is purified, is made potent. It is also this Agni whom meditating men discover hidden away when they murmur their *mantra* fashioned in the heart.[76] He, the knower of the classes of beings (*jātavedas*), 'the one ocean, the foundation of riches, the one of many births, shines forth from our heart'.[77] Inspired bards (*dhīrāsaḥ* . . . *kavayaḥ*), each by himself keeping watch in his heart (*nānā hṛdā rakṣamānāḥ*), take the everlasting one to his own realm (*padaṃ* . . . *nayanti* . . . *ajuryam*); by such bards the sun was made manifest for men (*āvir ebhyo abhavat sūryo nṛn*, I.146.4). Meditation in the heart over the sacred fire which underlies the ocean of being results in the bringing to birth of the sun of illumination. Agni, in mythological terms, brings forth the sun into the heavens (*cf.* X.3.2, X.7.3 and X.88.11). *Fire* and *sun* are expressions of one fundamental state. Agni, the fire, stands as the guardian and the gateway to that light immortal vouchsafed by the patriarchs (X.107.1) to which these found the path (I.71.2), which 'Sūrya as he rises spreads with his rays' (Ath.v. XII.1.15), that 'undying flame in beings without which nought can be done' (Yj. v. v.s. 34.3). The same kind of inspiring and releasing power is ascribed to Soma.[78] Soma too finds the access to prayer, that is, opens up the way to the release of the *brahman* (IX.96.10 *vidad gātuṃ brahmaṇe*) for it exalts the worshipper as it is quaffed in his heart.[79] Its juice is *svarvidaḥ* (IX.107.14), heaven finding or light bestowing. In Soma the *brahman* exalts Indra

(I.80.1) creating exhilaration (*cakāra vardhanam*). Spiritual knowledge is born of exaltation and the swelling of the heart.

With 'heart and mind' (*hṛdā ... manasā*) united the sages (*vipaścitaḥ*) behold the flying bird (*pataṅgaṃ ... paśyanti* X.177.1), or the 'one fine-winged bird' (*ekaḥ suparṇaḥ* X.114.4), or sun-bird, or solar or supernal ray, as this *suparṇa* could also be translated; it is 'anointed with the asura's magic power' (*aktam asurasya māyayā* X.177.1) and envelops all things (*viśvaṃ bhuvanaṃ vi caṣṭe* X.114.4), pervading the ocean (*samudram ā viveśa* X.114.4) immersed in its depth (*samudre antaḥ* X.177.1). The verb √*vi cakṣ*, to perceive but also to shine and √*paś* to see, coupled with *antitas* near, imply an observing at close quarters and this perception, we are told, is effected by means of a simple mind (*pākena manasā*), a mind unspoiled. The overtones of genuineness, sincerity, spontaneity, contained in *pāka*[80] accentuate the quality of seership, a pure, genuine insight untrammelled by the paraphernalia of intellect, its logic or prejudices and limitations. Such a mention is a direct pointer to the fact that the seeing is of a supra-rational kind and that an intellectual type of mind is not needed to contact that particular truth which is open only to spiritual vision.

Similar in insight and resulting vision, both these stanzas express the mystical experience of immanence, the one pervading ray or bird enfolding, because pervading, abiding in, all things, and yet having its own centre, *pada*, the fountain-source whence emerge its rays (*marīcīnāṃ padam*), the object of the sages' longing (*icchanti vadhasaḥ* X.177.1).[81]

The intuitive insight (*manīṣā*) into the nature of the all-pervading light symbolised as the winged bird (*suparṇaḥ*) or solar ray which in pervading the ocean has penetrated all things is described in X.177.2 as bright as lightning (*dyotamānā*) as well as *svarya*.[82] This is illumination. The lightning-like flash of insight, whether caused by Soma, the elixir of immortality, or by *brahman*, the Vedic prayer, revealing something hitherto unknown, grants an uplifting or ecstatic experience which elsewhere made the bards exclaim: 'We have seen the gods, we have become immortal' (VIII.48.3). The constant use of epithets denoting sunny, shining, bright, lightning, fiery, heavenly, with regard to prayer, meditation, absorption, vision, is significant of the quality of the poet's visionary life.

IV. THE SUN AND ILLUMINATION IN VEDIC MEDITATION

Spiritual knowledge is a result of illumination and illumination finds its full expression in the Vedic conception of the sun. The particular role which Sūrya plays in the Ṛgveda assumes unprecedented importance when considered psychologically. He is the eye or insight of the gods,[83] and also of men as he is common to all men. His meaning is not half as simple as early scholars had set out to demonstrate. He is the organ of perception with which the gods view manifested existence: from the throne (*garta*) of Sūrya, Mitra and Varuṇa behold the infinite and the finite (V.62.8 *aditiṃ ditiṃ ca*); through that *eye* Indra looks upon the world (VII.98.6). 'Through the gods' intelligence (*kratu*) that eye was originally created' (VII.76.1 *kratvā devānām ajaniṣṭa cakṣuḥ cf.* VII.77.3). Thus *kratu* which for want of a better term we are translating as intelligence is responsible for the bringing about of perception, hence of the *eye*. This generating of Sūrya by the gods[84] is important, not in the ordinary sense in which it may be and has been taken, namely that Sūrya is thereby secondary to the gods, but rather that he is the very instrument of their vision and omniscience which they themselves have forged; he belongs to their inner nature and is a sign of their divinity. He is not merely the star out in the sky, but a tool, an organ of perception, a symbol as well as a god in his own right. This is where we catch a glimpse of the complexity of the gods' function in the Vedic thought. They are both principles working in men and entities working in the cosmos. Sūrya, like Agni, being common to all men (VII.63.1: *sādhāraṇaḥ sūryo mānuṣānām*) impels them (*janāḥ sūryena prasūtāḥ*) to action (*kṛṇavann apāṃsi* VII.63.4). Does this mean solely that in shining from above upon all men, upon the just and the unjust as the New Testament puts it,[85] all men can see the sun and in that sense alone he is common to all, dear to all (*viśvajanya* VII.76.1)? We believe not. The Atharvaveda describes Sūrya as 'the one eye of what exists which looks beyond (*ati paś*) the sky, the earth, the waters'.[86] It is also worth observing that Sūryạ 'impels' men to action. In the human constitution the mind is the great impeller to activity. But Sūrya stands beyond the mind since he looks into the darkness into which the mind cannot look. The mind is but his instrument.

No conclusion was drawn either by J. Muir or A. A. Macdonell or A. B. Keith (or A. Bergaigne, A. Kaegi, M. Winternitz and so on) as to Sūrya's essential (apart from any obvious) function, a function which links gods and men and points to a clear-eyed perception or vision, a spiritual insight, as proper to gods and as hidden but to be developed in men—and as having been so developed in those ancestors who gained immortality—this being the inner significance of Sūrya. Sight which transcends both sky and earth, as made clear in the Atharvaveda verse already quoted, is not physical. The light which Sūrya bestows from the sky upon the earth can be taken as a mirror of the spiritual light he engenders or arouses in both heart and mind.[87]

For J. Muir[88] in the many passages that he quotes from the Ṛgveda

> . . . the grand luminary becomes little more than a part of nature, created and controlled by those spiritual powers which exist above and beyond all material phenomena.

For A. B. Keith[89]

> the chief feat of Sūrya is his shining for the world, for gods, and men: he smites away the darkness and triumphs over the powers of darkness and witches; he prolongs the lives of men and drives away sickness, disease and evil dreams. He is also the divine priest of the gods . . .

Sūrya is certainly not 'little more than a part of nature', but the very expression of vision, insight, the personification of divine knowledge, the deity whose all illuminating gaze makes of the 'spiritual powers' that generate it the all-seeing, all-knowing and all-wise gods that the Vedas describe them as being, and makes of men eventually gods.

There is no real confusion between the idea of 'shining' and that of 'seeing' as claimed by A. Bergaigne:[90]

The confusion between the idea of shining and the idea of seeing, frequent in Vedic mythology, has not only been responsible for assimilating the sun to an eye but has also referred the origin of the eye to the Sun IX.10.8; *cf.* X.158.3 or inversely that of the sun to the mystical eye of Purusha, X.90.13.

Just as the same word 'perception' is used for perceiving physically and mentally, the one instance meaning to see and the other to understand, so Bergaigne completely missed the point that spiritual perception is an illumination and therefore a shining from within, hence the connection, not the confusion, between shining and seeing, luminosity and spiritual insight. Those who gain this perception are therefore sun-eyed (as the Ṛbhus). The verse cited by Bergaigne (IX.10.8) states that Soma, working from his central point (*nābhā*) receives us in his centre (*nābhiṃ na ā dade*) and places the eye with the sun (*cakṣuś cit sūrye sacā*), i.e. in awakening man's inner perception Soma makes human insight equivalent to Sūrya's divine gaze, in other words, Soma helps to 'illuminate' man, to render him 'sun-eyed'. Since Sūrya is the organ of the gods' spiritual insight and therefore of enlightenment he is naturally born from the eye of the divine man, *puruṣa* (X.90.13)[91] and is the 'overlord of sights' in every sense (Ath.v. V.24.9). Sūrya thus signifies and at the same time symbolises spiritual insight.

Only J. Gonda in his exhaustive study,[92] examining the epithets *viśvacakṣas* the "all-seeing" used of Sūrya (I.50.2, VII.63.1), of Viśvakarman and Soma, and also *urucakṣas* (wide-visioned) and *vicakṣana* (widely observant)[93] draws the conclusion that these:

. . . illustrate the belief in an omniscience which is based essentially on the power of sight; a knowing which comes from, or is intimately connected with, an unusual and supra normal faculty of seeing . . . 'Visual omniscience' is the specific attribute of deities and not, or not primarily, of deities in general, but of those gods who are somehow connected with the heavenly realms of light . . . these deities are all knowing because all seeing and all-seeing because they are luminous.[94]

We have here a recognition of the Vedic seership with its undertones of luminosity and the Vedic knowledge of the possibility of illumination with its implication of omniscience.

As the function of the eye is closely connected with the sun in the Ṛgveda its essential meaning should be clarified. Going back to 'origins' we find that the 'Father of the eye' (*cakṣuṣaḥ pitā*) is the 'all-creator' *viśvakarman*, he who is 'wise in mind' (*manasā hi dhīraḥ*, X.82.1) and thus promoter of wise insight as *cakṣuṣaḥ pitā* could be interpreted. The 'all-seeing' (*viśvacakṣas*) and 'all-creator' (*viśvakarman*) are one, and Sūrya, as the eye or visionary instrument of the far-sighted gods (*urucakṣāḥ*, VIII.101.2) who, true to law (*ṛtāvāna ṛtajātā*, VII.66.13) are themselves subservient to the *ṛta*,[95] partakes in this creative process.

Two words are used as may be seen from the examples: *cakṣu* which means 'eye' but is equivalent to internal or spiritual perception (in addition to physical sight) and *cakṣas* which has both connotations of 'eye' and 'brilliance'. The sun, the 'far-sighted' or 'wide-visioned one' (*urucakṣas*) (VII.35.8 & 63.4) as the gods' eye is the divine insight into all things—a combination of vision and wisdom and represents the gods' omniscience. Through Sūrya their knowledge of truth and falsehood[96] remains infallible,[97] they are undeceivable,[98] for in perceiving all creatures (*abhi yo viśvā bhuvanāni caṣṭe*) Sūrya has insight into the *manyu* or spirit of mortals.[99]

But man, not having sufficiently developed this inherent insight—let us remember the sun is common to both men and gods (VII.63.1)—is often deluded and not capable of distinguishing between the true and the false or of knowing the divine nature[100] and begs for guidance from the gods to reach the 'fearless light' (*jyotir abhayam* VI.47.8 & II.27.11), the 'wide world' (*uruṃ lokam*),[101] the world of freedom and light, the world of *svar*. Meditation on truth, as IV.23.8 implies, help him to gain this insight; illumined apprehension of *ṛta* (*ṛtasya dhītiḥ*) removes obstructions.[102]

From the 'Father of the eye' man has inherited *manas*, his mental insight, his superior understanding which marks him out among all creatures, *manas* that 'eye' by means of which the seer perceives internally (*paśyan ... manasā cakṣasā* X.130.6) the sacrifice performed of old and grasps its fundamental significance. Wisdom, clear-sightedness and seeing or insight which are necessary elements of deep understanding, are closely associated in the Ṛgveda where the act of 'seeing' implies far more than mere physical sight.[103] Similarly Agni is considered the eye (*cakṣu*) that bestirs devotional thought (V.8.6 *cakṣuḥ ... codayan-mati*).[104] This plainly points to the psychological aspect of the word and of the god who is the inner eye that keeps vigil during the dark stage of the unillumined mind—as well as the fire that illuminates the night.

This is the kind of eye[105] or far-reaching insight into truth for which the poet longs (X.87.12), a celestial light (*jyotiṣā daivyena*) which enabled the sage Atharva, as the verse continues, to consume the untruthful.

The other word *cakṣas*[106] is used with the dual sense of radiance, clearness and of sight and eye. The adjective *vicakṣaṇa*, 'widely observant, clear-sighted' (√*vicakṣ* meaning to shine as well as to appear) also shows the internal link between shining far and wide and perceiving in depth. Like Sūrya (I.50.8) Savitṛ is the clear sighted one or wide-eyed (IV.53.2) *vicakṣaṇaḥ*, like Agni, Soma and Indra, to whom the epithet also applies. All have insights into men's souls.[107] Resourcefulness, ingenuity, all aspects of intelligence (*kratu*) and this shining perception akin to illumination are juxtaposed as attributes of Soma in IX.107.3 (*kratur indur vicakṣaṇaḥ*) for Soma is the 'far-seeing one who causes illumination' (IX.39.3 *vicakṣāṇo virocayan*). This alone demonstrates that illuminating insight or far seeing illumination as here quoted, granted by the gods, whether Sūrya or Soma, is of the nature of transcendental perception, hence *enstasis.* So Agni is begged to 'shine' his auspicious gifts upon the worshippers (*saubhagā didīhi*) that 'we may reach supreme understanding' (VII.3.10): the substantive (*kratum*), adjective (*sucetasam*) and verb (*api vatema*), emphasising the idea of apprehending in depth, point to the essentially psychological quality of the boon 'shined'—or as we would now say 'showered'—upon the devotee as 'riches'.

This shining from within makes the wise ones who foster truth (VII.66.10 *bahavaḥ ṛtavṛdhaḥ*) 'sun-eyed' (*sūra-cakṣaḥ*)[108] and 'flame-tongued' (*agnijihvaḥ*) (*cf.* I.89.7). The gods are thus able to see by the light of heaven (*svardṛśaḥ*), o be sun-eyed (*sūracakṣuḥ*), indeed enlightened.

The epithet *svardṛś* translated in accordance with J. Gonda's commentaries,[109] is a common qualifying epithet.[110] Sūrya beholds all things becuse of his own inherent divine light (I.50.5: *pratyañ viśvaṃ svardṛśe*). *Svar* and *Sūrya* are not only etymologically related but have a common meaning, sun-light. The terms derived from them, *svardṛś*,[111] beholding by heaven, or spiritual insight, and *sūracakṣu*, sun-eyed, have equally a common meaning and refer to those whose divine eye, the sun-eye, is open. So the Ṛbhus who through their intelligence, ingenuity, artistic skill, are finally granted immortality when they reach the home of Savitṛ, are described as sun-eyed (I.110.2–4), and Agni, in so far as he sees by the light of heaven (*svardṛś* V.26.2) is its 'sign' (III.2.14 *svardṛśaṃ ketuṃ divaḥ*) as well as the seal of immortality (VI.7.6). Similarly, Mitra-Varuṇa, in beholding by means of the sun or sunlight, the world and ruling it from that platform, evidence in the eyes of the *ṛṣis*, their divine insight and thus kingship.[112]

Whether the poets or seers projected their state of illuminated consciousness upon their mental screen in the form of the golden orb, Sūrya-Savitṛ, or the golden juice, Soma, or the well-winged one (*suparṇaḥ*), the sun-bird or solar ray (X.114.4 & X.177.1.2), or anything else, is secondary. Bṛhaspati, the lord of prayer, is asked for that splendour which shines with power and is resourceful among men.[113] This is the same 'splendour' or illumination as is personified in the sun. All spiritual insights being accompanied by light and enlightenment, a tearing of the veil, and a feeling of increase and invigoration, were explained in terms of light, splendour and shining. As light is the nature of the sun, the latter was the great luminary of enlightenment, the sun of truth which Indra sought and found dwelling in darkness (III.39.5 *satyam . . . sūryaṃ viveda tamasi kṣiyantam*). The essential idea behind the many Vedic statements centers around the one fact of shining illumination which forms the core of mystical experiences which have been depicted in terms of dazzling or solar or fiery light—whether those described in antiquity, or by Christians and Muslims.[114]

In the state of heightened awareness as was familiar to the Vedic sages they beheld the 'golden one' (*apaśyāma hiraṇyayam* I.139.2) not with visionary thoughts or mental insight (*dibhiś cana manasā*) but 'with the very eyes of Soma [our] very eyes' (*svebhir akṣabhiḥ somasya svebhi akṣabhiḥ*) or as the verse could also be translated 'with the very eyes of Soma, indeed its very eyes', the meaning being the same, as 'its very eyes' become the eyes of the seers. These 'eyes' may mean the perception granted through ecstasy, since after drinking Soma the bards could exclaim 'we have become immortal, we have come to the light, we have found the gods' (VIII.48.3), the juxtaposition of gods (i.e. divinity), of light (i.e. enlightenment) and immortality (i.e. the abolition of limitation) expressing the gradation of the rapture experienced. The direct mention that here is no mental visioning but an actual realisation through the eyes granted by Soma, the insight of the god intoxicated spirit, lifts up the vision to a higher level than that so far considered. It is also remarkable that the eyes of Soma are equated with 'very eyes' as it can be taken that the essence of the seer's perception or 'eyes' is one with Soma. From this may be easily inferred that the eyes of the immortal spirit which are the real eyes, are referred to here.[115]

There is no certainty among Western scholars as to what exactly is the 'golden one'. It may mean the sun, the personification of the divine light and life-giver, not necessarily because of the epithet 'golden'. There is evidence (I.50.10) that the transcendent reality was expressed by the *ṛṣis* as the sun, though the latter is also the immanent soul, the *ātman* of all things (I.115.1). The sun in the Ṛgveda is not only the luminous orb out in the sky, but it is the living embodiment of the light of illumination, the goal of human life.[116] It is a concrete representation of the Vedic idea of Deity no less valid than any subsequent anthropomorphic conception. The all too obvious link traceable between Agni and Sūrya—both being promoters of enlightenment, Agni whose light kindled by the worshipper merges into the sun as the latter rises (X.88.11)[117] and whose lofty face is honoured in heaven as the light of

Sūrya (X.7.3),[118] who is the beautiful face of truth (VI.51.1)[119]—has its origin in this striving after light, in this constant endeavour to express the ever widening vision of truth in terms of light, of blaze, of fire. Whether the 'golden one' applies to the 'throne'[120] of deity, or to the sun, or to Soma who elsewhere is described as the 'far-sighted' one (*vicakṣaṇa* IX.86.23, 37.2, 107.3, 106.5) and the 'thousand-eyed' (*sahasra cakṣas* IX.60.1) is of no primary importance. As shown above it essentially refers to an all illuminating vision-rapture. That Soma is closely connected with Sūrya in certain respects is brought out in IX.75.1 where Soma is said to mount on Sūrya's chariot or in IX.107.7 where he makes Sūrya ascend to heaven and in IX.85.9 where he, as ever far-sighted, is rising in the sky, shining by means of the sun (IX.2.6), assuming for his robes the rays of Sūrya (IX.86.32: *sa sūryasya raśmibhiḥ pari vyata*),[121] and his drops are *svarvidaḥ*, light-bestowing (IX.104.14). The implied identification of both is due to their representing clear-eyed perception whether granted through inspiration or illumination (*soma* and *sūrya*), both being sparked off by Soma's stimulating effect.

V. ILLUMINATION (SOLAR ENLIGHTENMENT) AND BRAHMAN

The epitome of this quest of solar enlightenment and divine illumination finds its fit expression in VIII.6.10 and V.40.6:

aham id hi pitus pari medhām ṛtasya jagrabha ahaṃ sūrya iva ajani	'Having received from my father the perception of truth I was born even a sun (VIII.6.10)

We recognise here the second birth of all great religions, the twice born of the Brāhmaṇas. The *ṛṣi*, in his spiritual awakening, was a son of the sun and through illumination consequent upon meditation (*dhī*) resulting in *brahman*, strove to return to his solar origin. For Manu, the first man, and Yama, the first who gave up his own body and found for men the way to heaven, are sons of Vivasvant the shining one, the solar splendour. This solar origin of the human race is significant of its spiritual grounding and confirmed by the [second] birth alluded to in VIII.6.10 and clearly stated in X.61.19: 'twice born am I' (*dvijā aha*).[122] The return to the solar source, the divine illumined life represents the Vedic conception of immortality, unlimited or all-round consciousness, 'all-seeing' (*viśva-cakṣas*) and shining because illumined from within. This enlightenment, or sungaze or insight, as implied in VIII.48.3, is fruitful of something beyond the quality of vision, knowledge and understanding. (*cf.* YS III.55). The sun is not merely the eye of the gods as their omniscient gaze but, as the eye of Agni Vaiśvānara, it is the hall-mark of immortality (*amṛtasya ketu* VI.7.6). Enlightenment, the vision of the golden one, *svar* or heaven, all point to a supraterrestrial state wherein freedom from limitation and therefore from time is known.

Somewhat like his counterpart in the Egyptian rite of old wherein the neophyte stands between hawk-headed Osiris, the sun, and ibis-headed Mercury, and on his head both pour the waters of life, so the *ṛṣi* claimed his heritage, to be united to the sun.[123]

Hence the *ṛṣi's* ascension to the summit of the 'ruddy one' (VIII.69.7 *ud bradnasya viṣṭapaṃ gṛham*) which he undertakes with Indra's help—obviously a form of meditation. So the devoted sages, the followers of the law, having become what they are through spiritual exertion (*tapasvato . . . tapojān*) act as 'protectors of the sun' (*gopāyanti sūryam* X.154.5), grant light to men (X.107.2) and among those who have passed beyond some have entered into the sun[124] (*ni anyā arkam abhito viviśre* VIII.101.14), just as the patriarchs of old were united to the rays of the sun (I.109.7).

The significance of Ṛgveda V.40.6 bears upon the Vedic approach to meditation which L. Renou clearly recognised.[125] It hints at the meaning of the symbol of the sun, that 'immortal light' (*jyotir amṛtam*) which the Yajurveda claims 'abides in all living beings' (Yj.v.s.34.3).

It was during 'the fourth degree of prayer' that the ancient sage 'Atri found the "sun" [till then] immersed in gloom':

> *gūḷhaṃ sūryaṃ tamasā apavratena turīyeṇa brahmaṇā avindad atrih.* (V.40.6)

This verse was taken by A. Ludwig to refer purely and simply to an eclipse which he even identified with that which must have occurred on 20 April 1001 B.C.[126] A. Bergaigne devotes an article[127] to refuting Ludwig's theory of solar eclipses[128] and seems to treat the information of the *fourth brahman* given in V.40.6 as not much better than a reference to magic or, worse, legerdemain. He inclines, if any sense could be made of it, towards a mythological explanation. The so-called demon Svarbhānu is said to have caused the obscuration. Two questions arise: is Svarbhānu, in the Ṛgveda, really a demon? Is a temporary obscuration really meant? To which another question may give an indirect answer: is not the obscuration in line with all other Ṛgvedic myths of the hidden sun brought to sight either by Indra, or the patriarchs through their songs or, in this case, Atri by his fourth prayer?[129] It should be kept in mind that ancient man did not consider the celestial and the terrestrial order of things as separate as modern man, but to him every earthly phenomenon was underlined by a divine something which was but the result of spiritual laws and the action of godly beings. Myths then may be interpreted at different levels and the one that is of interest to us here is the spiritual level to which the words *turīyaṃ brahman* give the clue. During his fourth degree of prayer the ancient sage Atri (who is also a form of Agni)[130] found the sun till then hidden away by Svarbhānu,[131] the 'skylight', whereas others, says verse 9, could not do so. This is significant enough. The finding of the sun is due to the reaching of a certain degree of prayer.

The Atharvaveda gives a clue as to the process only hinted at in the usual veiled way in the Ṛgveda:

> They either who by meditation led the beginning (*agra*) of speech, or who by mind spoke righteous things (*ṛta*) they, increasing with the third incantation (*brahman*) perceived (*man*) with the fourth the name of the milch cow. (VII.1.1).[132] (Whitney's Translation).

This stanza, as many another, was quite unintelligible to W. D. Whitney.[133] Nevertheless keywords are given showing steps in the progress of meditation, the idea of 'increase' or exhilaration (*vṛdh*) being notable and pointing to that exalted fulfilment which contemplation brought to its practitioner, a state of consciousness completely missed by nineteenth century Western exegesis. Meditation, thence absorption into truth (*ṛta*) lead to the 'third incantation', thence to the fourth whence the supreme mystery is revealed, or the sun is found, or the name of the cow is known.[134] We surely have here what might be called a sacerdotal language, and we have to come to the twentieth century, to L. Renou, to find a suitable analysis of the meaning of this strange jargon:

The fourth brahman is '... the end of an inner progressive realisation, the stages of which are marked out by *dhītī*, "intuition" ... *manasā*, "reflection" ... *tṛtīyena brahmaṇā*, "the third *brahman*" (that which "enhances" [increases or gives added worth] *vāvṛdhānaḥ*); last, *turīyena*, the final stage which grants the right to "think the name of the cow"'.[135]

that is, to realise, in our rational consciousness, the full meaning of the mystery. L. Renou adds: 'It is not accidental if in a RV hymn (X.67.1) Bṛhaspati, i.e. "the master of *brahman*" has also "engendered" the "fourth" by similar stages'.[136]

The fourth brahman is thus a state of consciousness known to the Vedic *ṛṣis*, but the technique of its achievement was systematically analysed only in the Upaniṣads. The full meaning of this fourth stage is not found in the Ṛgveda. We have to turn to the Upaniṣads for further elucidations. Of the four conditions of the human being which Indian philosophy describes as the awakened state, the dream state, deep sleep when the mind is at perfect rest (equivalent to *dhyāna*) and beyond sleep when it has awakened to a new state of being which later speculation called *samādhi*, the fourth is considered the greater. Entrance into the hall of brahma, claims the Maitrī Upaniṣad, can be effected only by killing the door-keeper *ahamkara* or self-consciousness. Thence the 'fourfold sheath of brahma' should be dispersed. This consists of the four *kośas* or sheaths of the human constitution explained as 'food' (i.e.

body), 'breath' (i.e. *prāṇa*), mind (*manas*) and 'understanding', to which the Vedantic fivefold classification applies: *annamayakośa* or physical body with which the unevolved person is wholly identified; *prāṇamayakośa*, the field of the hatha yogin's exploration; *manomayakośa* over which the *munis* or ascetics have dominion; *vijñanamayakośa* or buddhi consciousness into which the *ṛṣis,* through their visionary insights, gained entrance. The last *kośa*, or *anandamayakośa* is that state of supreme bliss to which alone the *paramahamsa* has access. One may infer that some *ṛṣis* caught glimpses of it (*cf.* I.164.21, V.40.6, I.50.10).

Only when these envelopes or sheaths of consciousness are dropped away can there be any transcendental experience. The Vedic *ṛṣis* symbolised the latter as the sun which they called the soul or *ātman* 'of what moves and moves not', the 'splendid face of the gods' (I.115.1) which only the divine in man can behold: 'O mortals you behold it not' (I.105.16); it is discovered as the loftiest light beyond darkness (I.50.10) in the *fourth brahman* (V.40.6). Ṛgv. I.115.1 is extremely important in so far as it clearly identifies the sun with the *ātman* or self of all: *sūrya ātmā jagatas tasthuṣaś ca*. That self in all which the Atharvaveda described as 'desireless, wise, immortal, self-existent, contented with the essence, lacking nothing, is He. One fears not death who has known him, the *ātmā*—serene, ageless, youthful' (Ath.v. X.8.44 Whitney's translation) is the divine sun. This is confirmed in the Upaniṣads.[137] The Maṇḍūkya Upaniṣad gives a further hint: 'Ungraspable ... unthinkable ... one with the self (*ekātman*) ... benign, without a second (*advaita*) [such] they think is the fourth. He is the Self [*ātman*].[138]

Since Atri found the sun in the fourth *brahman* he merged with his own *ātman*.

The Upaniṣads give us a ground for a better understanding. Turning back to the Ṛgveda we may yet find further hints revealing the depth of insight of the *ṛṣis* which enabled their descendants to express these philosophically in the Upaniṣads.

The fourth *brahman* seems to have been the culmination of the Vedic quest for truth and seems to have signified that stage of deepest absorption when human consciousness actually reaches full illumination and merges in the supreme consciousness. For prayer, it should be clear by now, is not a mere recitation of words or incantation or orison. It is a process implying stages of deepening absorption—with or without the use of words—requiring purification of the whole being (*cf.* IX.67.23), and culminating in illuminating upliftment and *enstasis*. This is the fourth *brahman*.

Such meditative states fruitful of transcendental insights mean that the flow of consciousness in one chosen direction remains unbroken, whether contemplation of a god, or of cosmic problems is used as a focus, the thought-image leading to the vision, to heightened awareness and spiritual realisation, a flow which according to Patañjali's Yoga-sūtra (III.2) is *dhyāna*. The latter takes one a stage further than simple meditation or concentration upon any particular object or abstract idea, for in its intensification all thought modifications cease and perfect stillness ensues, the acme of which is deep contemplative absorption and abstraction; only during such absolute quietude does the transformation or transmuting process take place, for the mind is then being slowly transcended. Such a state is referred to in one of the many riddles of the Atharvaveda, a stanza which was not understood until J. Gonda who mentions it and evidences an inkling as to its real significance:[139]

brahma jajñānaṃ pratha-
maṃ purastād vi sīmataḥ
suruco vena āvah

sa budhnyā upamā asya
viṣṭhāḥ sataś ca yonim
viṣṭāḥ sataś ca yonim
asataś ca vi vaḥī

The brahman that of old
first manifested from the
luminous border-line, the
seer has uncovered;
its loftiest station, fathom-
less, he has uncovered
as the womb of the mani-
fest and the unmanifest.
(Trans. J. M.)

(Ath.v. IV.1.1, similarly quoted in V.6.1, and also in Śat. Br. VII.4.1.14, XIV.1.3.3 and elsewhere).

This is an near a description of *dhyāna* as may be found in the four Vedas. It shows that meditation was already well known in Vedic times. Several factors are worth observing and keeping in mind for they are part of the meditative process as known then and now. Into the darkness and void of the inner silence which is a matrix palpitating with potential power, the meditator penetrates even to the 'dividing line', that which separates the known from the unknown, the mind from the beyond. In deep *dhyāna* he crosses over that boundary line. This is not yet *samādhi* but a step towards it. We should notice the quality of luminosity which marks the entrance into another state of consciousness (*suruc* shining brightly). From that matrix where lies concealed the zero point or the edge between the outer and the inner worlds, the phenomenal and the transcendent, the conscious and the supra-conscious, the *brahman*, the power of the spirit, looms upon the horizon of consciousness, flashes forth (like lightning, *cf.* Indra's bolt which severs the mountain rock or the confiner, or Agni's bolt which dwells in the ocean) and fills the meditator's whole being with light, knowledge, illumination, and thence disappears back again into the womb whence the manifest emerged—the borderline of the mysterious.

We may now, perhaps, better understand Aurobindo's[140] definition of the brahman given on p. 48 and also grasp how, plunged in their heart-searching contemplation the Vedic seers discovered 'the link between the created and the uncreate' (X.129.4). Without any insight into *dhyāna* these words remain meaningless.[141] In such states of perfect absorption the Vedic seers would go back in time to the origin of the cosmos:

The Unmanifest was not then, or the Manifest;
spatial depths or heaven beyond were not.
What encompassed, where, who nurtured it?
What ocean, profound, unfathomable, pervaded?

Death was not then or immortality.
Neither night's nor day's confine existed.
Undisturbed, self-moved, pulsated the One alone.
And beyond that, other than that, was naught.

Darkness there was; at first hidden in darkness
this all was undifferentiated depth.
Enwrapped in voidness, that which flame-power
Kindled to existence emerged. . . .

Desire, primordial seed of mind, in
the beginning arose in That.
Seers, searching in their heart's wisdom,
discovered the kinship of the created with the uncreate.
(Ṛgv. X.129.1–4)[142]

They thus conceived the Absolute as beyond the manifest and the unmanifest, beyond life and death, beyond the shadow of death and the shadow of immortality (Ṛgv. X.121.2),[143] beyond all speculation and left it at this unreachable height. There was no question of degrading the Absolute, but between man and those dizzy heights they discovered that which links both and raises man to Deity, to the 'highest immortality' (*amṛtatve uttame* I.31.7), Agni, the flame divine abiding in every human tabernacle,[144] whom 'from the supreme Father was brought for' men (I.141.4).[145]

The further question of *samādhi*, a word which does not appear in the Ṛgveda, is best considered in the light of the solar element around which cluster most of the hymns and praises addressed to Indra, the conqueror of the sun. Patañjali's laconic description of *samādhi*—an intenser continuation of *dhyāna*, a plunging into the very essence of the object contemplated, is in terms of shining forth or illuminating (*nirbhās*).[146] It is almost certain that the *ṛṣis* experienced *samādhi* but they did not analyse this in terms used in later ages as Patañjali was to do; its culmination meant for them contemplation of and perhaps mergence with the sun as evidenced in the quotations considered above (V.40.6, I.50.10, *cf.* also I.164.21). There is no direct statement that the beholding of the 'golden one' becomes a blending of the beholder and the object perceived but the knowledge of immortality which is part of the experience of *samādhi* is clearly stated in VIII.48.3. A hint as to god-possession may be found in I.164.21:

yatrā suparṇā amṛtasya bhāgam animeṣaṃ vidathā abhi svaranti ino viśvasya bhuvanasya gopāḥ sa ma dhīraḥ pākam atra viveśa.

Where those fine winged-birds sing to their share of immortality and of rites there is the lordly herdsman of the whole universe, the enlightened one who has entered into me the simple.

The seer is no longer himself but is pervaded by the spirit of the Lord and since this is the universe's guardian (in line with the loftiest overseer of the empyrean of X.129.7) this kind of divine possession seems to be of a higher order than that expressed in X.136.2.[147]

We have touched the height and depth of Vedic meditation, for all subsequent expressions are but variations on the theme so far expounded. The transcendent side of the vision or 'light beyond the darkness' recognised in Sūrya (Ṛgv. I.50.10 & Ath.v.VII.53.7), so finely sung in the Īśā Upaniṣad as the 'face of truth ... veiled by the effulgent chalice' which the 'only seer, deliverer, sun' is begged to remove so that the inner splendour may be known, for that 'divine man is I' (15 & 16) is rooted in the certainty of the divine immanence. Immanence and transcendence meet in man's recognition of oneness and his own intrinsic link with the cosmos and its heart. Such knowledge goes back to the Ṛgvedic affirmation of the all enfolding 'golden one', whether bird, ray, sun[148]—the *ātman* of what moves and moves not (1.70.2)[149] the herdsman of immortality (VI.7.7, and VI.9.3. *amṛtasya gopaḥ*). 'The wise one has arrayed himself in every form' sings the poet of Savitṛ (V.81.2), but equally of Agni,[150] and equally reminds us that all worlds are comprised in the solar god, Viṣṇu's three strides (I.154.2), all creatures rest in Savitṛ's lap (I.35.5).

No deeper depth can be reached by communion than this vision of oneness, of immanence, of all enfolding protection, no greater certainty can be attained of the everlasting presence, no more powerful knowledge can be bestowed by prayer—the certainty of the impossibility of falling out, or erring far away since all is in the one, the assurance of a divine ground to our being, the knowledge of a divine origin and therefore a divine return.

This is the *ṛṣis*' gift to the world, a prayer as great in its kind in point of visionary knowledge, poetic inspiration and uplifting yearning as any of the finest psalms of the Old Testament. That it has been misunderstood or missed by early Western scholarship is due more to our lack of insight than to any obscurity of Vedic language. Obscure some of the references definitely are, but the language on the whole is simple. The overwhelming impression is one of sunlight, radiant exaltation, of an elevating certainty of the divine ground on which all things are based, perhaps at times, on the one hand, somewhat naive to the sophisticated, modern, unbelieving mind, in its formulation, and on the other, obscure only because our minds work differently and can with difficulty find the key to a perfect understanding of ancient man's mythological thought and language. Between that language and our modern conceptions lies a gap which only a willingness to uncondition our minds and enter into a completely different mental attitude can bridge.

NOTES

1. *cf.* Ṛgv. II.21.7.
2. *yuje vāṃ brahma pūrvyaṃ namobhiḥ*. *cf.* III.2.14. To Agni the poets turn with homage *tam īmahe namasā*.
3. Other words are also used such as *uktha*, *śloka*, *sāman*, *ukta*, but the ones listed above are of a peculiar interest and importance.
4. For a discussion of *matis*, *manma*, *manīṣā* see L. Renou. 'Les pouvoirs de la parole dans le Ṛgveda, *Études véd pān*. I. fasc. 1, p. 1 ff. (1955).
5. *cf.* the Oriental hearing of quarter tones. Something of the ancient response to sound is still found in the reaction of Arabic audiences to readings from the Koran which, not through the meanings of words but their sounds, casts a spell over them. Likewise Gregorian chants affect those who are particularly sensitive to that kind of plainsong. *cf.* also the various effects various types of music have on various people.
6. *cf.* W. N. Brown. 'Theories of creation in the Rig Veda', J.A.O.S. **85,** 1, pp. 23–34 (1965): 'The close relation between ritual and magic leads to what is essentially an ascription of creative action to the power of words or sound. That is, the potency of words is considered to be the effective creative force. When the gods utter the names of things, at the time of the first sacrifice, these things come into existence (RV. 10.71.1; 10.82.3).'
7. St. John 1:1.
8. *cf.* Śrī Aurobindo: '... the Word is a power, the Word creates. For all creation is expression, everything exists already in the secret abode of the infinite, *guhā hitam* ... By expression we form, by affirmation we establish. As a power

f expression the word is termed *gih* or *vacas*; as a power of affirmation, *stoma*. In ther aspect it is named *manma* or *mantra*, expression of thought in mind, and ·*ahman*, expression of the heart or the soul,—for this seems to have been the ırlier sense of the word *brahman* . . .' *On the Veda* (Pondicherry, 1964) p. 284–5. *ee also* L. Renou, '*Les pouvoirs de la parole dans le Ṛgveda*', *Études véd. pān.* fasc. 1 (1955). 'Les spéculations védiques . . . reposent sur une sorte de primat e la parole . . . un mot tel que *vāc* n'est autre que l'équivalent de logos: c'est prototype de la notion d'*ātman-brahman*', p. 1.

9. I.164.45: *catvāri vāk parimitā padāni tāni vidur brāhmaṇā ye manīṣinaḥ uhā trīṇi nihitā nā ingayanti turīyaṃ vāco manuṣyā vadanti.* See also D. S. Ruegg. La spéculation linguistique dans le Véda' in *Contributions ā l'histoire de la hilosophie linguistique indienne* (Paris, 1959).

10. For a short discussion of the various meanings ascribed to this word see . Bergaigne, *Études sur le Lexique du Rig-Véda*, pp. 7–11 (Paris, 1884). Also . Renou, 'Les pouvoirs de la parole dans le Ṛgveda' *Etudes véd pān*, I, fasc. 1, p. 9–10 (1955).

11. The milch cow which the gods gave to the Aṅgirasāḥ (I.139.7) which they assed on to their descendants, is according to Bergaigne's interpretation, prayer. ee *La Religion Védique*, tome III, p. 95. In VIII.101.16, Aditi admits that smallinded mortals have turned to her, the arouser of speech and vision, as to a cow. Iere is a plain reference to the symbolic meaning of the cow. *cf.* VI.28.5 where he cows are the gods.

12. *akṣareṇa prati mima etām ṛtasya nābhau adhi sam punāmi.*

13. *ṛc* or *ṛk* connected with *arka* is according to Śrī Aurobindo the word consilered as a power or realisation in the illuminating consciousness.

14. *cf. svṛ* or *svar* 'to sound, resound, to sing, praise, to shine'; *svar*, ind. light, lustre, heaven'.

15. *cf.* D. S. Ruegg, *Contributions à l'histoire de la philosophie linguistique ndienne*. 'La spéculation linguistique dans le Véda' (Paris, 1959) and L. Renou, Les pouvoirs de la parole dans le Ṛgvéda', *Études véd. pān*, I, fasc. 1, pp. 6–7 1955) for a discussion of *arka*. 'Le mot *arka* . . . est ambigu entre les valeurs de 'lumière" et de "chant".' Also 'Les hymnes à l'Aurore du Ṛgvéda'. *Études véd. ān*, III, fasc. 4, p. 34 (1957) where he discusses the meaning of *arcanti* as 'they sing' with the possibility of 'they shine'. Also A. Bergaigne, *Études sur le lexique lu Rig-Véda*, pp. 82–3 (Paris, 1884), also p. 178 under *arka*: '. . . la racine du mot . . . a incontestablement les deux sens de "chanter" et de "briller".'

16. *Études sur le lexique du Rig-Véda*, p. 179 (Paris, 1884).

17. Both Agni (I.74.3; VI.16.14.48) and Soma (IX.89.7) as well as Indra are called Vṛtra slayer (*cf.* also the Aśvins called Vṛtra slayers VIII.8.9); they are the Inspirers, Agni and Soma exalting men to the light of Sūrya, Indra breaking through the stall of heaven and setting up the sun on high. *cf.* V.14.4 which is related of Agni but applies constantly to Indra.

18. *cf.* also VIII.6.11 'I beautify my songs with the ancient expression of thought (*pratnema manmanā giraḥ śuṃbhāmi*) even like Kaṅva whereby Indra himself gains vigour.'!

19. $\sqrt{man}$ to think. Monier Williams, dictionary gives the meaning as, thought, devotion, prayer, hymn, perception, understanding'.

20. Inspired insight is also referred to the action of Soma (VI.47.3). *cf.* IX.95.1. and IX.96.5 & 10. He is also the lord of song (IX.99.6) since his action is exalting (*cf.* IX.103.4).

21. *patango vācaṃ manasā bibharti tāṃ gandharvo avardad garbhe antaḥ taṃ dyotamānāṃ svaryaṃ manīṣām ṛtasya pade kavayo ni panti.*

22. A. A. Macdonell and A. B. Keith. *Vedic Index of Names and Subjects*, p. 213 (London, 1912).

23. On the subject of the wheel *cakra* see J. Gonda 'Ancient Indian kingshi in *Numen*, **4,** 2, pp. 144–9 (April 1957). 'It is . . . beyond doubt that the wheel h already at an early period, what is sometimes incorrectly qualified as a met phorical or symbolical value, that is to say that it involved conceptions of a ritu or magico-religious order'. p. 145.

24. *cf.* the cows which are rescued from the dark cave (IV.1.13) and Chāndog Upaniṣad 'that which existeth within mankind is of a truth the space (*ākāś* which existed [sic] within the heart. It is omnipresent and eternal. He who knowe this attains eternal and all sufficient treasures'. III.12.8. Trans. by Rajendra Mitra (Calcutta, 1862).

25. *cf.* X.13.3: 'I purify in the hub of truth.' *ṛtasya nābham adhi saṃ punān*

26. It is only recently that the notion of colour in music has been given cons deration. The blend of colour and sound however is not possible at the physic level, but *synaesthesia* as 'intersensorial transfer' is a common tool among poet visionaries, etc.

27. Two meanings are ascribed to *dīdhiti* ($\sqrt{}$*dīdhī* to shine); brightness, sple dour and religious devotion, inspiration—the Vedic idea of shining inspiratio *cf.* also IX.102.8 where Soma is begged to speed on the inspiration of truth, the splendour of the ritual *ṛtasya dīdhitim.*

28. *śukra* in conjunction with *manīṣā* is described by L. Renou as "claire" . . c'est a dire "pure" (de tout élément incorrect, avec nuance religieuse). *Étud Védiques et Pāṇinéennes*, IV, p. 92 & V, p. 38 (Paris, 1955–.).

29. *cf.* also *dhiyaṃ ghṛtācīm* (I.2.7) and *cf. śukrebhir akṣabhiḥ* (IX.102. 'with the radiant eyes' of Soma who is asked to open the heaven's pen.

30. V.45.11: *dhiyam vo apsu dadhiṣe svarṣām. cf.* I.61.3.

31. X.114.1: *divas payo didhiṣāno aveṣan vidur devāḥ saha sāmānam arkan cf.* VIII.32.27: 'sing forth the prayer which gods have given' *devattaṃ brahm gāyata. cf.* also I.37.4.

32. *cf.* VIII.6.28: *dhiyā vipro ajāyata.*

33. *cf.* I.61.16: *dhiyā vasur jagamyāt. cf.* also I.61.3.

34. *vardhantu no giraḥ*, VIII.44.19. *cf.* also X.49.1 and V.17.3.

35. *añjantu* VI.69.3. *cf.* also V.73.10 and X.65.14 where the poet wishes tha the gods might enjoy his heaven-grounded songs, his prayer, his eloquenc (*svargiro brahma sūktam*).

36. V.13.1: *arcantas tvā havamahe arcantaḥ sam idhīmahi agne arcanta utay*

37. I.60.3: *hṛda ā jāyamānaṃ asmat sukīrtiḥ. cf.* also V.11.5.

38. III.34.1: *brahmajūtas tanvā vāvṛdhāno bhūri dātraḥ*
X.50.4: *bhuvas tvam indra brahmaṇā mahān. cf.* VIII.6.21.

39. *cf.* VI.23.6: *brahmāṇi hi cakṛṣe vardhanāni tavat.*

40. *cf.* also IV.20.9; 21.1; VII.93; VI.19.10; VIII.6.23, etc.

41. There is also the imploration for mercy which characterises the hymn to Varuṇa and some addressed to other gods (*cf.* Rudra, Agni). *cf.* I.25.3: *mṛlīkāya te mano rathīr aśvaṃ na samditaṃ gīrbhir varuṇa sīmahi.* 'For the sak of thy compassion O Varuṇa, with songs let us bind thy mind even as the chario teer his tied up steed.'

See also C. W. J. van der Linden. *The concept of deva in the Vedic age* (Utrech 1954): '. . . sacrifice has a power over the devas and they themselves are dependen on this sacrifice . . . *cf.* I.164.50; X.90.16; 124.6' (p. 25).

42. Śrī Aurobindo defines the *mantra* as: 'Expression of thought in mind' but it '. . . is not a creation of the intellect. To be sacred and effective it must com as an inspiration from *ṛtam*—the Truth-plane'. *Śrī Aurobindo's Vedic Glossary* Compiled by A. B. Purani, p. 69–70 (Pondicherry, 1962). This gives the reasor for the great emphasis on the *mantra* in Vedic meditation: it wells up from the

depths of the heart and is thus an expression of truth.

43. *cf.* I.67.2: *hṛdā yat taṣṭān mantrān aśamsan.*

44. *mantraṃ vadati ukthyaṃ yasmin . . . devā okānsi cakrire.*

45. *cf.* I.164.34: 'I ask of lofty heaven where dwells the word'.

46. *cf.* VII.7.6: *ete dyumnebhir viśvam ā atiranta mantraṃ ye vā araṃ naryā atakṣan pra ye viśas tiranta śroṣamāṇā ā ye me asya dīdhayan ṛtasya.*

47. This stanza shows a remarkable wish. The seven *ṛṣis* are requested by the bards: 'May we give birth, through the mother, Dawn, to pious men. May we be sons of heaven and with our shining forth (*śucantaḥ*) may we break through the treasure-holding rock'. We suspect that the engendering referred to, specifically described as taking place through Dawn, is nothing other than *paraṃparā*, the handing down from *ṛṣi* to *ṛṣi* or priest to priest of the secret knowledge. This is emphasized by the request 'may we be sons of heaven', 'may we break through the rock' of matter, i.e. may we be worthy of receiving the divine wisdom and passing it on to later generations.

48. The translation of *dhīmahi* as 'meditate' is according to the traditional Indian idea. Originally, according to J. Gonda the meaning was no doubt 'receive'. In *The Vision of the Vedic Poets* he writes: 'The injunctive *dhīmahi* being indifferent as to mood and tense should, also in connection with the following subjunctive, be best translated by an expression stating a wish or hope: "we should like (we hope) to obtain that desirable (excellent) radiance (light, brightness) of savitar (the "generator" or divine "stimulator" the light of heaven in its dynamic moving and mobile aspect, the divine "motor" which impels the sun with which it is sometimes identified 5.81.2–3), who will . . . excite (stimulate, inspire, urge on) our "visions".' (p. 98).

49. *acikitvān cikituṣaś cid atra kavīn pṛchāmi vidmane na vidvān.*

50. *cf.* V.22.1: light purifies (*arca pāvaka śociṣe*).

51. *cf.* V.22.3: *cikitvinmanas*, IV.10.2, I.96.1, I.127.9, I.128.4, I.77.3 and VI.7.4. See also VIII.95.5.

52. *cf.* I.154.5 and X.56.2 *divīva jyotiḥ svam ā mimīyaḥ.*

53. *cf.* VI.9.3 where Agni is called the herdsman of immortality *amṛtasya gopaḥ.*

54. *cf.* VIII.100.9: *samudre antar śayata udnā vajro abhīvṛtaḥ bharanty asmai samyataḥ puraḥ prasravaṇā balim.* See p. 31 for the myth of the bolt in the ocean.

55. *suparṇaṃ viprāḥ kavayo vacobhir ekaṃ santaṃ bahudhā kalpayanti.*

56. *cf.* Agni in VII.13.3 and Varuṇa I.105.15.

57. *cf.* Indra VII.97.3; Agni VII.13.3.

58. *cf.* VII.66.12, 36.1; V.81.1; III.39.1; X.189.3; I.31.5.

59. *cf.* also III.3.3: Sages glorify Agni with their thoughts *cittibhiḥ.*

60. This verse could be translated thus: when may that principle of thy godhood (*devasya cetanam*) be made unceasingly manifest.

61. *parā me yanti dhītayo gāvo na gavyūtīr anu icchantiḥ*, I.25.16.

62. *cf.* I.164.37: *na vi jānāmi yad iva idam asmi niṇyaḥ saṃnaddho manasā carāmi yadā mā ā agan prathamajā ṛtasya ād id vāco aśnuve bhāgam asyāḥ*, which Griffith renders thus: 'What thing I truly am I know not clearly; mysterious, fettered in my mind I wander. When the first-born of holy Law approached me, then of this speech I first obtain a portion.'

63. *cf.* VI.28.5: 'I long for Indra with my heart and mind.' *ichāmi id hṛdā manasā cid indram.*

64. I.61.2: *indrayā hṛdā manasā manīṣā pratnāya patye dhiyo marśanta.*

65. *vi cakṣur vi idaṃ jyotir hṛdaye ā hitaṃ yat*, VI.9.6. *cf.* Yoga-sūtra III.35. *hṛdaye citta saṃvit.*

66. Many a time we notice that the poet is not quite sure what is all this about!

cf. I.164.37 quoted in fn. 62. *cf.* also the different nuances of the various Sanskri words usually lost in translation but surely denoting extreme subtlety of though on the part of the poets: *citti, cetas, dhī, dhiṣaṇa, dhiṣṇya, matis, manīsā* (whicl could be the Vedic equivalent to *buddhi*), *manma, manyu, codayanmati, cikitvin manas, kratu.* The bringing to birth of the sun within the human being changes hi state from that of unillumined mind to that of illumined mind and thus to that of wise man. This is the gist of the Vedic doctrine.

67. J. Gonda defines *kratu* thus: '. . . a kind of effective mental power o intelligence, mental energy and determination, which enables its possessor t have solutions for preponderantely practical difficulties . . .' *op. cit.* p. 18 The fact that this intelligent apprehension is stated to be placed in the heart b the divine powers means that it combines the ratiocinative as well as emotiona intuitive aspects of the human psyche and that therefore *kratu* means far mor than intelligence in our ordinary sense of the word. *cf.* Ṛgv. VIII.100.5. See als *Epithets in the Ṛgveda* ('*S*-Gravenhage, 1959) by the same author, p. 37 ff. Sı Aurobindo has this to say on kratu: '*Kratu* means, in Sanskrit, work or actio and especially work in the sense of the sacrifice but it means also power or strengt (the Greek *kratos*) effective of action. Psychologically this power effective o action is the will. The word may also mean mind or intellect and Sayana admit thought or knowledge as a possible sense for *kratu*.' *On the Veda*, p. 67 (Pondi cherry, 1964).

68. A. B. Keith writes: 'It is probable that the conception later prevalent tha the mind has its abode in the heart was already developed.' *op. cit.* p. 404.

69. *cf.* X.47.7 and VII.101.5 *cf.* also VII.86.2.

70. *samyak sravanti sarito na dhenā antar hṛdā manasā pūyamānāḥ. cf.* Ṛgv I.60.3 *taṃ navyasī hṛda ā jāyamānam asmat sukīrtir madhujihvam asyāḥ*, wher the new heart-felt praise is hoped to reach the honey-tongued god.

71. *hṛdā taṣṭeṣu manaso javeṣu yad brāhmaṇāḥ samyajante sakhāyaḥ atra aha tvaṃ vi jahur vedyābhir īha brahmāṇo vi caranti u tve.* X.71.8.

72. *cf.* IV.43.1, VII.86.8.

73. *cf.* VIII.43.31.

74. IV.11.3: *tvad agne kāvyā tvan manīṣāḥ.*

75. III.26.8: *hṛdā matiṃ jyotir anu prajānan.*

76. I.67.2: *hṛdā yat taṣṭān mantrān aśamsan.*

77. *ekaḥ samudro dharuṇo rayīṇām asmad hṛdo bhūrijanmā vi caṣṭe*, X.5.1.

78. *cf.* Ṛgv. VI.47.3: *maṇīṣām uśatīm ajīgaḥ.*

79. *cf.* I.179.5: *hṛtsu pītam*, and X.25.2 'In all thy conditions, Soma, thou art heart-touching' (*hṛdispṛśas ta āsate viśveṣu soma dhāmasu*).

80. With this idea should be compared I.164.21 where the wise herdsman of immortality has entered into the 'simple' (*pāka*) seer and IV.5.2 where the deity vouchsafes hidden knowledge on to the simple mortal.

81. *cf.* Bhagavad-Gītā. 'Having pervaded this vast universe with a fragment of myself, I remain.' 10:42.

82. *cf.* the two verbs $\sqrt{svar}$ to sound and $\sqrt{svar}$ to shine and the fact that to the *ṛṣi* that which is sounded shines and is made visible. They 'saw' the Veda.

83. *cf.* VII.77.3; I.115.1; I.50.6; VII.76.1; X.37.1, etc.

84. Sūrya is generated by Soma (IX.96.5)—Soma grants exaltation and inner perception as will be seen, hence generates Sūrya; by Indra-Viṣṇu (VII.99.4); by Agni (X.3.2) etc. He is lifted up from his ocean dwelling (X.72.7) and set on high in the sky (X.88.11), etc.

85. Matthew V. 45.

86. XIII.1.45:

sūryo dyāṃ sūryaḥ pṛthivīṃ sūrya āpo 'ti paśyati
sūryo bhūtasya ekaṃ cakṣurā ruroha divaṃ mahīm.

cf. Agni who in Ṛgv. I.94.7 sees even through night's gloom (*rātryāścid andho ati . . . paśyasi*).

87. *cf.* Agni's 'bringing to birth within the heart a thought as light', *hṛdā matiṃ jyotir anu prajānan*, III.26.8, and the function of the heart in the Ṛgveda.

88. O.S.T. vol. V, p. 159 (London, 1868).

89. *The Religion and Philosophy of the Veda and Upanishads*. Harvard Oriental Series. **31,** p. 105 (Cambridge, Mass., 1925).

90. *La Religion Védique*. (Paris, 1878) 1, p. 82. (École des Hautes Études. Bibliothèque. fasc. 35) Trans. J. M.

91. Similarly the eye of the dead goes to the sun (X.16.3) the outer connection between the sun and the eye being found in their power to make all things visible.

92. *op. cit.*

93. *vi* +$\sqrt{}$*cakṣ* 'to appear, shine, be conspicuous, splendid, clear-sighted.'

94. p. 193. *cf.* also p. 274 and 31.

95. They both obey, and are lords of, its statutes. *cf.* Mitra-Varuṇa 'lords of the light of truth' (*ṛtasya jyotiṣas pati*, I.23.5) i.e., as this may be interpreted, 'lords of enlightenment'.

96. *cf.* VIII.18.15, where the gods are said to be on the side of the simple, guileless or sincere ones, *pākatrā*, and to know in their hearts who is honest or not.

97. *cf.* *cakṣur adabdham*, that infallible eye of Mitra-Varuṇa, VI.51.1.

98. *cf.* *adābhyaḥ*, and *adabdhāsaḥ* in VIII.67.13. *cf.* also Ath.v. XVII.1.12, *adabdhena brahmaṇā vāvṛdhānaḥ*.

99. VII.61.1: *sa manyuṃ martyeṣvā ciketa*. *manyu* is given in Monier-Williams as 'spirit, mind, mood, mettle', also 'passion and wrath'.

100. *cf.* V.48.5: *na tasya vidma puruṣatvatā vayam*, 'nought by our human nature do we know of him' (Varuṇa).

101. See J. Gonda's *Loka. World and Heaven in the Veda* (Amsterdam, 1966) for further elucidations.

102. *cf.* I.23.22 & 25.1.

103. *cf.* *kratunā paśyate* IX.71.9.

104. Indra is likewise called *codayanmati* VIII.46.9.

105. *cf.* the heavenly eye *divyaṃ cakṣuḥ* to which man could have access to perceive spiritual truth in Arjuna's vision (Bhagavad-Gītā XL.8).

106. For a comment on certain functions of the eye as expressed in the word *cakṣas* see J. Gonda's *The Vision of the Vedic Poets*, p. 33.

107. *cf.* VI.51.2: *veda yas trīṇi vidathāni eṣāṃ devānāṃ janma sanutarā ca vipraḥ ṛju marteṣu vṛjinā ca paśyann abhi caṣṭe sūro arya evān*, 'where the inspired sage, the sun, who knows all orders and generations of the gods, beholds the righteous and unrighteous among humans and regards the pious with favour'.

108. *cf.* I.16.1; I.110.4: *ṛbhavaḥ sūracakṣasaḥ*.

109. *op. cit.* p. 30. J. Gonda does not agree with Grassmann's translation of it as 'Himmelslicht schauend' or Monier-Williams' 'seeing light or the sun', but explains it as 'seeing by (means of) the light of heaven (the sun)'. He brings forward an analogical example '*namovṛdh*' 'growing by adoration'. This would confirm the present interpretation of the sun as spiritual insight. *cf.* *mano-yuj* yoked at will; *yāma hū* called by entreaties. *cf.* also *ṛtāvṛdh* which may be translated as 'increasing *ṛta*' and equally as 'increasing by the ṛta.'

110. *cf.* I.44.9, VII.37.2.

111. For *svar* and *svardṛś* see also L. Renou, *Sur quelques mots du Ṛgveda*, J.A.O.S. **85**, 1, pp. 83–84 (1965).

112. *cf.* V.63.2: *sam rājāv asya bhuvanasya rājasthe mitrāvaruṇā vidathe svardṛśā*. 'Together ye rule in council as kings of this world O Mitra-Varuṇa, ye heaven-beholders'.

113. *cf.* II.23.15: *dyumad vibhāti kratumaj janeṣu yad dīdayac chavasā*. *cf.* also

dyumnaṃ svarvat VI.19.9 and VI.35.2 and VIII.19.15.

114. *cf.* the transfiguration: Math. 17.2: 'And his face did shine as the sun and his raiment was white as the light.'

115. Such a declaration constitutes one of the nearest of Ṛgvedic approaches to Yoga-Sūtra III.3.

116. *cf.* VIII.101.14: *prajā ha tisro aty āyam īyur ni anyā arkam abhito viviśre.* 'Three generations indeed have gone into the beyond. Others have entered into the presence of the sun'.

117. *cf.* X.156.4 where Agni makes the sun ascend into the sky.

118. *agner anīkaṃ bṛhataḥ saparyaṃ divi śukraṃ yajataṃ sūryasya.*

119. *ṛtasya suci darśatam anīkam.* Here again we observe how all phenomena are rooted in that ultimate abstract notion of truth to which even the gods are subservient.

120. This is J. Gonda's tentative interpretation. *op. cit.* p. 69. The vast improvement in the understanding of this stanza is noticeable in his translation as against Griffith's, but we do not quite agree with J. Gonda's point of view that the seers are not certain as to whether they owe their privilege of seership to their *dhiyaḥ* and mind or to the 'special visual faculty granted by Soma'. *dibhiś cana manasā* brings out the fact that they know this is a loftier vision than the usual one caused by *dhī* or *manas.*

121. *cf.* IX.65.1 where the sun is identified with Soma and IX.101.7, 57.2.

122. This stanza is thought to be spoken by Agni. But as Agni abides in every human being (*cf.* Ṛgv. I.67.2 & X.45.1; I.31.7 & IV.1.20) he, as the inner sun, causes the second birth. *cf.* Agni's epithet Vaiśvānara 'who belongs to all men'.

123. *cf.* I.109.7: 'these are the sun-beams by means of which our fathers were made one'. *ime nu te raśmayaḥ sūryasya yebhiḥ sapitvaṃ pitaro na āsan. cf.* Ath.v. 16.9.3.

124. The word *arka* is here tentatively translated as the 'sun' for want of a precise word to express its full meaning. *cf.* the section on mantric meditation.

125. *See* his 'Sur la notion de brahman,' *Journal Asiatique* (Paris, 1949) tome 237, pp. 7–46.

126. See *Sitzungsberichte d. böhmischen Gesell. d. Wiss.* 1885.

In accordance with the six vedāṅgas, we do not deny a possible astronomical meaning. But the verse has definitely an underlying spiritual meaning brought out by the words *turīyeṇa brahmaṇā.* For the astronomical aspect see V. G. Rahurkar's 'The solar eclipse in the Ṛgveda', in the *Poona Orientalist,* **23,** 1 (January, 1958).

127. *Journal Asiatique* (Paris), ser. 8, tome VI.1885, 'M. Ludwig et la chronologie du Rig-Véda.' p. 372 ff., especially p. 383.

128. See also W. D. Whitney, J.A.O.S. **13,** p. lxi & ff., 'On Professor Ludwig's views respecting total Eclipses of the Sun as noticed in the Rig-Veda.'

129. *cf.* also Ṛgv. I.50.10 where Sūrya is reached beyond the darkness, and III.39.5 where Indra seeking the cattle on his knees *abhijñu* discovers the 'sun lying hidden in the darkness'.

130. Bergaigne, *Religion Védique.* II, p. 467 suggests that Atri is really in origin Agni (*√ad to devour*). If this be correct we have again an example of a myth woven around the central idea of the divine flame finding the sun of transcendence or truth.

131. *cf.* Ṛgv. V.40.5 where the verse perfectly lends itself to the eclipse thesis. This seems to us typical of Vedic ambiguity, a different, spiritual meaning hidden behind a natural phenomenon.

132. *dhītī vā ye anayan vāco agraṃ manasā vā ye vadann ṛtāni*
tṛtīyena brahmaṇā vavṛdhānās turīyeṇā amanvata nāma dhenoḥ.

J. Gonda translates as follows: 'they who by vision led the beginning of speech

. . . or they who by mind . . . spoke truths . . . having increased by the third brahman, perceived with the fourth the name of the milch-cow.' (*op. cit.* p. 228).

133. See *Atharvaveda Saṃhitā* Translated . . . by W. D. Whitney, Cambridge, Mass., 1905, p. 389 (Harvard Oriental Series, vol. 7).

134. The milch cow which the gods gave to the patriarchs is according to A. Bergaigne's interpretation 'prayer'. (*Religion Védique*. vol. III, p. 95, Paris, 1883.) The gods generated it as the divine speech (*devīṃ vācam ajanayanta*, VIII.100.11). However, in VIII.101.16 it is identified with Aditi and described as arousing speech and vision in mortal man, these being the end or by-product of the *brahman*. It is thus a many-sided symbolic expression, varying in exact meaning in various contexts, but here referring to the fourth state of consciousness, the treasure hidden in darkness, the mystery the probing of which gives the right to formulate the truth.

135. *op. cit.* p. 11. See also note 24 on p. 23.

136. In this verse X.67.1 Ayasya after discovering the seven-headed thought born of truth 'engendered the fourth eulogy'—(*turīyam . . . janayad . . . uktham*). See J. Gonda's quite different interpretation: *The Vision of the Vedic Poets* pp. 77–8 (The Hague, 1963).

137. See e.g. Maitrī Up. 6.7, 16 & 17 and the whole of sect. 7.

138. *cf.* Maitrī Up. 'That which is non-thought, which stands in the midst of thought, the unthinkable supreme mystery. Thereon let one concentrate his thought and the subtle body too, without support' (6.19). With this compare Ath.v. IV.1.1, quoted on p. 98.

139. *op. cit.* p. 357.

140. *cf.* Śrī Aurobindo, *The Life Divine*. Śrī Aurobindo Library Inc. (New York, 1951). 'For at the gates of the Transcendent stands that mere and perfect Spirit described in the Upanishads, luminous, pure, sustaining the world but inactive in it, without sinews of energy, without flaw of duality, without scar of division, unique, identical, free from all appearance of relation and of multiplicity,—the pure Self of the Adwaitins, the inactive Brahman, the transcendent Silence' (chapter 3, p. 23).

141. They were meaningless to W. D. Whitney. See 'The Cosmogonic Hymn, Ṛgveda X.129.' p. xl J.A.O.S. (May, 1882).

142. For an analysis of this hymn see G. Feuerstein and J. Miller, *A Reappraisal of Yoga*; *essays in Indian philosophy* (London, 1971).

143. *yasya chāyā amṛtaṃ yasya mṛtyuḥ*.

144. *cf.* also Ath.v. IV.16.2 & 5: 'What two, sitting down together, talk, king Varuṇa, as third, knows that' (2); 'All this king Varuṇa beholds—what is between the two firmaments, what beyond; numbered of him are winkings of people' (5) (Whitney's translation). *cf.* N.T. Math. 10.30 and Luke 12.7.

145. *pra yat pituḥ paramān nīyate*.

146. *tad eva artha mātra nirbhāṣāṃ svarūpa sūnyam iva samādhiḥ* (*Yoga-sūtra*, III.3).

147. 'The wind-girt sages have donned the yellow robe of dust. Along the wind's course they glide when the gods have penetrated them.' X.136.2.

148. The sun is a bird (Ṛgv. X.189.3, IV.5.8), a flying falcon (Ṛgv. VII.63.5) or ruddy bird *arusaḥ suparṇaḥ* (Ṛgv. V.47.3) or bird and bull and ocean (V.47.3) or as here *pataṅga*, X.177.1 or *suparṇa* X.114.4.

In VIII.69.7 the sun is *bradhna*, the ruddy or yellowish or mighty. The word used in VIII.101.14 and III.26.8 is *arka*. See explanatory notes to *arka* on p. 68. *arka* developed the meaning of 'sun' in classical Sanskrit.

149. I.70.2: *garbhaś ca sthātāṃ garbhaś carathāṃ*. *cf.* VII.101.4 addressed to Parjanya.

150. *cf.* the magnificent hymn to Agni II.1.

PART III

Vedic Prayer and Western Scholarship

In the light of these investigations it is not possible to subscribe to any of the past scholars' verdicts on Vedic prayer. A. B. Keith's remarks are far too sweeping and completely lacking in depth of insight:

> It is undeniable that the prayers are nearly always for material objects, and that the occasional expressions of desire for spiritual goods are in the extreme exceptional . . . The hymns often remind the god [sic] of their ancestral connexion and in the pride of their production and of the value which the gods must attach to them are extremely naive.[1]

If we remember that most of the hymns are the final stage or voiced expression of a long process of visual meditation culminating in communion or deep abstraction, that their essence is the poet's own divination, their form his own fashioning, that the words, their meaning, the rhythm, all play a most important part in the final production, and all are more than partially lost on alien ears, we shall not find anything naive in the bards' pride of workmanship. Moreover, to judge the poet's unquestioning belief (there are indeed a few traces of scepticism) against the modern sceptical attitude as naive, can have no place in this book since we are examining the religious ideas as they stood in the eyes of their protagonists, not as they appear to a much later, sophisticated, unbelieving generation. Furthermore, we should always keep in mind that the bards of Vedic India *believed* because they *saw* because their psycho-mental constitution was different from ours. They wielded their thought power to visualisation. On this seership rests the whole fabric of Vedic doctrine and subsequent Hindu philosophy. It matters not whether the gods are named in one age Varuṇa, Rudra, Indra and disappear in the next to reappear under different names, Śiva, Brahma, etc.; the idea of active agents in the cosmos remains one and the same, the name, form, attribute, function may vary. Let us also recall that behind this multiplicity of cosmic agents which bewilders the simple minded, ever stood the Eternal One, *tad*, 'That' which breathed breathlessly by Itself before this universe and its multiplicity of gods, men and creatures appeared. This is the immovable basis on which manifestation is projected and this is a Vedic concept arrived at through contemplation.[2]

The charge that the prayers are mostly for material benefits also evidences lack of insight into Vedic imagery and want of analysis. Sufficient examples have already been brought forward, we hope, to show that the great boon desired of the gods by the poets was spiritual enlightenment. The desire of many of the prayers is essentially for light, wisdom, heaven, bliss, immortality, and even those verses which ask for 'kine', 'sons' and 'wealth' are susceptible of a dual meaning. Uninspired translations, wholly missing the point of Vedic imagery which though it may appear mixed up yet shows consistency in significance, have given countenance to the erroneous idea that the Vedic *ṛṣis* prayed only for material prosperity. Their *solar* language rendered their thought unintelligible. However the charge, as laid by Keith, ought to be met with further investigations.

All the gods are lords of wealth, they are *vasu*, the good, beneficent, bright gods, rich in bounties of all kinds, for all things in nature are their gifts, rich in light, in knowledge, in blessings. Through their action all things work according to the law (*ṛta*) and he who lives according to the *ṛta* will receive the favour of the gods. Mortals are exhorted to disregard (*pari mamanyāt*) material wealth (*draviṇa*) and to desire to win the path to truth through obeisance, to commune with their deeper insight with mind intent on grasping the light from their own superior discernment (X.31.2).[3]

Considering groups of gods separately, we find that the wealth generally attributed to them may fall under two headings: glory, whether expressed as splendour, richness, brightness, and might or courage usually expressed as *vāja*[4] (also *ūrja* and *vīrya*) which itself is closely connected with glory.

The Aśvins or twin gods of the dawn are lords of splendour (*śubhaspatī* I.120.6 & VIII.22.4) whose treasure or bounty is that vigorous quality which means courage and heroism (*vājaratnā* IV.43.7 & 44; *vājinīvasū* VIII.8.10 & 22.7. *cf.* VIII.35.11 *ūrjaṃ no dhattam*). Indeed the Aśvins are the gods of succour par excellence who are called upon in moments of danger and always perform heroic deeds. They bestow all sorts of blessings (VII.70.1 *viśvavārā*) on their devotees. They are rich in the sun, says VII.68.3 (*sūryāvasū*). In the light of the explanation given in this chapter as to the intrinsic meaning of the Vedic sun there should be no difficulty in understanding the significance of the sun with regard to the Aśvins' wealth. An interesting verse (I.117.21) leaves a wide margin of interpretation: through the plough and the sowing, the Aśvins gave food to man, through the blasting away of the demon they gave the wide light to the Aryans, in other words, they provided by their examples and teachings for the physical and spiritual well-being of the people. Their wealth in cattle and horses (VII.71.1 & 72.1 etc.) which belong to the celestial realm may be the Vedic metaphor for light and energy (*go* in the plural meaning rays of light) which would agree with the constant emphasis laid upon the solar brightness (or enlightenment) and manliness, vigour or courage[5] which characterise the gifts of these gods. Through the Aśvins' aid men's thoughts are directed to good deeds (I.112.2 *dhiyo 'vathaḥ karmann iṣṭaye*).

With regard to valour the Maruts, commonly considered the storm gods, stand in a similar position to the Aśvins, if not in an even stronger one. Most of the prayers to the Maruts who are 'all possessing in wealth' (I.64.10 *viśvavedaso rayibhiḥ*) and peerless in courage (*taviṣībhiḥ*) are for mighty power, and those who invoke them surpass all others in vigour. (*cf.* I.64.13,14.15). They themselves are unlimited in their might (*apāro mahimā*) and towering strength (*vṛddhaśavasas*) (V.87.6), they are sure friends of adamant standing (V.52.2). All the hymns addressed to these heroes of the Vedic pantheon show the utmost admiration for their power and beauty—possibly as expressed in the storm, lightning and thunder. We find here evidence of the *ṛṣis*' own mastery of descriptive language. But in the midst of this array of might and warlike valour as well as joyous wonder at, and enjoyment of, nature's terrifying phenomena, a reminder startles us and sets us realising that this power so much requested has its spiritual aspect and that it is connected with the *brahman*, itself the greatest power on which the human being can draw:

Give us O Maruts that outreaching winged-stallion as a chariot, daily stimulating prayer; that ambrosial reward for your praisers in our holy-grounds and for your singer flawless wisdom and unconquerable might. (II.34.7).[6]

The sun-eyed Ṛbhus are equally rich in the treasure of *vāja* (IV.35.5 *vājaratnāḥ*). Bards are invited to drink with the treasure-bestowing Ṛbhus.[7] The same imagery of cattle (*go*) and emphasis on vigour (*vāja*) are found in descriptions of the Ṛbhus' wealth—the boon begged of them (IV.34.11) (*ratnadheyāya*). They are rich in kine (*gomantam* or rays of light), in vigour (*vājavantam*), in hero-power (*suvīram*), in food (*purukṣum*); they possess all manner of blessings (*vasumantam* IV.34.10). Again, since they are conversant with all human needs and desires (IV.36.8), they are asked to 'fashion' (*takṣata*) for men that splendid vigour (*dyumantaṃ vājam*), that mightiest courage (*vṛṣaśuṣmam uttamam*) that energy (*vayas*) which constitutes their fortune (*rayim*).

The Ṛgveda gives voice to many a message, but that of courage and heroism is certainly of outstanding importance and heralds Kriṣṇa's command to Arjuna in the Bhagavad-Gītā: Stand up and fight, and in more recent times, the mighty work of Acharia Pranavananda who sought to restore to India's youth the ancient valour and heroism in selfless work. Sloth, timidity, lack of purpose, inertia, laziness, despondency, can find no room in the Vedic outlook and the Vedic code of morals.

The Ṛbhus are perfect examples of courageous activity, of ingenuity of mind and artistic skill. These, we are repeatedly told, won them the boon of immortality (*cf.* IV.33.4 & I.110.3–6). They are asked for blessings (*vasūni*) to be granted in the third libation (*tṛtīye* . . . *savane*) which is offered them (IV.33.11), this same libation 'treasure-bestowing' (*ratnadheyam*) which, by their skilfulness (*svapasyā*), they performed (IV.35.9). Is it to be understood that in this third outpouring, taking place in the sacrifical rite, they won a certain boon which their descendants are now asking the Ṛbhus to vouchsafe to them? This treasure seems, to all appearances, to be the ecstasy of exaltation which accompanies the drinking of Soma and made the bards exclaim 'we have seen the gods', 'we have become immortal' (VIII.48.3). Men offer up the soma, the Ṛbhus give in return the ecstasy.

Looking at indivual gods we find the same emphasis being laid upon a wealth which is not purely of a material type. The bards pray to Indra the lord of riches,[8] the ram, knower or finder of heaven (I.52.1 *meṣam* . . . *svarvidam*) protector of the weak.[9] He is the all powerful one who confers wealth of thought,[10] who is begged to bestow that thought vision duly elaborated with beauty.[11] They pray for that bright or resplendent wealth which is heaven-finding or heaven-bestowing[12] and is his to give. Incidentally, this verse throws quite a clear light on what the wealth is about. Similarly they pray for those 'riches of his, nourishment plenteous, virile, fit for men, profuse, ageless, celestial' (VI.22.3). We may ask, what kind of food is that which is fit for men (*puruvīra nṛvat*) and also without age (*ajara*) and heaven-finding (*svarvat*)? Heaven, however, is not easy to gain. The coveted ecstasy which shatters every kind of constriction[13] demands those fearless qualities (VIII.46.7) which win heaven as though through heroic deeds.[14]

Present in Indra are all those characteristics of valour, courage, heroism summed up as fearless (VIII.46.7 *viśvā abhīravaḥ*) which are the hallmark of manliness and form the constant petition of, and the ideal held up to, Vedic man. We are reminded of the Christian tenet that the kingdom of heaven suffereth violence. Indra leads his devotee to that wide world (*uruṃ lokam*) full of splendour, the kingdom of heaven, to the fearless light which means freedom from the shackles of mortality, the world encompassed by Indra's mighty arms: 'Lead us . . . to heavenly light (*svarvaj*), the fearless light (*jyotir abhayam*), to well-being (*svasti*) that we may find protection in the shelter of thine ample arms' (VI.47.8).[15] This demands that vigour of spirit so typical of Indra and his band of Maruts, and courage or heroic power (*suvīrya*) which in VIII.3.9 is identified with *brahman*: 'I implore of thee that blessed heroic power (*suvīryam*) that *brahman*' (*tad brahma*). Hence that wealth destructive (*prabhangam*) of evil-minded people (*durmatīnām*) is asked of Indra the thought bestirrer (*codayanmati* VIII.46.19).

Likewise Soma, guardian of the community, possessor of heaven and the waters [of life] (*svarṣām apsāṃ vṛjanasya gopām*, I.91.21), is a lord of valour (*īśiṣe vīryasya* I.91.23) and is asked for a share of his riches (*rāyo bhagam* I.91.23). 'Bring us that resplendent courage, heaven finding'.[16] Through his much desired and prolific juice[17] abundance reaches out to the worshipper. What is that abundance? The perfect state of being, denoted by words such as *ajiti* and *ahati* (a state of being uninjured) in IX.96.4 which is being asked of the rich god, should give a clue as to the trend of the bard's thought. It implies wholeness and well-being or prosperity (*svasti*). These, coupled with the very word *sarvata* (wholeness) itself (IX.96.4)[18] point to a certain psychological state of fullness.

The *cow* and the *fleet steed*, the gifts of Soma (I.91.20), are as we have seen, capable of a dual meaning. The same verse lists as further petitions those manly actions (*vīraṃ karmaṇyam*) as are worthy of the home, the religious assembly, the council, and worthy of a father—noble riches indeed.[19] Soma's blessings are described in VIII.79. 2–5: he covers nakedness, makes the blind see, the lame walk, etc. His drops, in their exhilaration (*matsarāsaḥ*), bestow intuitive perception (*manīṣiṇaḥ*) and heavenly light (*svarvidaḥ*: IX.107.14. *cf.* IX.21.1). They find for man the light of heaven for his are the eyes that grant illumination (*cf.* I.139.2 & VIII.48.3). 'Like kindled fire' begs the poet of Soma 'inflame me; illumine me; make us more than *vasu* (√*vas* to shine)' (VIII.48.6). 'In thine exaltation', the verse goes on, 'I consider myself wealthy' (*revān*).

Men call on Agni who shines with bounties as heaven's envoy (X.3.2: *vasubhir vi bhāti*) to be the bearer of their gifts to the gods (I.45.6). What are these? They form part of the sacrificial ritual and consist of the lighting of the fire, the use of the *ghṛta* or ghee, the pressing of the Soma and its preparation, and the offering of songs of praise which magnify the gods.[20] Agni is asked by the worshippers to 'shine wealth' upon them through their well-fashioned praise, fine invocation[21] or peerless vision,[22] these being as it were vessels framed and offered up by man and filled up by the god and returned enriched. Through their songs and homage, through their visionary thoughts (V.25.4 *dhībhiḥ*) there occurs a meeting point between them and the gods, there is fashioned a receptacle receptive of the divine influences. 'Through these our flashing songs, do thou turn towards us like heaven's radiance'.[23] The emphasis lies on blessings poured out through the power of visions and of offerings sent to the gods through that same power.[24] Hence the importance of visionary meditation. The action is reciprocal and is summed up in the sacrificial chariot travelling hither and thither (V.18.3). 'Songs and praises mount (*giraḥ stomāsa īrate*) like conquering chariots (*vājayanto rathā iva*) gaining wealth, giving aid' (VIII.3.15). Hymns, thought-visions and aspirations, rise upwards to the gods upon the sacrificial flames of Agni.[25] His chariot, through wise discernment (*kratvā*) travels between men and gods laden with wealth.[26]

The heart-felt oblation is brought to Agni, as though it were an offer of cattle,[27] cattle that wealth of the community fittingly used as a simile. Aspirations or thought-visions are offered up as the wealth desired of the god. Heart and mind, being tuned inwardly to the divine, produce a realisation of a lofty state of being, those riches of men pleasing to the gods, those riches for which the poet yearns that he may enter the gods' assembly (VII.84.5 & 85.5).[28]

So the priest who is the minister or go-between of gods and men is the wise man, adept at the apprehension of the truth;[29] with his gifts and worship[30] he brings his influence to bear upon the gods that they may help men.[31] It is his function to offer up his thoughts[32] and by means of these which he fashions into songs he makes the god manifest to man.[33] So the giver (*dāḥ*) who tends the flame is rich (*sureknāḥ*) in mental power (*kratvā* VI.16.26).

We have uncovered certain points worth deeper investigations. The question at issue concerns the many shades of meaning which the Vedic bards ascribed to the words *rayi* and *rai*[34] (given out in dictionaries as 'property, wealth', etc.) which do not merely refer to wealth of a material order such as cattle, sons, corn, long life, the usual terrestrial requests, but as often as not to those of a psychological and spiritual order—if we take the uplifting visionary ecstasy and the knowledge of the divine order gained thereby as belonging to the latter category. In a hymn (VII.86) where the poet gives vent to his pining after communion with Varuṇa, his bewilderment as to what sin he could have committed to incur the god's anger and withdrawal of his presence, he admits that the 'noble-god' (*devo aryaḥ*) causes the thoughtless to think (*acetayad acitaḥ*) and in his deeper wisdom (*kavitaraḥ*) impels the wise or experienced man (*gṛtsa*) to wealth (*rāye* VII.86.7). The tone of the whole poem, as indeed of all those addressed to Varuṇa, is highly ethical. The word *rai*, wealth, here surely denotes spiritual bounteousness or blessing, that richer life of the spirit for which no terrestrial wealth compensates.[35]

The use of *rayi* with verbs denoting shining (e.g. $\sqrt{vi}$ *bhā śuc*) and with such nouns as *dyumna* and *śravas* certainly gives cause for deeper consideration of this Vedic concept of shining wealth as the reward of prayer. What kind of riches can these be? Right conditions fostering wholeness of being, resulting from communion bringing about right living and subsequently all the boons of well-being, abundance, could be an answer to this question: 'Grant us those riches that cause prosperity for all'.[36] 'Shine these blessings upon us, Agni that we may reach supreme undertanding',[37] is unequivocal. So also is the following prayer: We solicit wholeness and the boundless' or as could equally be translated 'perfect happiness and freedom' X.100.1: *ā sarvatātim aditiṃ vṛṇīmahe*), the accent being on completeness which is spiritual achievement.[38]

Agni thus shines with blessings.[39] He is rich in nourishment (I.141.2 *pitumān*),[40] i.e. material well-being as well as spiritual food (*cf.* 'Give us this day our daily bread'); he, the generous, opens the door of riches[41] for of these he is the lord,[42] he grants his devotee exhaustless boons.[43] His bounty is his splendour, his richness is his light,[44] it shines like Sūrya (VIII.43.32). This is the gift the poet prays for (VIII.43.33) the exhaustless, treasured bounty.[45] No exact definition of the wealth is ever found but the allusions certainly point to the imparting of shining visions which is a granting of illumination. This is Agni's blessing, and also the gods' bounteousness. That splendour Agni is begged to bring to the worshipper[46] that the demons might be overcome.[47] He is implored to drive away transgressions by the force of his flame,[48] to remove hostility that the evil of mortals may be overcome (V.9.6). The verb *śuc* used here in the intensive form together with the preposition *apa* implies the scorching or burning off (shining away) of any impurity, immediately after which comes the request 'shine wealth upon us' (*śuśugdhi ā rayim*). In a similar trend of thought we are told that Agni won over the *ṛṣi* Atri to great riches by making him *perceive*.[49] That these riches or blessings are not necessarily material may yet again be understood from another verse:

Whoever watches the flow of truth has perceived him (Agni) lying hidden away; whoever release [plural] him, serving the rites of truth, to such does he proclaim blessings. (I.67.4)[50]

Sitting vigilant for the approaches of truth can mean nothing other than meditating on truth or the order of reality. In such a state of absorption the *ṛṣi* discovers the—otherwise hidden—presence of the flame divine which, if properly fed by right living and devotion, waxes ever stronger, showers blessings upon the human being and illuminates him with its own wisdom and vision. (*cf.* V.15.5 cited above and VI.16.26).

He who in sacrifice, claims the poet (VI.5.5) worship Agni by means of flashing songs and praises, shines im mortal among mortals with riches, with splendour, wit glory.[51] In other words, he is an illumined man of the gods The bard of IV.10.1 offers up his own resourcefulnes (*kratu*) through his praises, for he knows that this wil touch the god's heart (*hṛdispṛśam*), as Agni himself is th charioteer of blessed intelligence and unerring menta ability[52] and is implored for that *kratu* which is an unfailin source of blessing for man;[53] that being his fundamenta treasure, he towers above every mental activity[54] an fosters the intuitive perception of the pious.[55] Agni's ow *kratu* is most glorious (*dyumnintama* I.127.9). The connota tion of resplendence once again allies the understanding t illumination. Agni is thus the bestower of enlightenment He is the illumined sages' inspiration, the granter of intui tions, of songs of praises (*cf.* II.9.4) and of that wealt wrought with heroic power (or wealth that adorns heroi valour *vīrapeśāḥ* IV.11.3). It becomes apparent that Agn is himself the wealth offered up in the service of the gods.[5 He, the vehicle of the transcendent (I.77.3 *adbhutasy rathī*), alone can act as perfect messenger between heave and earth, between immortals and mortals.

Courage also finds its fit embodiment in the god of th flame. *Vayas*, *vīrya* and *vāja*,[57] in their emphasis upo force, all denote some form of what may be summed u as soul heroism. Such valour (*suvīrya* V.16.4) often take as an imploration for plenty of heroic sons,[58] is not neces sarily meant in that particular concrete sense but rather a that quality of courage found in heroes. It is also Agni' peculiar gift, the essence of the flame divine: 'mighty powe is in this splendour' (V.16.1: *bṛhad vayo hi bhānave*).[59] I stimulating to visionary thought he impels to vigou (I.27.11: *dhiye vājāya hinvatu*). He wins vigour for whom soever will strive after immortality (III.25.2: *sanoti vājam amṛtāya bhūṣan*) for only the strong, only the brave, th valorous, can win that nectar. We find the same idea a was present in the Indra stories: the kingdom of heave suffereth violence.

We can no more agree with M. Winternitz's or Max

ǂüller's views concerning Vedic prayer. M. Winternitz[60] laims:

here is nowhere [in the Vedas] any thought of devotion or exaltation to ɪe divine, but [the word brahman] always means mere formulae and erses containing secret magic power, by which man desires to influence ivine beings, or to obtain, or even to force something from them.

ǂax Müller[61] declares:

hough the idea of prayer as swelling or exalted thought may be true vith us, there is little, if any, trace of such thoughts in the Veda. Most of he prayers there are very matter-of-fact petitions, and all that has been aid of the swelling of the heart, the elevation of the mind, the fervid npulse of the will, as expressed by the word Brahman, seems to me deciedly modern, and without any analogies in the Veda itself.

What of the offering fashioned in the heart (*havir hṛdā aṣṭam* VI.16.47) sent on the wings of song to Agni and the nany outpourings to the god of flame? What of the praise ashioned in heart and mind (*hṛdā taṣṭo manasā*) given to he Maruts (I.171.2, *cf.* X.65.14)? What of that exalted ɪeaven-winning song of praise submitted to the god's own glory?' (I.61.3). What of the contrite heart of the repentent vorshipper seeking communion with Varuṇa (VII.86 & 38), unable to understand what has brought him into lisgrace? What of the prayers for forgiveness which many bard sings to Varuṇa, Agni, Aditi, for union and harmony ımong men (X.191 to Agni, *cf.* I.31.5); what of the yearnings for blessings? What of the poet's longing to come nto touch with the wise in understanding (III.38.1, *cf.* V.66.6, VII.3.10)? What of his wonder at the god's favour or having filled him, the simple, with the divine presence ınd wisdom (IV.5.3, I.164.21, VI.9)? Nothing could be nore explicit than the following: 'O gods, I can discern neither the right nor the left, neither the east nor the west. in my simplicity, O bounteous ones, in my wisdom, I would be guided by you, I would reach the fearless light.' II.27.11).[62] These and many other examples are surely expressions of the devotions of the heart, indeed formulated n a simple, even matter-of-fact way because of that perfect sincerity which characterises the Ṛgveda and is touching in its humanity.

M. Winternitz furthermore completely missed the

fundamental meaning of the *brahman*, the drawing fro the depth of the innermost self, of that power, dynamic an creative of visions and songs of shining words, the divin exaltation. The very frequent use of derivatives and des derative forms of the verb *vṛdh* to 'increase' goes again M. Müller's sweeping assertion—though he does acknow ledge that such forms are used but for some unknow reason of his thinks they are of little consequence. On th contrary, they are the Vedic formulation of that ver feeling denied by M. Müller.

Exhilaration, yielding a feeling of increase and fulfilmen finds expression in I.80.1: the *brahman* there is said t produce exhilaration (*brahma cakāra vardhanam*) or 'in crease' with the help of Soma. L. Renou, commenting explains that the *brahman* 'creates invigoration'[63] whic is very close to the idea of the swelling of the heart whic M. Müller denies. Indra is addressed (VI.23.6) as havin made prayers for his own exaltation.[64] In X.49.1 th *brahman* is again the cause of *vardhana*: 'I have made th *brahman* invigorating for myself'.[65] The singers hope tha their 'exhilarating prayers' (*imā brahmāṇi vardhanā*) ma be pleasing to the Aśvins (V.73.10). Again, prayer is, a well as Soma and the sacrificial gift (the juxtaposition i important), the 'strengthener' of Indra.[66] The Soma drop are well known for their exhilarating (*matsarāsaḥ*)[67] an heaven-finding effect (*svarvidaḥ* IX.21.1). In these context prayer certainly exalts both gods and human beings an is used for that very purpose.

That light which is free from fear (*jyotir abhayam*) i thus revealed as the great goal of the Vedic seer, the priz to be won.[68] We find here a perfect example of the cris way in which the bards expressed themselves. Fear, a human emotion, cannot qualify light. The poet refers to that illumined state of consciousness which opens the wa to perfect understanding and all embracing insight i which there is, of course, no room for fear. The harnessin of the chariot of prayer is done with a view to reachin *svar*, that wide world (*uruṃ lokam*) full of spacious freedom and splendour (*svarvat*), that ultimate light (*jyotir uttaram* which the Yajurveda was to claim abides eternal in ever creature (Yj.v.34.3), which the Ṛgvedic *ṛṣi* discovers beyond the darkness and identifies with the sun (Ṛgv. I.50.10), which the seer Atri found as the sun of illumination in the fourth degree of prayer (V.40.6). This 'heavenly light' (*svarvaj jyotiḥ*) the sages yearn to obtain[69] as they proceed to the transcendent lord of the assembly[70] for that 'longed for gift' (*kāmyaṃ sanim*) which is wisdom or enlightenment (*medhā*). 'May we consciously share in this perfect resourcefulness'[71] prays the *ṛṣi* to Agni. Would that, in his immaturity, he be guided by the *Vasus*' wisdom (II.27.11) to attain the fearless light, to obtain that flawless understanding (*medhām ariṣṭam*) and unconquerable might (II.34.7 *duṣṭaraṃ sahaḥ*), that valour no obstacle can daunt. 'Would that we might reach the spacious mansion ye rule'.[72]

These are noble prayers, yearnings for the wisdom that enlightenment bestows, the cry of the human soul to know, to understand, to live in that wisdom. The Ṛgveda is the monument of ancient man's longing for illumination and the eternal bliss conferred thereby. Its message may be hidden for us beneath obscure references and imagery, a mythological language out of touch with our modern outlook, but a little digging will bring it out in all its pristine purity. We can no longer afford to pass it by or disdainfully brush it away as has been done in the past, but should pause and consider the antiquity of man's aspiration for something beyond himself, for a state of ecstasy in which the bounds of everyday life recede and the heart and mind expand beyond expectation, a communion with the *numinous* which he discovered he could reach through certain practices, indeed a desire to surpass his ordinary self to touch his greater self.

NOTES

1. '*Religion and Philosophy of the Veda and Upanishads*, p. 311, Harvard Oriental Series, vol. 31 (Cambridge, Mass. 1925).
2. *cf.* X.129 and VIII.58.2 (= Val. 10.2).
3. *pari cin marto draviṇaṃ mamanyād ṛtasya pathā namasā ā vivāset.*
   uta svena kratunā saṃ vadeta śreyānsaṃ dakṣaṃ manasā jagṛbhyāt.

4. J. Gonda defines *vāja* as 'a general term for the specific power-substanc of the generative potency which manifests itself in vegetation, cattle, horse men, etc. and by which new food, new subsistence, new resources, new life i gained' (*op. cit.* p. 150). See also *Epithets in the Ṛgveda* by the same autho p. 145 ('S-Gravenhage, 1959) *cf.* A. C. Bose, *Hymns from the Vedas* (Londo 1966). 'Certain orientalists have persuaded themselves to believe that *vāja* (power means "booty", "loot". So when the *Rigveda* says "Let us leave here those who ar evil-minded, and cross over to powers that are beneficent", we are asked to thin that the words for "beneficent powers" (*śivān vājan*) should mean "plenty o booty", though "śivān", "beneficent" can never mean "plentiful". Similarly when Sarasvatī, Goddess of learning, the "inspirer of *dhī*, the higher intellect is said to be possessing "Vāja" (power) (Ṛgv. VI.4) we are expected to imagin that she had collected "booty"' (p. 37).

cf. Griffith's translation of *vājaratnā* (IV.44.7 & IV.43.7) as rich in booty.

5. *cf.* VIII.35.10–12: *ūrjaṃ no dhattam*, 'grant us vigorous strength' 22–24 *dhattaṃ ratnānī dāśuṣe*, 'give treasures to the devotee.'

6. *tam no dāta maruto vājinaṃ ratha āpānaṃ brahma citayad dive dive*
iṣaṃ stotṛbhyo vṛjaneṣu kārave saniṃ medhāṃ ariṣṭāṃ duṣṭaraṃ sahaḥ

See J. Gonda, *Epithets in the Ṛgveda*, p. 145 ('S-Gravenhage, 1959) on *vāja* and *vājin*.

7. IV.35.7: *sam ṛbhubhiḥ pibasva ratnadhebhiḥ*.

8. VIII.46.6: *iśānaṃ rāya īmahe*.

9. *cf.* I.51.14 & VIII.45.36.

10. VI.44.2: *tuviśagma te rāyo dāmā matīnām*.

11. I.61.16: *viśvapeśasaṃ dhiyaṃ dhāḥ*.

12. VIII.13.5: *rayiṃ naś citram ā bharā svarvidam*.

13. *cf.* VIII.46.8, the Vṛtra slaying: *mado vareṇyo ... vṛtahantamaḥ*.

14. *cf.* VIII.46.8: *ādadiḥ svarnṛbhiḥ*.

15. *cf.* VIII.13.5: *rayiṃ nas ... ā bharā svarvidam*, translated by J. Gonda a 'bring us wealth consisting in light (to live in)'. *Loka*, etc. p. 79.

16. IX.106.4: *dyumantaṃ śuṣmam ā bhara svarvidam*.

17. *rayiṃ ... bahulaṃ puruspṛham ... abhy arṣasi* IX.107.21.

18. *ajitaye ahataye pavasva svastaye sarvatātaye bṛhate*
tad uśanti viśve ime sakhāyas tad ahaṃ vaśmi pavamāna soma.

Griffith translated as follows: 'Flow for prosperity and constant vigour, flow on for happiness and high perfection. This is the wish of all these friends assembled; this is my wish, O Soma Pavamana.'

19. *cf.* IX.86.29.

20. *cf.* I.139.5.

21. *rāyo didīhi naḥ suvṛktibhiḥ*, V.25.3.

22. *dhītī variṣṭhayā*, V.25.3. *cf.* I.93.10: 'shine forth profusely': *dīdayataṃ bṛhat*.

23. IV.10.3: *ebhir no arkair bhavā no arvāñc svarṇa jyotiḥ*.

24. *cf.* V.41.5: *rāya eṣe'vase dadhīta dhīḥ*.

25. *cf.* I.123.6 and I.143.4.

26. V.17.4: *asya kratvā vi cetaso dasmasya vasu ratha ā*.

27. VI.16.47: *ā te Agna ṛcā havirhṛdā taṣṭaṃ bharāmasi te bhavantu ukṣaṇo ṛṣabhāso vaśā uta*.

28. *cf.* I.64.10 where the Maruts are called lords of riches or all possessors (*viśvavedaso rayibhiḥ*) and (I.85.2) where they have made their seat in heaven (*divi ... adhi cakrire sadaḥ*).

29. *sukratur ṛtacid ... hotā*.

30. *namasvān ... haviṣmān*.

31. VII.85.4: *āvavartad avase vām.*
32. VIII.6.7: *imā abhi pra nīnemo vipām agreṣu dhītayaḥ.*
33. VIII.6.28: *dhiyā vipro ajāyata.*
34. *cf. draviṇa* in IV.11.3 and in I.96.1–3: 'the gods preserved the wealth-giving Agni' *devā agniṃ dhārayan draviṇodām.* What kind of 'property' can this be of which the gods partake unless it be of a celestial kind? *cf.* also *surekna* 'rich in possession', as in Monier Williams' dictionary, which in VI.16.26 seems rather to mean 'rich in insight'. *cf.* II.23.15 and see J. Gonda's comment in *The vision of the Vedic poets,* p. 203.
35. *cf.* also VII.86.8: *śaṃ naḥ kṣeme, śam u yoge no astu,* be propitious that we may be safe, be propitious that we may be in union.
36. I.79.9: *rayiṃ viśvāyu poṣasam. cf.* also V.20.1.
37. VII.3.10: *etā no agne saubhagā didīhi api kratuṃ sucetasaṃ vatema.*
38. *cf.* IX.96.4 with regard to Soma, p. 124, fn. 18.
39. X.3.2: *vasubhir . . . vibhāti.*
40. *cf.* I.70.1: 'May we win abundance through our intuition' (*vanema pūrvīr . . . manīṣā*) does not necessarily mean food but well-being resulting from illumined communion, abundant enlightenment. 'May resplendent Agni' the verse goes on 'reach out to all things'.
41. I.68.10: *vi rāya aurṇod duraḥ purukṣuḥ.*
42. I.68.4: *āsāṃ patī rayīṇām. cf.* I.72.1: *rayipatī . . . rayīṇām.*
43. I.72.1: *cakrāṇo amṛtāni viśvā.*
44. VIII.43.32: *vibhāvasuḥ*; I.44.10: *vibhāvaso dīdetha.*
45. VIII.43.33: *yan na upadasyati tvad agne vāryaṃ vasu.*
46. VIII.19.15: *tad agne dyumnam ā bhara.*
47. *cf.* X.87.12.
48. I.97.1: *apa naḥ śośucad agham.*
49. V.15.5: *maho rāye citayann atrim aspaḥ.*
50. *va īṃ ciketa guhā bhavantam ā yaḥ sasāda dhārām ṛtasya*
vi ye cṛtanty ṛtā sapanta ād id vasūni pra vavāca asmai.
51. *sa martyeṣu amṛta pracetā rayā dyumnena śravasā vi bhāti,* VI.5.5.
52. *krator bhadrasya dakṣasya sādhoḥ,* IV.10.2.
53. I.123.13: *bhadraṃ bhadraṃ kratum.*
54. IV.6.1: *tvaṃ hi viśvam abhi asi manma.*
55. *pra vedhasaś cit tirasi manīṣām,* IV.6.1.
56. I.127.9: *jāyase devatātaye rayir na devatātaye.*
57. For a definition of *vāja* according to J. Gonda see fn. 4, p. 124.
58. *cf.* I.1.3 *vīravattama* and I.85.12 *suvīra.*
59. *cf.* VI.7.3: *tvad vipro jāyate vājy agne tvad vīrāso abhimātiṣāhaḥ.*
60. *History of Indian literature* vol. 1, p. 248 (Calcutta, 1927).
61. *The Six Systems of Indian Philosophy* p. 70 (London, 1899).
62. *na dakṣiṇā vi cikite na savyā na prācīnam ādityā na uta paścā*
pākyā cid vasavo dhīryā cid yuṣmānīto abhayaṃ jyotir aśyām.
63. *op. cit.* p. 16.
64. *brahmāṇi hi cakṛṣe vardhanāṃ tāvat.*
65. *ahaṃ brahma kṛṇavaṃ mahyaṃ vardhanam.*
66. *yasya brahma vardhanaṃ yasya somo yasya idam rādhaḥ,* II.12.14.
67. *cf.* I.14.4, I.15.1 and VI.17.4.
68. IX.4.2: *sanā jyotiḥ sanā svarviśvā.*
69. X.36.3: *naśīmahi. cf.* VI.47.8 & VII.88.2.
70. I.18.6: *sadasas patim adbhutam.*
71. VII.3.10: *api kratuṃ sucetasam vatema.* This verse lends itself to

different interpretations. According to P. Thieme, *Festschrift F. Weller*, p. 657 (Leipzig, 1954) *api-vat* means 'to blow, fan'. The poet would thus be fanning Agni. According to J. Gonda the verse would rather mean 'direct my inspiration to'.

72. V.66.6. *cf.* also X.100.1 earlier quoted.

SECTION III

Vedic Eschatology

Introduction

Vedic eschatology may be considered under its two main themes apparent in the Ṛgveda and further developed in the Atharvaveda and the Yajurveda: the belief in an after-death life of which detailed descriptions are extant in the *saṃhitās*, with the implications resulting therefrom; and the avowed knowledge of a reality beyond death, not necessarily identical with common after-death states, but transcending these, and expressing the essence of immortality. This latter field of Vedic thought Western exegesis has so far completely failed to differentiate from the former and therefore to probe in depth.

Passing through the gates of death signified to the Vedic people only the extension of existence, though without the physical body, an existence in a heightened state of awareness whose keynote is joy; this being the legacy left to mankind by Yama the king of the kingdom of the dead, the first of 'mortals' to have shuffled off the physical body. For men's sake he found and protected the way to heavenly 'pastures' (Ṛgv. X.14.2). Immortality, on the other hand, throughout the Vedic age, meant far more than mere survival. It meant attaining the status of the gods and thereby gaining divine insight or seeing by means of the solar splendour (*svardṛś*), the meaning of which was omniscience and omnipresence.

PART I
Death

I. GENERAL MEANING AND VEDIC ATTITUDE TO LIFE AND DEATH

That death was but the crossing from one level of existence to another is all too obvious from the Ṛgveda itself: The question of survival does not seem to have aroused the slightest doubt.[1] This is a far cry from the scepticism recorded in Job: 'Man lieth down and riseth not. Till the heaven be no more they shall not awake' (14.12) or in Psalm 115.17: 'The dead praise not the Lord, neither any that go down into silence.' Such a melancholy note as is here struck is quite alien to the Vedas which breathe an atmosphere of vigour, optimism, sunshine.

That the soul of the departed, if good, awakens on the other side, after due rites of purification by fire, to a land of sunshine and honey, or a state of joy and sweetness, is also fully evident in both the Ṛgveda and the Atharvaveda; that, if bad, due punishment is meted out to the offender may be inferred from the hints of the deep dark pit, the bottomless darkness into which the evil-doer is plunged.[2] Characteristically, the hell aspect of the after-death state is not emphasised in the Ṛgveda.[3] The hymns show that the bards of those early days had a pronounced preference for an optimistic outlook in so far as eschatological problems are concerned. In contrast to later generations they hardly indulged in morbid speculations, and powerful imprecations of which Ṛgv. VII.104 is a good example, are uncommon. These, however, are customary in the Atharvaveda. Spells indeed were used to ward off demons or even death when it was not wanted or rather when it was deemed too premature, but these are not of primary import. The keynote is on the whole one of vigour of spirit and *joie de vivre*. The heaven contemplated for average humanity is a 'fountain full of honey in the highest step of Viṣṇu, where rejoice those who are devoted to the gods' (Ṛgv. I.154.5).[4] This heaven is essentially the world resulting from what has been well accomplished, *sukṛtasya lokaḥ* (the world of good works Ath.v. VI.120.1 & XVIII.3.71) or the world of the deserving, *sukṛtāṃ lokaḥ* (Ṛgv. X.16.4).[5]

Two trends of thought are perceptible:

The wish for life on earth with its corrolary avoidance of death;[6] the wish for immortality and the equal avoidance of death—even though physical life and immortality are generally not equivalent.[7] The quest of the latter was ultimately the quest of every mortal. In the meanwhile the ordinary man was content with a full life of a hundred years of vitality, a boon for which one finds many a prayer;[8] hence, one step at a time sums up the attitude: enjoyment of this earthly life first, then the heavenly reward. Typically the Ath.v. XII.2.45 begs: 'Do thou Agni, prolong the lives of living creatures and may those who are dead go to the world of the Fathers.'[9]

Perfect acceptance of conditions, such as they are, is reflected in the following prayer:

> Well knowing I have bound me horse-like to the pole ... I seek for no release, no turning back therefrom. May He who knows the way, the leader, guide me straight.[10]

Contentment with what is, admission of one's responsibility for what befalls one's self; agreement to play one's full part without seeking escape—the sole request being for guidance upon the straight path—in other words, acquiescence to fate and recognition of one's part in it, these are the elements that form the keynote of this remarkable prayer. Yet it evinces a positive spirit, ready to face life as it is, that spirit typical of the Vedic people shying at asking anything that might lie beyond their present capacity of understanding.

But sooner or later the inevitable end must come and evidence points to requests that death might 'keep to that path which is thine O death, and is not the way of the gods' (Ṛgv. X.18.1)[11]—the typical human wish to avoid the unpleasant. However, a more curious request is found in Ṛgv. VII.59.12: 'like the cucumber from its stem, even so may I be released from death, not from immortality.'[12] Noteworthy are these verses in so far as they posit the unexplored problem of the difference between death which is survival and immortality which is more than survival[13] and therefore not merely equivalent to it. Taking for granted that death, to the Vedic people, did not mean extinction, the wish for release from it assumes an unusual significance. If, at the end of one life, there be but one death which leads to such a pleasant state as that of the Vedic paradise, why the wish to be set free from it?[14] Moreover, what is the difference between that state of paradise and of immortality from which the poet would 'not be released'? Death being the abolition of physical shackles and the entrance into a joyous state of existence could not but be in itself attractive. Even if the transition period from one kind of life to another was considered unpleasant,[15] or the final uncertainty of what might happen during the transit led to anxiety, nevertheless that period was short and of unique occurrence. It therefore could not account for the desire for release from death or for the longing for immortality in heaven (Ṛgv. IX.113). Would death not be used as a collective singular indicative of death in general and repeated deaths in particular[16] which the poet would terminate by entering into the state of immortality? The latter being beyond birth and death and thus beyond their shackles would indeed effectively release him from mortality altogether. This is a field of Vedic thought worth a deeper investigation than has hitherto been accorded to it.

II. THE PROCESS OF DEATH

1. THE HUMAN CONSTITUTION

Dying does not seem to have been thought of as a simple process. The human being is a composite creature. As early as the Ṛgveda the *ṛṣis* were aware of the complexity of human nature. Both the Ṛgveda and the Atharvaveda imply the idea of the scattering at death of man's various constituents. Such is borne out in several Ṛgvedic verses and in the enigmatic Atharvaveda verse:

By the first dying[17] it goes apart dividing threefold. Yonder goes it with one [part]; yonder goes it with one; here with one it dwells. (Ath.v. XI.8.33 Whitney's translation).

The word 'it' seems to stand for the human constitution. The previous stanza (XI.8.32) had pointed out that 'all deities [i.e. constituent elements] are seated in' man 'as cows in a cow-stall'. Death means the falling apart of the constituents or the scattering away of the 'cows'. The dividing threefold thus seems rather to refer to the separation of each component part which occurs at death, the grosser part going to the grosser elements, the subtler to the subtler, this being confirmed in Ṛgv. X.16.3. Western exegesis does not credit Vedic India with the doctrine of the *kośas* or *śarīras* of the later schools of philosophy. Nevertheless these doctrines are found in germ in the Vedas, and we have here at least a hint, if nothing more, of the threefold division of the human constitution.

Further details may be gathered from Ṛgv. X.16.3:[18]

Let the eye go to the sun, the spirit to the wind; go thou, according to thy nature to heaven and earth. Or go to the waters . . . take thy stand with thy body among the plants.

This verse does not mean that the departed one is going as a complete entity to either the waters, or the plants, or the sun, as Western commentators have generally understood, but that in him which has affinity to these will eventually find its way there.[19] The connection with the sun, for example, has been ill-understood. The eye in all ancient civilisations has been deemed the window of the inner being whether the latter be called soul or spirit; the *ātman* or spiritual principle[20] in man shines through the eye. In the Ṛgveda the sun is stated to be 'the *ātmā* of what moves and what moves not' (Ṛgv. I.115.1),[21] it is the universal soul manifesting through all things. The gods observe the world through the sun which is their spiritual insight. They are sun-eyed.[22] Any *ṛṣi* becomes sun-eyed when spiritual perception welling up from within himself illumines his whole being and, as a result, the whole world. He now 'sees' in a different, in a transcendent light. In this illumination, or enlightenment, is found the link between the eye and the sun so closely related in Ṛgvedic thought but so completely misunderstood in Western exegesis. As the sun is the light and life-giver of all things on earth—the *ātman* of the world—so the eye is the organ through which the light and life-giver, *ātman* (the *aja* or unborn of the Ṛgveda) looks out upon the physical world, as well as that into which the light of the world is received. According to the Atharvaveda 'Sūrya is the superintending lord of the eyes'.[23]

The next part of the verse under consideration (Ṛgv. X.16.3) sends the *ātman* to the wind. As this involves the meaning of *ātman* which implies breath and essence as well as innermost self it will be treated in the last part of this study. The *ātman* here refers to the impalpable breath which must return to the impalpable wind.

The doctrine that each part returns to its respective source finds its origin and confirmation in Ṛgv. X.16.3 as well as in the following verse (Ṛgv. X.16.4) which furthermore explicitly states that there is in the human being an 'unborn' part or eternal principle which goes to heaven or to the world of the righteous:

As for his unborn part do thou (Agni) kindle it with thy heat, let thy flame and thy lustre kindle it . . . convey it to the world of the righteous' (Ṛgv. X.16.4 as translated by J. Muir, O.S.T. V.p. 298).[24]

The unborn (*aja*) goes to the abode of the blessed though a qualification is needed here, for that part seems to be still connected with *manas* which is credited with the ability of roaming at will at first[25] and with *asu* (the breath), as will be considered and discussed in due course. This doctrine of the dispersal of the parts is no alternative view as claimed by Keith:

The alternative view once found in the Rigveda (X.16.3), which sends th eye of the dead to the sun, the breath to the wind, bids him go to the heaven and the earth, or if he prefers to the waters, and to dwell among the plant with his members, cannot be treated as more than a mere deviation of no great consequence for the general view of Vedic religion.[26]

The Vedic idea according to Keith is that the whole body is to be restored on the other side, even though on this side the body is being burnt. The words 'go according to thy nature, to earth and heaven' (Ṛgv. X.16.3)[27] point out the real meaning: according to the law of its own being, each part will automatically return to its corresponding source each but follows the law of which it is an expression. J Muir translates appropriately as 'according to (the) nature of (thy several parts)'.[28]

The word *aja* in Ṛgv. X.16.4 has given rise to more misunderstanding. Griffith, taking it to mean 'goat' translates the verse as follows: 'thy portion is the goat with heat consume him' giving a different and at first reading senseless significance to this otherwise explicit stanza. The difficulty arose from such passages as Ath.v IX.5.1–3 where the mention of 'hoofs' made Western scholars take *aja* as goat. But as J. Muir recognised 'some of the expressions seem more properly applicable' to the sense of *unborn* than of goat.[29] Both Ath.v. IX.5.1 and 3 repeat the words: 'let him, understanding (*prajānan*)[30] go to the world of the righteous', an epithet which can only apply to a human entity. There is most probably a play upon the word *aja* and if any meaning of goat can be ascribed to it, it is certainly only in a sacrificial sense: that which during life has sacrificed will now receive due reward,[31] hence it goes up to heaven in the quality of the sacrificial animal whose hoofs need washing before it reaches there. So the verse runs: 'Wash his feet if he has committed wickedness; understanding, let him ascend with cleansed hoofs' (Ath.v. IX.5.3)[32] thereby confirming the fact that the fire ritual of burning the dead had, in addition to any other meaning, a purifying intent.

Apart from the purifying aspect, the question as to why

Agni should be called upon to kindle the defunct, as expressed in Ṛgv. X.16.4. is bound up with *tapas*, that intense concentration upon an inner focus which arouses the divine fire to action. Agni, link between heaven and earth, is the immortal spark in mortals, the flame that burns in human beings, as throughout the cosmos, and causes all things to come into manifestation and to withdraw therefrom.[33] But for the defunct to become conscious on the other side, Agni also must be kindled. So the Taittirīya Brāhmaṇa (II.4.2.6) gives a further clue which confirms Agni's role as the link between heaven and earth, between the mortal and the immortal: he is the bridge.

Thou Agni art our cord, and our bridge; thou art the path which conducts to the gods. By thee we may ascend to the summit (of heaven), and there live in joyful fellowship with the gods'. (Quoted in Muir V.p.299).

2. THE BODY

The problem which confronts Western scholars arises in the form of a paradox which, however, is only apparent: once the departed one enters into paradise he is called upon to unite himself with a body in every respect similar to his physical form. A. B. Keith took this literally, as though the defunct is to recover his actual physical body[34] yet it is clear that the physical body is being burnt on the funeral pyre and, as a result, its components are scattered away. To complicate the question the Atharvaveda refers to the care taken to avoid injury to the body of the dead, even when it was being burnt. Keith explains: 'He has in the next world to unite himself with his body'.[35] Yet both Ṛgv. X.16.5 and X.14.8 do not speak of his own body but merely *tanū*: a body, or form, or self. 'Putting on life (enduring[36] life as a vesture—*āyur vasāṇaḥ*) rejoin a form' (X.16.5)[37] and 'unite with a form of splendour' (X.14.8).[38] The latter verse is rendered by J. Muir thus: 'become united to a body and clothed in a shining form'[39] which gives the spirit of the original. But the word *tanū* also means self,[40] the reflexive pronoun. It is noteworthy that when on the one hand, Agni is entreated to seize and burn the body of the defunct (Ath.v. XVIII.3.71) or, on the other hand, nc to dissolve it (Ṛgv. X.16.1) the word used in either case i *śarīra*, not *tanū*. But when the departed one is asked t unite himself with a 'body' the word used is *tanū* (Ṛgv X.16.5 and X.14.8). A conclusion could be drawn tha *śarīra* connotes a tangible envelope, therefore an objectiv body, whereas *tanū* refers to the subjective form[41] whic cannot be burnt away but now becomes the outer envelop of the dead when he has shed his physical sheath. T translate *tanū* as body may lead to misconceptions. Th shining form is apparently the Vedic expression for wha was later to be called *linga-śarīra* or it may even includ the *prāṇa* and *manomayakośa* of later thought. This i confirmed by the fact that heaven is the realm of eterna light (*jyotir ajasram* Ṛgv. IX.113.7–11) and that th departed are 'endowed with lustre' like that of the gods a Keith himself noticed:[42] 'with what light the gods went u to the sky . . . to the world of the well-done, with that ma we go to the world of the well-done . . .'[43]

The protean nature of *tanū* is exemplified in Ṛgv. X.15.14 'along with those (fathers) . . . grant us this (higher) vitality (*asunīti*) and a body according to our desire'.[44] This verse is addressed either to Agni, or to Yama in his close connection with Agni. It could also be rendered thus: 'along with these (the fathers) . . . adapt (prepare or fit) a body (or form) (*tanvaṃ kalpayasva*) for this ethereal life (*asunītim*) according to thy (or our) wish (*yathāvaśam*).[45] The Ath.v. XVIII.3.59 has a similar request: 'may he [the ruler] prepare (or fashion) our forms according to his wish' (or according to our wish).[46] This is quite consonant with the gods' capacity to mould their ethereal appearance according to their desire as we learn from Ṛgv. III.48.4b 'he [Indra] fashioned his appearance even as he pleased'[47] and VII.101.3b where the very same words are used of Parjanya which Griffith translates thus: 'even as he willeth doth he change his figure'.[48]

Three lights are ascribed to the human being in Ṛgv. X.56.1:

idaṃ ta ekaṃ This one [light is] thine

para ū ta ekaṃ	yonder [is] one for thee too
tṛtiyena jyotiṣā saṃ viśạsva	with the third light unite thyself
saṃveśane tanvaś	in mergence with thyself
cārur edhi priyo devānāṃ	be thou beloved and cherished of the gods
parame janitre.	in the highest birthplace.

This verse should be compared with the Atharvaveda verse already quoted:

> By the first dying, it goes apart dividing threefold; yonder goes it with one [part]; yonder goes it with one; here with one it dwells (*ni* + *sev*). (Ath.v. XI.8.33)

Here again the threefold division is inferred from the enumeration of the three lights which may pertain to the physical, mental and spiritual aspects of the human constitution and may also be interpreted as the three types of consciousness, the mere physical awareness which 'is thine', the mental or intellectual, and the third or spiritual insight with which the defunct is to unite in the highest place of origin. As *saṃveśana* means 'union with', the defunct is to assume complete control of his subtler form and to enter into that state of consciousness which is typical of heaven.

What is that self or principle which is to be united with the third light? One presumes this is the focus of consciousness or thinking principle *manas* which during the life time was centered in the physical brain and now must find its new centre. The word birth-place (*janitra* Ṛgv. X.56.1) points to the origin of both gods and men: the third light, being the highest (*parama*) must be in the third step of Viṣṇu (Ṛgv. I.154.5) or third heaven.

The burning of the physical body[49] is to be taken as symbolical of the purifying of the inner being as is easily surmised from Ṛgv. X.16.1, the clue to this interpretation being: 'When thou hast matured him (or made him viable as Coomaraswami[50] translates *śritam*) then send him on his way to the fathers.' The 'maturing' process assumes great significance when it is considered figuratively: for the complete burning of a body merely leaves ashes; the kindling of the inner being (as though a flickering flame) of which the outer burning is but the symbol, brings about the dropping of all psychological dross or moral defects (*mala*) until only that which is pure remains. The mature soul is one who has gone through the fire of life, the battlefield of the spirit.[51] The link between the self (*tanū*) and sacrifice is found in Ath.v. XVIII.2.17: 'they who fight in the contests, who are self-sacrificing (*tanūtyaj*) heroes ... unto them do thou go' (Whitney's translation).

There is thus no real deviation from the main doctrine that like returns to like whilst the form, or self (*tanū*) is fashioned of the substance of the heaven realm which is *light*,[52] espousing the shape of the discarded physical counterpart, but a subtler replica of it, and is, as hinted at in Ṛgv. X.135.3, the result of the more spiritual thought entertained during life which at death provides a *ratha* or 'vehicle' for taking the defunct to heaven. All these Ṛgvedic and Atharvavedic references contain in more than germ the doctrine of sheaths and subtler levels of later ages. Passing references without explanation would rather point to a body of doctrine already well established and cannot be dismissed either as meaningless or as without any future purport in point of doctrine.

3. THE CHARIOT OF DEATH

Any examination of the transition from earthly life to the life beyond should take into consideration the 'sober'[53] but difficult hymn Ṛgv. X.135 which holds one or two keys to the understanding of the Vedic conception of death. Despite its very simple language this hymn refers to certain mysterious after-death states which only the priests could understand. Also, the connection between the first two stanzas and the third is not very apparent. For these reasons this is one of the most cryptic hymns of the whole collection. However, it deals with the death of a boy, the transition from life to the other world (described in stanza 3) and part of the funeral rite.

yaṃ kumāra navaṃ ratham	The new, wheelless, one-poled car
acakraṃ manasā akṛṇoḥ	facing in all directions
ekeṣaṃ viśvataḥ prāñcam	which thou didst make O youth by means of mind,
apaśyann adhi tiṣṭhasi.	thou now ascendest unconsciously (seeing not).

X.135.3.

That part of the human being which is to go to Yama's kingdom at death, unconsciously mounts upon a vehicle which thoughts have fashioned during life. This revelation has not called for any commentary on the part of Western scholars who, like Renou, dismiss it as purely a figure of speech. True, but Vedic figures of speech have specific meanings each peculiar to itself. The important point is that since this imaginary vehicle which is used for the transit between this earthly life and the next, was built up of thoughts, or fashioned in the mind (*manasākṛṇoḥ*) and obviously during life, it is the expression, even the result, of the thoughts entertained during life, the thoughts themselves being both cause and effect of the kind of life lived. The description is specific: wheel-less, *acakra*, furnished with only one pole, *ekeṣa*; facing all directions *viśvataḥ*. This confirms that no earthly vehicle is meant here; its facing all directions surely implies a mental capacity for viewing or taking in all surrounding objects or many different concepts at once. It is new for, though fashioned during existence, it is used only after death, and in a peculiar sense resembles the *ratha* of the ritual which wafts the essence of the sacrifice to the gods. In other words, it is the representation of the *essence* of the previous life, of that alone which can take the defunct to paradise. It may be inferred from the next stanza that the funeral rite helps it on its onward journey, but the *ratha* is not equivalent to the rite. L. Renou[54] claims: '. . . the images car-ship-sacrifice coincide in all the hymns'. This does not imply equivalence in all cases. The Vedic bards delighted in metaphoric language. A striking example occurs in Ṛgv. X.85.8: 'hymns were the crossbars of the pole, *kurīra* metre decked the car'.[55]

That the youth ascends the car without seeing it (*apaśyan*) is not because he is 'dead' as Macdonell explains[56] but because he is unconscious. The centre of consciousness has not yet focussed itself properly upon the new level of existence, there is unconsciousness for a while during the transition period, any action such as the 'mounting' of a vehicle being automatic. This state may account for that region of gloom which the soul must cross on its way to heaven (Ath.v. IX.5.1)[57] and for the prayers said on behalf of the dead that he may awaken soon to his new condition and to an understanding of it. 'Let him go, foreknowing', says Ath.v. IX.5.1 'unto the world of the well doing'. So the Taittirīya Brāhmaṇa explains: 'One man departing from this world knows himself that "this is I myself" (*ayam aham asmi*). Another does not recognise his own world' (III.10.11.1), thereby implying that not everyone becomes unconscious when crossing through the gates of death. Ṛgv. X.135.5 asks curious questions:

kaḥ kumāram ajanayad?	Who generated the youth?
rathaṃ ko nir avartayat?	Who rolled out his car?
kaḥ svit tad adya no brū-yād	Who indeed could tell us this to-day?
anudeyī yathā abhavat?	How his equipment was?

There seems to be a doubt as to who or what caused the death of the youth. Furthermore, what did the boy take over with him? The important word is *anudeyī*[58] translated by Macdonell as 'equipment' and by Renou as 'chargement' which has a similar meaning of cargo or loading—a very materialistic connotation. The sense of 'that which is to be handed over or given back', is clear though the exact significance which Macdonell qualifies as 'uncertain' is elusive. Kunhan Raja[59] explains *anudeyī* as a technical term referring to the presents brought by the bride to the bridegroom. In this wheel-less chariot is thus to be placed the harvest yield of life so that the *ratha* bears the essence of the preceding life, the word *manasā* in stanza 3 pointing out that this harvest is reaped and stored up at the mental level. This interpretation is in line with stanza 3 which makes it plain that the chariot is the product of the thought life and the bridge which links earth life to paradise and therefore contains that which is to be offered to Yama as a present.[60] With this also could be brought together the idea of all the sacrifices performed on earth and stored up in heaven, the boon restored to the worshipper.[61]

The next stanza (6)—is even more curious. L. Renou[62] renders it as follows (as translated from the French):

yathā abhavad anudeyī	How was his equipment [chargement]
tato agram ajāyata	Thence was born the origin [of things].
purastād budhna ātataḥ	First the foundation is laid.
paścān nirayaṇaṃ kṛtam.	Then the egress is made.

In his translation of the second line Renou brings in a cosmic significance which we do not think applies here. On this basis he believes the hymn has a cosmogonic intent. The word *agra* means 'beginning, summit, front', so Renou chose the sense of 'origin' of things, and Macdonell that of 'top' as if applicable to a physical vehicle, translating the line thus: 'as the equipment was, so the top arose'.[63] The widely different appreciation and the evident failure to understand the exact meaning show the intrinsic difficulty of the two lines each of which consists of only three words. Yet whichever way the verse is considered, there is an underlying common factor. The word *agra* may simply refer to the origin of the particular departed soul described in the hymn: 'according to the harvest's yield so was it originally manifest' (*agram ajāyata*), implying thereby that even at the beginning of the youth's life it was possible to foretell what his life would be like and what he would reap from it. The stanza could then be paraphrased as follows: according as the foundation was laid in the beginning[64]—the ground (*budhna*) of everyday experience—

so will the way out be subsequently contrived by the human being. As we live, so we die, remembering the injunction to think nobly is to live nobly and die nobly.

To take *agram* as top and *budhna* as bottom, as Macdonell does, is to give the description a purely concrete or materialistic connotation, not in line with a *ratha* which is not physical but made of the stuff of thought, and which is therefore a symbol expressive of life's ingress and egress.

One word which has given rise to controversy holds one key to a better understanding of Vedic after-death conceptions: *asunīti*, used in Ṛgv. X.15.14 and X.16.2. A combination of *asu* 'breath', 'life', 'vitality', and *nīti*, 'guidance', 'wisdom' ($\sqrt{ni}$ to 'conduct, guide or to place' [in a certain condition]), it seems to point to that state, or immaterial condition, in which the defunct is placed after the transition period and to which, one may deduce, he must grow accustomed. It bears evidence to the fact that heaven or the after-death state was not conceived as one of material bliss, at least in the Ṛgvedic period, but rather as one of ethereal being, such as the word *asu* can convey, blissful ethereal counterpart of earthly joy, materialistic descriptions being an accretion of later times, as may be gathered from the Atharvaveda itself—a condoning of human weakness. *Asu*,[65] the life-breath or vital energy, that which animated the whole person during life, goes to the kingdom of the dead. This is beyond doubt from the wish expressed in the Atharvaveda that the *asu* may not depart to Yama (XVIII.3.62): 'let death go away; let what is immortal come to us; let [him] defend these men until old age; let not their life-breaths [*asu*] go to Yama' (Whitney). Similarly the *aja* or unborn part goes the same way. (Ṛgv. X.16.4). Are the two identical? No. *Aja*, being the 'unborn', must be equivalent to the later use of *ātman*. The *asu* belongs to the unborn part; when the latter withdraws its breath, the physical body decays, but the breath of life element remains with the *aja*. As explained in *A Reappraisal of Yoga*[66] breath is the very essence of existence. When it is withdrawn from the form which it animates the latter whithers. Breath is the pulse or heart-beat of the cosmos and therefore of the spirit—*aja* the unborn. It cannot be separated, yet *asu* is not *aja*, but only its expression, its one activity, its breath.[67] According to Ṛgv. X.15.1 (Ath.v. XVIII.1.44)[68] *asu* expresses life in its sublimated aspect, life beyond death, and as is easily gathered from the context, it is that state enjoyed in heaven: 'those who went to life' *asu*, or those who reached spiritual being *asum ya iyuḥ* (Ṛgv. X.15.1). The *manas* also goes to heaven (Ṛgv. X.58.1) 'thy mind that went far away to Yama'[69] so that the defunct is still a composite being of *aja*, *asu* and *manas* after the 'first dying'. Ath.v. VIII.1.3 enumerates his parts: *asu, prāṇa, ayus, manas.*[70]

Is there a further casting off of 'veils' (*āvaraṇa*) on the way to paradise? The only hints we gather from the *saṃhitas* seem to point out that if any further discarding is necessary, it would be done within heaven and would be connected with the three spheres in the third of which the elixir of immortality is hidden.[71] Are only the few who reach immortality capable of casting off the last veils, or of going through the second dying, whereas average mankind does not, and thus does not qualify for the boon of immortality? These are questions to which no definite answer is given and hardly any hints on which any theory may be built.

NOTES

1. Glasenapp, *Immortality and salvation in Indian religions* (Calcutta, 1963) is of the opinion that because '. . . the number of the passages in the Ṛgveda, concerned with the life to come, is not very great, and . . . the ideas developed in them are dim and little defined' (p. 13) the importance which was attached 'to life after death seems to have been only relatively small.' (p. 13). We do not agree with this.

2. *cf.* Ṛgv. VII.104.3, 11, 12; II.29.6; IX.73.8.9; Ath.v. XVIII.2.28, etc. Because of the paucity of such references J. Muir (O.S.T. V, p. 302, London, 1870) thought that the hymns contain 'no prominent mention of any such penal retribution'. For a discussion of this aspect see W. N. Brown's article 'The Rigvedic equivalent for hell' in the J.A.O.S. **61,** pp. 76–80 (Baltimore, June 1941). A full translation and commentary of Ṛgv. VII.104 is there found.

3. See also S. Bhattacharji. *The Indian theogony*, pp. 66–7 (Cambridge, 1970).

4. *naro yatra devayavo madanti . . . Viṣṇoḥ pade parame madhva utsaḥ.*

5. For a complete study of the word *loka* see J. Gonda's *Loka. World and Heaven in the Veda* (Amsterdam, 1966). See pp. 115–143 for an analysis of *sukṛt*.

6. *cf.* P. Masson-Oursel, *Ancient India and Indian civilization* (London, 1934). 'All that the Ṛgveda wanted was that the pious man should live out his full life without premature death ' (p. 135). *cf.* Ṛgv. X.97.16. 'Free me from Yama's

fetter' *muñcantu mā ... Yamasya paḍbiśāt*. Is death Yama's fetter? But, if it is to enter into such a pleasant state of life as paradise, why is it a fetter? *cf.* Ath.v. VIII.7.28: 'I have taken thee up out of ... Yama's fetter' and Ṛgv. I.38.5 'nor should he go on Yama's path'.

7. It is occasionally difficult to pinpoint whether the desire expressed is for immortality in the spirit or in the body. There are two doubtful passages where (Ath.v. VIII.7.22) *amṛta* or immortality seems to be taken as an elixir of long life ('of this amṛta we make this man to drink the strength; now do I make a remedy, that he may be one of a hundred years'), and where (Ath.v. XVIII.3.62) the wish is expressed that 'death may pass away and deathlessness come to us' with preservation from decay or old age. *Cf.* also Ath.v. V.30. Nevertheless Ṛgv. IX.113.7–11 expresses the wish for immortality in heaven.

8. *cf.* Ṛgv. X.18.4 & 6, Ath.v. XVIII.2.29 & VI.41.3.

9. *Jīvānām āyuḥ pra tira tvam Agne pitṛṇāṃ lokam api gachantu ye mṛtāḥ*. J. Muir's translation, O.S.T. V, p. 300.

10. Ṛgv. V.46.1. Griffith's translation of *hayo na vidvān ayuji svayaṃ dhuri tāṃ vahāmi prataraṇīm avasyuvam na asyā vaśmi vimucaṃ na āvṛtaṃ punar vidvān pathaḥ pura eta ṛju neṣati*.

11. *paraṃ mṛtyo anu parā ihi panthāṃ yas te sva itaro devayānāt*.

12. *urvārukam iva bandhanān mṛtyor mukṣīya mā amṛtāt*.

13. *cf.* also Ath.v. XVIII.3.62 quoted above, note 7.

14. See also the curious explanation in P. Masson-Oursel, *Ancient India and Indian Civilization* (London, 1934): 'Just as the offering of *soma* maintains the life of the gods, certain offerings secure for the dead "non-re-death" (*a-mritā*), an expression which should not be translated as "immortality" for the cult must be kept up for ever if the deceased are to continue to exist' (p. 136).

15. As could be gathered from Ṛgv. X.14.10–12 or even X.135.1–3.

16. And therefore successive incarnations references to which will be examined later on. With regard to the singular use of death *cf.* A. Bergaigne's discussion of the use of the singular for the plural in connection with *amṛta*, the immortal for the immortals (I.35.2) in *Études sur le lexique du Rig-Véda*, p. 135 (Paris, 1884).

17. *prathamena pramāreṇa tredhā viṣvaṇ vi gachati ada ekena gachaty ada ekena gachati iha ekena ni śevate*. Is there a second dying and if so a third one as well? L. Renou in his *Hymnes spéculatifs du Véda* (Paris, 1956) makes no comment on this idea. For him three paths are here understood to await man after death. He has the following note to the whole verse: '33. doubtless the path of the gods, that which leads to the other world without return (and which appears here in two divisions) and the path of the fathers which brings back the defunct to earthly life; a well attested Upaniṣadic conception', p. 268 (Trans. J. M.). The subject of the two paths which already appears in the Ṛgveda will be taken up in due course.

18. *Sūryaṃ cakṣur gachatu vātam ātmā dyāṃ ca gacha pṛthivīṃ ca dharmaṇā apovā gacha ... oṣadhīṣu prati tiṣṭhā śarīraiḥ*.

19. *cf.* Ath.v. XVIII.2.23. 'Let thy soul go to its own (*svān*); and hasten to the Fathers.' This is J. Muir's translation of *svān gachatu te mano adhā pitṛn upa drava* (O.S.T. V, p. 306). W. D. Whitney renders the verse thus: 'Let thy mind go to its own [pl.] then run unto the Fathers'. The commentator, adds Whitney, supplies *tanum* to qualify *svān*. This would mean that the verse was interpreted by the Indian Scholiasts as 'let thy mind go to its own form'.

20. In Ṛgvedic hymns the *aja* or 'unborn' is equivalent to the *ātman* of the Upaniṣads.

21. *cf.* Ṛgv. IX.37.8 & 9.

22. See the section on Vedic meditation.

23. J. Muir's translation of Ath.v. V.24.9: *sūryaś cakṣurṣām adhipatih.* (O.S.T. V, p. 298). The latter quotes from Greek literature to show how prevalent was this ancient idea: 'I regard it [the eye] as of all the organs of sensation, possessing the most affinity to the sun. (Plato, Republic, VI.18).' *op. cit.* V, p. 298.

cf. Ṛgv. X.158.3 & 4 where Savitṛ and the creator are begged to grant sight (the 'eye') and to grant insight unto the eye (4) *cakṣur no dhehi cakṣuse.* The sun is the celestial eye surveying the whole world. The human eye is a miniature edition of it. Here may be found the root of the later idea of the spirit as witness (*sākṣin*) looking on impartially, beholding the *pratyayas* or presented ideas of the mind (Yoga-sutra).

24. *ajo bhagas tapasā taṃ tapasva taṃ te śochis tapatu taṃ te arciḥ . . . vahainaṃ sukṛtām u lokam.*

25. *cf.* Ṛgv. X.58.

26. A. B. Keith, *The Religion and Philosophy of the Veda and Upanishads*, H.O.S vol. 32, p. 405 (Cambridge, 1925).

27. *dharmaṇā* which Griffith translates as 'as thy merit is' thus bringing in the question of reward and punishment.

28. *op. cit.* V, p. 298.

29. *op. cit.* V, p. 304.

30. *sukṛtāṃ lokam api gachatu prajānan.*

31. *cf.* Ath.v. XVIII.4.10: 'Ye O Agni, having become back-carrying horses, shall with most healthful forms (*tanū*) carry him that has sacrificed unto the heavenly (*svarga*) world, where they revel in common revelry with the gods' (Whitney's translation). Agni, like a beast of burden, will take the dead to heaven and in the process of the burning the form will be transmuted.

32. J. Muir's translation. *op. cit.* V, p. 304.

33. *cf.* Ṛgv. I.146.1.

34. Keith was perhaps influenced by the Christian doctrine of the resurrection of the body.

35. *op. cit.* p. 405.

36. This word is used by A. Coomaraswamy, *The Ṛgveda as Land-Náma-Bók* p. 23 (London, 1935).

37. *āyur vasāṇaḥ upa vetu śeṣaḥ sangachatāṃ tanvā.*

38. *saṃ gachasva tanvā suyarcāḥ.* su + varcas, *varcas* being explained by Monier-Williams as 'the illuminating power of fire or the sun, i.e. brilliance, lustre, light'. This line could also be translated as 'unite with thy more glorious self'. M. Bloomfield (*The Religion of the Veda*, N.Y. and London, 1908) is of the opinion that 'the corpse is addressed' in this line (p. 194). We are of the opinion that the Vedic priests were not as senseless as to address a corpse, but rather the *aja* or 'unborn', as is also apparent in Ṛgv. X.16.4: 'As for his unborn part, Agni, kindle it . . . convey it to the world of the good'.

39. *op. cit.* V, p. 293.

40. *cf.* Ṛgv. VII.86.2 'And thus with myself do I converse' *uta svayā tanvā saṃ vade tat*'. *cf.* also verse 5 and Ath.v. IV.25.5 where *tanū* would be better translated by self rather than body.

41. *cf.* Ṛgv. IV.51.9, the radiant bodies or rather forms of the dawns, and Ath.v. XVIII.4.10 'most healthful forms'.

42. *op. cit.* p. 406.

43. Ath.v. XI.1.37. Whitney's translation. *cf.* also Ṛgv. X.14.8 *tanvā suvarcāḥ*, the body of light.

44. Trans. J. Muir, *op. cit.* V. p. 297. *tebhiḥ svarāḷ asunītim etāṃ yathāvaśaṃ tanvaṃ kalpayasva.*

45. Griswold, *The Religion of the Rigveda* (London, 1923) p. 315, gives a

slightly different rendering: 'Along with these prepare according to thy power as sovereign ruler this spirit-guidance (to heaven) and a body'. The Śat. Br. XIII.2.7.11 explains the idea as 'assume thyself the form thou desirest'.

46. This verse is translated rather meaninglessly by W. D. Whitney: 'for them may the autocratic (*svarāj*) second life today shape our bodies as he will'. *no adya yathāvaśaṃ tanvaḥ kalpayāti.*

47. *yathāvaśaṃ tanvaṃ cakra eṣaḥ.* Griffith translates as follows: 'he framed his body even as he listed'.

48. *cf.* Ṛgv. II.35.13.

49. The fear, evidenced in the Atharvaveda, that any injury to the physical body might be reflected on its subtler counterpart could have arisen in course of time either because of the close interconnection between the two, or when the 'light' or ethereal nature of the replica was lost sight of, or for some other inscrutable reason! *cf.* Ath.v. XVIII.2.4: 'Do not O Agni burn him up; do not be hot upon (*abhiśuc*) him; do not warp (*kṣip*) his skin nor his body; when thou shalt make him done O Jatavedas, then send him forward unto the Fathers' (Whitney's translation). *cf.* also Ath.v. XVIII.2.36.

50. *The Ṛgveda as Land-náma-bók*, p. 23 (London, 1935).

51. For A. B. Keith 'The connexion of this journey of the souls with the actual burning of the body is always a vague one' (*op. cit.* p. 406).

52. *cf.* Chānd, Up. III.13.7: 'the light which shines above this heaven . . . that is the same as that which is here within the person', as quoted in J. Gonda. *The Vision of the Vedic Poets*, 1963, p. 270. J. Gonda also draws attention to Bār. Up. 1.5.12 where 'heaven is considered to be the body of "mind" and the sun its "light form"' (*athaitasya manaso dyauḥ śarīraṃ jyotīrūpam asāv ādityaḥ*).

53. L. Renou, *Hymnes spéculatifs du Véda*, p. 255 (Paris, 1956).

54. *op. cit.* p. 256.

55. Griffith's translation of *stomā āsan pratidhayaḥ kurīraṃ chanda opaśaḥ.*

56. *Vedic Reader*, p. 214 (London, 1960).

57. . . . *ā naya etam ā rabhasva sukṛtāṃ lokam api gachatu prajānan tīrtvā tamāṃsi bahudhā mahānti aja nākam ākramatāṃ tṛtīvam.*

58. Explained as a feminine of *anudeya, deya* (gerund of $\sqrt{dā}$ given as 'present' in Monier-Williams.

59. *Poet-philosophers of the Ṛgveda*, p. 136 (Madras, 1963).

60. Macdonell, in his explanation of *anudeyī*, comes near to this point of view without realising the implications when he writes: 'It not improbably means that with which the deceased was supplied for the journey to Yama's abode' (*Vedic Reader*, p. 215). The 'present' with which the youth is supplied is the fruit of his earthly life.

61. *cf.* Matthew VI.19 & 20. 19 'Lay not up for yourselves treasures upon earth . . . 20. But lay up for yourselves treasures in heaven . . .'

62. *op. cit.* p. 130.

63. *Vedic Reader*, p. 125 (1960).

64. Max Müller renders this line as 'the abyss is stretched out in the East, the outgoing is in the West'. *Lectures on the Science of Language, delivered* . . . 1863. 2nd series, p. 516 (London, 1864). The East denotes entrance into life (*purastāt* = before, in front, in the beginning, in or from the East), the West departure therefrom (*paścāt* = from behind, in the rear, in the West, afterwards, hereafter etc.). This would agree with the idea which seems to be expressed here that as it was at the beginning of life, or as the seed was sown, so it is at the end. But the application is here to the particular individual, not to the cosmic process.

65. Śat. Br. identifies *prāṇa* with *asu* (VI.6.2.6).

66. G. Feuerstein and J. Miller, *A Reappraisal of Yoga*, p. 71 (London, 1971).

67. *cf.* Ath.v. VIII.2.1 a recall to life: 'I restore to thee breath and life' *asuṃ ta āyuḥ punar ā bharāmi.* The word *ātma* as used in the Ṛgveda may be equivalent to *asu*. Yet it may also stand for the equivalent or *prāṇa* or even be a combination of *aja* and *asu*. Ṛgv. I.66.1 identifies life with *prāṇa*: 'like the sun's glance, like prāṇa which is life' *āyur na prāṇo*. Ṛgvedic terminology is still rather fluidic or else our modern understanding of it is deficient.

68. Ath.v. XVIII.1.44: 'they who went to life (*asu*) unharmed (*avṛka*) right-knowing' *cf.* Ṛgv. X.15.1: *asuṃ ya īyur avṛkā ṛtajnāḥ*.

69. *yat te yamam . . . mano jagāma dūrakam.*

70. Ath.v. VIII.1.3 'Here [*be*] thy life, here breath, here life-time, here thy mind' (Whitney). *iha te 'sur iha prāṇa iha āyur iha te manaḥ.*

71. Ṛgv. VI.44.23.

PART II

Paradise and its Opposite

INTRODUCTION

Once heaven is reached bliss is assured.

Certain important points do not seem to have occurred to Western Sanskritists. The idea and meaning of paradise throughout the ages as rooted in the depth of the human *psyche* manifests as a projection of that longing for satisfaction and perfect happiness which cannot find fulfilment under earthly conditions and physical trammels. The average person's heaven, as conceived in his imagination, is always the ideal replica of his life. The more restricted the mental and spiritual aspirations the more limited the idea of paradise. The opposite is also true. Robert Browning evidenced his depth of understanding in the following lines:

All we have willed or hoped or dreamed of good, shall exist;
Not its semblance, but itself; no beauty, nor good, nor power
Whose voice has gone forth, but each survives for the melodist,
When eternity affirms the conception of an hour.
The high that proved too high, the heroic for earth too hard,
The passion that left the ground to lose itself in the sky,
Are music sent up to God by the lover and the bard;
Enough that he heard it once: we shall heart it by and by.

('Abt Vogler', Dramatics Personae, 1864.)

Beyond paradise there has always been another conception incomprehensible and therefore unacceptable to the average person: the beatific vision or union of th Christian mystic, the *ātman* realisation or liberation o the Hindu, the Ṣūfī's *fana* or self-annihilation in the Be loved with its corollary *baqa* or self-perpetuation in th Godhead, the *nirvāṇa* of the Buddhist so incomprehensibl to the European scholars that at first they argued it mean total extinction.[1] In Vedic India it is found in tha permanent union with the sun which Keith mention without drawing the proper conclusions and least of al suspecting that he had touched upon an aspect of Vedi thought unexplored by Western exegesis. Paradise an immortality should therefore not be lumped together a has been done without any discrimination.

It is characteristic that, in the *Kaṭha Upaniṣad*, to th one question which Naciketas has at heart to find a reply Yama three times evades the answer and tries to lure th inquirer away with promises of sensuous well-bein (I.23.25) thereby testing his sincerity and persistence i seeking the ultimate truth. For his is the deepest questio ever framed by the human soul and it does not concer mere survival but centres upon the meaning of liberation some say man exists: others that he exists no more (I.20) The same paradox was debated over *nirvāṇa* and th misunderstanding still persists. It is again characteristi that Yama yields to Naciketas's entreaty only after he ha ascertained that the latter is not to be deluded by th passing glories of the world of *māyā*. The paradises o humanity are not the ultimate reality of the truth seekers that reality as envisaged by the sages of all ages, includin the Vedic age. That truth is found at a transcendenta level to which the *ṛṣis* had access, but which the averag mind or the average person with all his passions is in capable of touching, let alone of fathoming out, and indeed has no wish to do so.

I. THE TREE OF LIFE

A further lack of insight on the part of Western scholar as to the importance and deep significance of Vedic imager s again evidenced in Keith's note to the mention of the g-tree in paradise: 'It is implausible to see any mytholo-ical importance in this tree which seems merely the reflex f the tree of the Indian village under which sit the elders'.[2] On the contrary, the tree under which Yama[3] and the ead ones revel is the tree of life such as is present in all nythologies, a tree which can be traced right to the Chris-ian Revelation (22.2) the leaves of which are there said o heal the nations. The Norse ash tree or yggdrasil, the 'zite tree of the Popol Vuk, the Tibetan Zambu, the holy ree of Ahura Mazda,[4] the sycamore of the Egyptian, the umerian tree whose foliage is the couch of the great nother and the Vedic *aśvattha* (Ṛgv. I.24.7. I.164.20 X.135.1 and Ath.v. V.4.3) are examples among many and ne in their inner significance: they are all the tree of life nd of knowledge and wisdom.[5] The only superficial yet onetheless important and interesting difference between ll these trees and the Vedic one is that the latter, as des-ribed in both the Ṛgveda and the Kaṭha Upaniṣad (6.1) tands 'with root above and branches below . . . that is he pure, the Brahman, that is called the deathless', thus dentifying this conception with the antique myth of the ree of life whence all creatures, in heaven and on earth, lerive their sustenance, the tree drawing its life from the piritual realm, hence its roots, in the Vedas, merge into eaven rather than into the earth. 'It comprises all the vorlds' goes on the Kaṭha Upaniṣad 'none ever goes eyond it'. (6.1) The same tree is described in Ṛgv. I.24.7:

> Varuṇa . . . sustaineth erect the tree's stem in the base-less region. Its ays, whose root is high above, stream downward. Deep may they sink within us and be hidden. (Griffith's translation)

The rays (or branches) of the tree of life sustained by no ess a god than Varuṇa, the lord of righteousness, pervade every human being who is thus intrinsically connected with everyone else and with the very source of spiritual ife. The import of this verse is obvious and meets that in Revelation.[6] The tree of life and of knowledge of the Old Testament is the direct descendant of the Vedic tree. In the shadow of this sacred tree the souls of the dead take their rest in Yama's kingdom. There they stand closer t its roots and thus to the fountain-source of existenc Hence their rest implies invigoration. On this same tre (Ṛgv. I.164.20) two birds have found a refuge, one eatin the fruit thereof, the other looking on, a graphic descrip tion of divine and human nature, one partaking c experience, the other observing.[7]

Furthermore, the Atharvaveda gives some mor interesting details:

> The *aśvattha*, seat of the gods, in the third heaven from here; there th gods won the *kuṣṭha*, the sight (*cakṣaṇa*) of immortality (*amṛta*). (Ath. V.4.3. Whitney's translation)

The *kuṣṭha* is a plant which according to Ath.v. V.4.1 i the remover (*nāśana*) of fever (*takman*). It is found o snow-topped lofty mountains (V.4.2) and is obviousl indicative of purity. This plant in the next verse (V.4.4) i called *kuṣṭha*, the flower of immortality.[8] This flower th gods won in the third heaven, under the *aśvattha* tree Having risen to the third sphere, to their seat which vers 3 identifies with the *aśvattha*, the gods won that plan which removes fever and they became immortal. If ther were any doubts as to a metaphorical meaning, the tw words *nāśana* and *takman* connected with the gods shoul dispel it. Fever is surely symbolical of earthly or huma passions which must be discarded before immortality ma be attained.

II. THE ṚGVEDIC HEAVEN

The Vedic heaven, as rightly pointed out by Keith,[9] is no the heaven of a war-like people. His surprise at this can onl be attributed to the prejudice of the nineteenth centur which considered the Vedic tribes as warrior barbarians Nevertheless he drew somewhat erroneous conclusions The Vedic paradise may represent the wish-fulfilment o the community at large as voiced through the priests, bu not necessarily be the complete priestly idea. The projectio of inner longings into a concrete representation of fulfilment, even if only imaginary, is the never failing mirror of the soul of a people. We find the paradises of Christians and Muslims and Hindus alike pander to the weaknesses of human nature and therefore show a mixture of the lofty and the low. They may be formulated by the priests and the prophets themselves, but they remain the best that human comprehension at large can grasp because they mirror in themselves the essence of human longing. Heaven is therefore the land of heart's desire where every wish finds its fulfilment. These very words are expressed in Ṛgv. IX.113.9–11:

> Make me immortal in that realm where they move even as they list, in the third sphere of inmost heaven where lucid worlds are full of light . . .
>
> Make me immortal in that realm of eager wish and strong desire, the region of the radiant moon, where food and full delight are found . . .
>
> Make me immortal in that realm where happiness and transports, where joys and felicities combine, and longing wishes are fulfilled . . .[10]

For the average mortal paradise is the undecaying world of everlasting lustre (Ṛgv. IX.113.7), the place of happiness and unalloyed harmony where one may join parents and children who have passed on (Ath.v. XII.3.17) and rejoice with the 'gracious-minded fathers' (Ṛgv. X.14.10):

> Where the well-hearted, well-doing revel, having abandoned disease of their own selves, not lame . . . undamaged in heaven (*svarga*) there may we see [our] parents and sons. (Ath.v. VI.130.3. Whitney's translation).[11]

Such is the typical yearning of the average person and such it was of the Vedic people. At the hour of death, or even of loneliness, fear of the unknown grips the person and he falls back on his love of family or nucleus of safety and asks only for that. Moreover in both the Ṛgveda and Atharvaveda the emphasis is on wholeness—no disease, no sin but reunion with the loved ones, i.e. fullness in ever respect. The Vedic paradise may be interpreted accordin to the frame of mind of the commentator, either alon spiritual lines as is evidenced in Griswold[12] or along purel materialistic lines as is seen in Keith,[13] Macdonell[14] an others.

However, doubt arises as to the permanence for huma beings of this sojourn in heavenly realms. Certain verse in both the Ṛgveda and the Atharvaveda make such permanence highly questionable:

> Having gone to my relatives, let me not fall (*mā v patsi lokāt*)[15] down from [their or that] world! (Ath.v VI.120.2)

As there is no sin or blemish in that world, as we sha learn presently, why should there be a fall? Verse 3 'wher the well-hearted . . . revel . . . there may we see our parent has been taken as proof of the Vedic belief in persona immortality whereas it is nothing of the sort. Since th possibility of a 'fall' is clearly enunciated the verse merel proves personal survival, a different conception. There i no evidence here as to an eternal sojourn in paradise fo human beings.

Ṛgv. X.14.8 enjoins the departed soul to 'go back to th home' *punar astam ehi*, the emphatic word *punar* (again giving rise to the question: why 'again'? Has the defunc been to heaven before that he should turn back agai thither? Why is heaven called a 'home' if he is to reach i for the first time only. This would at least imply that heave is the place of origination (the *janitra* of Ṛgv. X.56.1) o humans and this in turn would imply pre-existence i nothing more. Further, whether we translate the verse a Roth[16] does, as 'enter thy home, laying down again a imperfection', or as M. Müller[17] does, as 'leave evil there then return home', the idea of recurrence (or at least o pre-existence and of having done this once before) canno be dismissed. Such an idea obviously present here doe not seem to trouble the commentators; neither Grisworld[1 nor Bloomfield[19] (neither Roth, nor Whitney nor Mac donell) pass any remark, Griswold merely interpreting the phrase as going 'back home—to his true home as it were'.[20] Muir, on the other hand, is of the opinion that Max Müller's 'rendering appears to make the departed return to this world to resume his body, though in a glorified state, which does not seem to bring out a good sense'.[21] Whatever 'a good sense' would be is not made clear. Muir himself translates the verse thus: 'throwing off all imperfections again go to thy house', a rendering which emphasises the idea of recurrence. Keith has a very poor explanation: 'The heaven is called also the home, but the idea can hardly be pressed to the view that the going to heaven is a return home; it is rather that the man reaches in the highest heaven a new and abiding home'.[22] On the contrary, the verse seems to emphasise the thought of returning home. The 'reaching a new and abiding home' throws no light whatsoever on the word *punar* but the 'abiding home' contradicts the fear of falling therefrom expressed in Ath.v. VI.120.2. Why it cannot be viewed as evidence of an implied[23] pre-existence of the human soul and its repeated sojourns in heaven—the length of the latter depending upon the value of the good deeds performed when on earth—is far from clear unless indeed the Christian disbelief in such doctrines militated against any understanding. Similar evidence of the idea of recurrence appears in Ṛgv. X.16.5: 'Give up again Agni, to the Fathers, him who comes offered to thee with oblations'.[24] This could be superficially interpreted as the fact that Agni is constantly giving up thousands of souls to the fathers. Nevertheless, the reference is not to any one in general, but to the particular person, 'him who comes offered to thee' upon the funeral pyre and no one else; whether we translate *ava sṛja* as 'give up', 'cast off' or 'set free', it is coupled with *punar* which yields the meaning 'set free again' or 'once more'.

Furthermore, it is clearly stated in the Ṛgveda and the Atharvaveda that there are various categories of 'fathers', those who 'departed first and last' (Ṛgv. X.15.2), 'who take their dwelling in terrestrial spheres' (*pārthive rajasi*) and those who take their dwelling 'in fair abodes' (*suvṛ-*

janāsu vikṣu) which Muir renders as 'among the powerful races' (the gods). Griffith explains the former as 'the firmament nearest to the earth', yet the expression used is *pārthiva*, pertaining to earth or terrestrial. In any case, the distinction is made between the earthly and the heavenly or godly.

The Atharvaveda has an even clearer reference to these categories: 'Let us worship . . . those fathers who . . . have entered into the atmosphere, or who inhabit the earth or the sky' (Ath.v. XVIII.2.49).[25] The important point is the distinction of the three locations, *antarikṣa*, *pṛthivi*, *dyu*. In these three words is apparent the Vedic division of the world, not the physical world only as much as the psychological one: the material or cerebral consciousness and therefore earthly life; the intermediate or psycho-mental, and the spiritual or heavenly. The fathers are located in these three realms. What does the earthly realm or even the *antarikṣa* mean if not a pointer to our thesis that those who have not won immortality do not stay for ever in heaven. Some ancestors, such as the Ṛbhus, are expressly mentioned as having won immortality. This very fact ought to arouse doubt as to the equivalence of heaven and immortality in so far as human beings are concerned.[26] It is interesting to note in this connection that the *Mahābhārata* (Sabhāparvan 461) classifies the *pitṛs* into seven categories, four embodied, three formless. (Quoted in Muir O.S.T. p. 296).

Ṛgv. X.14.8[27] brings up yet another problem. The third *pada* begins with the philosophically important words: 'leaving imperfection behind' (*hitvāya avadyam*). Is transgression to be altogether forgotten or forgiven, perhaps melted in the ritual, purifying fire, though we are told that not all people were cremated (Ṛgv. X.15.14 'those cremated and those not cremated')? The words actually used are 'leaving behind'; they imply neither forgetting nor forgiving. Whether the whole verse is interpreted as 'once again leaving blemish behind, go home' or as 'leaving transgression behind, go back home' the idea of recurrence is as insistent as ever. Therefore the doubt arises: is not the meaning a leaving behind of transgression or sin as a seed to bear fruit in due course and operate the 'fall' from the state of bliss as hinted at in Ath.v. VI.120.2? It will be argued that this is a later doctrine. These verses nevertheless point to it in no uncertain terms.

The departed is, in the meantime, to 'unite with the reward of his sacrifices and good works' (*saṃ gachasva . . . iṣṭāpūrtena*) as well as with the patriarchs and Yama, leaving his transgressions on the threshold of paradise. *Iṣṭāpūrta* is the fruit of good deeds performed when on earth. Muir quotes Haug as explaining *iṣṭāpūrta* as 'what is sacrificed' and 'filled up to'. 'The words before us' sums up Muir, 'mean "rejoin thy sacrifices which were stored up"'.[28] This is the eternal religious idea that what we sacrifice here below we shall gain a hundredfold in heaven, and not a mere reference to the ritual sacrifice to be performed by the dutiful worshipper. The Atharvaveda has an enlightening verse: 'With my soul (*manasā*) I ascend after the great sacrifice as it goes dwelling with my austere fervour' (*tapasā sayoniḥ*) (Ath.v. VI.122.4).[29] There is here a hint as to the inner sacrifice which liberates the human being and enables him to rise beyond himself. Atharvan, the sage, it is declared in the Ṛgveda 'by sacrifices laid the paths' (Ṛgv. I.83.5).

If the fruit of good deeds is reaped in heaven as obvious from Ṛgv. X.14.8, what of the fruit of other deeds—not those of extreme evil which make the human being dig his own 'pit'[30] but those transgressions to which man is just too prone? The average person has neither just good nor just evil to his credit, the balance is seldom completely on one side only. The abandonment of disease and infirmities at the threshold of heaven (Ath.v. VI.120.1 & 3), the making whole of the human being (Ṛgv. X.14.8)—the 'physical' aspect being but the reflection of the psychological—imply that all imperfections are simply abandoned on the threshold but does not prove their obliteration. They are only discarded. There is undoubtedly a figurative meaning in the act that only the 'whole' in body reach heaven. Those who are blind or who have eyes but see not and equally those who are deaf to the call of truth, 'the wicked travel not the pathway of law' (Ṛgv. IX.73.6).[31]

We do not agree with Keith when he asserts:

> The idea of judgement of any sort is foreign to the Ṛgveda as to early Iran, and it is only in the Taittīriya Aranyaka that we have the express statement that the truthful and the untruthful are separated before Yama.[32]

Heaven and hell (or the pit) are in themselves ideas of reward and punishment although originally they may not have been clearly considered in that light. Likewise is the expression *iṣṭāpūrta*. Heaven is definitely the world of what has been well accomplished (*sukṛtasya lokam* Ath.v. VI. 120.1).[33] Ṛgv. IV.5.5 shows the belief that each one makes or mars his own future: 'They for themselves this deep place created', as translated by Griswold[34] or by Griffith 'they who are full of sin, untrue, unfaithful, they have engendered this abysmal station'.[35] The word 'engendered' (*jan*) confirms that they are the cause of their own undoing. Furthermore, Ṛgv. IX.13.8 states unequivocably that Soma, the purifier, the guardian of law, 'the knower, beholding all worlds, hurls the hated and irreligious into the abyss'.[36] This militates against Keith's statement which needs considerable qualification before it could be endorsed—if at all. He fails to account for e.g. the curious but very suggestive Atharvavedic statement (Ath.v. XVIII. 2.37): 'I bestow this resting place upon that man who has come here, *if he is mine*. Yama, having observed, admitted "he is mine, let him come here and prosper"'.[37] This verse at least implies judgement or mere sorting out. The doubt 'if he is mine' and Yama's consideration of the question, his acceptance of the defunct as his own, places him in the quality of arbiter. But the idea of arbitration seems to be more of a poetised or allegorical personification of the law of cause and effect than anything else. Again Ath.v. XVIII.2.25 'having found your place among the fathers prosper among Yama's subjects',[38] etc. being addressed to the departed one, indirectly points out that the 'finding' is the defunct's own action or business, with the implication that his deeds have led him to such conditions as will enable him to discover for himself his place in heaven.

There is thus really no reward or punishment meted out by an extra-cosmic deity in the Christian sense and this Christian doctrine may account for the scholars' apparent incapacity to detect the working of the impersonal law of cause and effect: the working of an intrinsic and inexorable law according to which a particular cause will create a particular effect quite in line with Indian philosophic thought.[39]

III. THE ṚGVEDIC HELL

Is the Vedic equivalent of hell annihilation as claimed by A. Weber,[40] R. Roth, and others? Rudolph Roth argues thus:

> Two possibilities here present themselves: the one, that after the death of the body the evil will live on for an indefinite time their evil life, in contrast to that of the blest in heaven; the other, that their individuality is extinguished by death ... Passages in the sacred writings ... speak in favor of the second supposition, of the annihilation of the wicked at death. We read there that Varuna, the supreme judge of the actions of men here and of their fate hereafter, thrusts those who displease him down into the depth. As their body into the grave, so they themselves sink into a dark abyss; *and with that, doubtless, their being is* at an end.[41] Herewith accords, too, the already mentioned doctrine that *immortality is a free gift from heaven*.[42] Whoever fails to receive it, ends his existence when his body dies. Of a hell this religion knows nothing, although the later Indians have imagined for themselves hell and its horrors, after the same manner as other nations.[43]

The whole problem is not as simple as imagined by Roth who here is drawing wrong conclusions based upon purely gratuitous assumptions. A dark abyss does not necessarily mean annihilation. 'Bottomless abysses' (*gūhamānā vavrān*) are mentioned in Ṛgv. VII.104.3 with reference to demons and a deep place (*padam ajanata gabhīram*) is produced for the sinners and evil ones (*pāpāsaḥ ... anṛtāḥ*) in Ṛgv. IV.5.5. Ṛgv. VII.104 is a rather vindictive incantation directed more towards demons and very evil men. It is thus not surprising to find there very strong language being used and imprecations sending the demons or the evil men to 'destruction' (*nirṛti* VII.104.9). 'Let those who employ charms of hate receive your destruction' (14) is clearly addressed to sorcerers who may have been regarded as the worse evil doers. Thus verse 8 speaks in no uncertain language:

> Whoever, when I am acting with pure and single heart, works against me with charms that are counter to the ṛta (*anṛta*), may he, O Indra, as he pronounces non-existence (*asat*), himself go to non-existence, like waters held in the fist.[44]

However, that kind of death wish, possibly pronounced in the heat of wrath, is not of common occurrence and by itself is not of sufficient evidence for drawing conclusions that annihilation awaits the wicked.

J. Muir, like all nineteenth century scholars, failed to grasp the psychological meaning of *andhaṃ tamas* (Ṛgv. X.103.12[45] and Ath.v. XVIII.3.3.[46]). '. . . It is not clear', he writes 'that in these passages the words denote a place of punishment'.[47] Once again we have here the Christian idea of punishment which prevents the scholar from grasping the Indian intent. Muir quotes Ath.v. V.30.11—one of those uncertain passages where darkness cannot mean punishment—where a sick man is called upon to 'rise up from deep death, even from the black darkness'.[48] Both words 'death' and 'darkness' here refer to unconsciousness. After the death of the physical body, as already discussed, there was considered to be a period of unconsciousness[49] equivalent to the coma state of a sick person, after which the defunct had to get his bearings and accustom himself to the new conditions. So the same word is used for both unconsciousness and darkness and this may account for the fear of death and the development of this idea into hell which, however, as rightly noted by Roth, shows no trace in Vedic times of the monstrous imaginings of later Hindu and Christian Medieval literature.

Tamas being both darkness and inertia points to the later *avīci* the waveless *loka* or hell, already somewhat present in the Ṛgvedic hell, the place of heaviness 'down below' the earth (Ath.v. II.14.3). It is a chasm, a pit of silence 'beneath all three earths' (Ṛgv. VII.104.11), a perfect forerunner of *avīci.* It is then not surprising to find that *tamas* as Muir[50] remarks is 'in Ath.v. VIII.1.10 . . . used by itself, apparently for the state of the dead' as against the 'light of the living' (*Jīvatāṃ jyotiḥ*). But there seems to be degrees or different spheres of hell just as there are three realms of heaven: 'they do not die there, nor go to the nethermost darkness', the nethermost darkness (*adhamaṃ tamaḥ*) pointing to a deeper state of gloom (Ath.v. VIII.2.24).

It should be realised that all these conceptions of darkness-heaviness and light-lightness are based upon the human *psyche*.[51] Growth, which is life, implies 'taking in' from outer sources and assimilating, whether at the physical or intellectual level; the child grows by taking; the man should grow by giving, the latter the result of his assimilation; he gives back to life and his surroundings what he has received, assimilated and coloured by his personality, that is, made his own. Both processes *add* something to life and belong to the *light* side of life: *expansion*, whether in the child or in the adult, means joy. The opposite, constriction, shrinking, atrophy, avarice, etc., takes away from life and therefore leads to separation, unhappiness, folly, darkness and death. Similarly, light (heaven) means knowledge, soul expansion, bliss, life. Darkness (hell) means ignorance, inertia, contraction, heaviness, death to the soul. The highest heaven is supreme light, enlightenment, therefore supreme consciousness, to fail to reach which does not mean annihilation but may mean to remain in darkness (with its various degrees) and this may be regarded as a punishment though, more correctly, it is only the direct effect of the cause created, namely lack of endeavour along certain lines. So we have two aspects of *tamas*, one referring to unconsciousness, and the other to soul-blindness and therefore darkness, heaviness, inertia, hell. J. Muir quotes appositely from the Viṣṇu Purāṇa and the Mahābhārata two most illuminating verses which better than any others reveal the true Indian meaning of heaven and hell:

> Heaven is that which delights the mind; hell is that which gives it pain; hence, vice is called hell; virtue

> is called heaven. (Viṣṇu Purāṇa, II.6.40).
>
> Falsehood is the embodiment of darkness (*tamas*); by darkness a man is carried downwards. Those who are seized by darkness, being enveloped in darkness, do not see the light. Heaven they say is light (*prakāśa*) and hell darkness (*tamas*). (Mahābhārata XII.6969 ff.)[52]

In other words heaven is illumination, hell blindness. Hell is an abyss of gloom, heaven a mountain of light. Hence the idea of flight and lightness, of 'ascension' to heaven, and, on the other hand, of heaviness, of falling and of 'descent' into hell. To live is to see eternal light, as one gathers from many a verse, e.g. Ṛgv. X.185.3 'the man on whom the sons of Aditi bestow eternal light that he may live' and Ath.v. VII.53.7: 'Up out of darkness have we, ascending the highest firmament, gone to the sun, god among the gods, highest light' (Whitney's translation) equivalent to Ṛgv. X.50.10. There the essence of light, of illumination, is the sun: 'We have gone to heaven (*svar*) . . . we have united (*saṃ-gam*) with the sun's light'. (Ath.v. XVI.9.3).

NOTES

1. *cf. The New Catechism. Catholic Faith for Adults* produced by the Higher Catechetical Institute at Nijmegen, 1967, which in its chapter on other religions describes *nirvāṇa* as 'the cessation of individual existence' (p. 29). The Buddhist idea that the drop becomes the ocean, the consciousness expands into the universal, carries a much deeper connotation than the mere 'extinction of individual existence', a definition which shows a marked lack of that profounder understanding so characteristic of Buddhism.
2. *op. cit.* p. 407, fn. 7.
3. *cf.* Ṛgv. X.135.1 and Ath.v. V.4.3.
4. *cf.* Vendidad Fargard XIX.2.18 (60) 'Go O Spitama Zarathustra towards that tree that is beautiful, high-growing and mighty amongst the high-growing trees'. The Vendidad, trans. by J. Darmesteter. S.B.E. vol. 4, p. 20 (Oxford, 1880).
5. For excellent studies of the whole idea *see* F. A. S. Butterworth, *The Tree at the Navel of the Earth* (Berlin, 1970) and O. Viennot, *Le Culte de l'arbre dans l'Inde ancienne* (Paris, 1954), especially pp. 25–37.
6. Revelation, 22.1: 'And he shewed me a pure river of water of life . . . 2. 'In the midst of the street of it, and on either side of the river, was there the tree of life, which bore twelve manner of fruits, and yielded her fruit every month; and the leaves of the tree were for the healing of the nations.'
7. *cf.* also Kaṭha Up. III.1.
8. *cf.* also Ath.v. XIX.39–1–8.
9. *op. cit.* p. 407: 'The total absence of anything which could be regarded as

natural in the heaven of warriors is a striking reminder that the conceptions of Vedic India . . . were the ideas of priests and not the whole community.' We fail to agree with the latter part of this quotation for reasons given above. Macdonell writes in the same vein: 'Heaven is a glorified world of material joys as pictured by the imagination not of warriors but of priests.' 'Vedic Mythology', *Grundriss der Indo-Arischen Philologie und Altertumskunde*. III. Band, 1. Heft A, p. 168 (Strassburg, 1897).

10. Griffith's translation. The Sanskrit of these verses is given on p. 199, fn. 2.

11. *cf.* also Ath.v. III.28.5: 'Where the good-hearted [and] well-doing revel, quitting disease of their own body', etc. (Whitney's trans.)

12. *Vedic eschatology* in *The Religion of the Rigveda* (London, 1923), pp. 314–318. '. . . the Rigvedic Heaven is a place of radiance inexhaustible and of living waters, of spirit-food and complete satisfaction, of movement glad and free . . . The grave and solemn tone of this Rigvedic hymn of Paradise [IX.113] reminds one of the similar utterance in Ṛgv. VII.16–17: 'they shall hunger no more neither thirst any more' etc.

13. *op. cit.* p. 407.

14. *op. cit.* p. 168 'Heaven is a glorified world of material joys as pictured by the imagination not of warriors but of priests', etc.

15. For a complete exegesis of the meaning of *loka* see J. Gonda's *Loka. World and Heaven in the Veda* (Amsterdam, 1966).

16. '. . . geh' ein Heimath alles Unvollkommene wieder ablegend'. 'Die Sage von Dschemschid' D.M.G.Z. Leipzig, 4, p. 428 (1850).

17. 'Die Todtenbestattung bei den Brahmanen'. D.M.G.Z. Band 9, p. xiv (Leipzig, 1855).

18. *op. cit.* pp. 315–16.

19. *The Religion of the Veda* (N.Y. and London, 1908), American lectures on the History of Religions, 7th series (1906–7). 'They have left all imperfections behind them on returning to their true home' (p. 251). *cf.* also p. 195.

20. *op. cit.* p. 316.

21. *op. cit.* V, p. 293–4, fn. 434.

22. *op. cit.* p. 406.

23. *cf.* Coomaraswami, '*The Ṛg Veda as Land-Nâma-Bók*', p. 21 (1935). '. . . where as reincarnation, not in the later and more literal (Buddhist) sense, but of the progenitive principles at the dawn of a new creation is implied'.

24. Muir's translation. *op. cit.* V, p. 298–9: *ava sṛja punar agne pitṛbhyo yas ta āhutaś carati svadhābhiḥ.*

25. . . . *ya āviviśur urv antarikṣaṃ ya ākṣiyanti pṛthivīm uta dyām* (Muir's translation, V, p. 296).

26. This subject will be discussed in due course. *cf.* A. Bergaigne, *La Religion Védique*, tome I, p. 83 (Paris, 1878), who considers there is a confusion between *antarikṣa* and *dyu*, but notices the existence of 'inferior fathers or those who inhabit the earth'. He adds 'they are certainly also dead . . . from certain texts it seems to come out that after having gone up to heaven the fathers descend thence to the earth' (p. 84). (Trans. J. M.)

27. The whole stanza runs as follows: *saṃ gachasva pitṛbhiḥ saṃ Yamena iṣṭāpūrtena parame vyoman hitvāyāvadyaṃ punar astam ehi saṃ gachasva tanvā suvarcāḥ. cf.* also Ath.v. XVIII.3.58: 'Unite thyself with the Fathers, with Yama, with thy sacred and charitable works in the highest firmament; abandoning what is reproachful, come again home;—let him unite with a body, very splendid' (Whitney's translation). The same idea of a return home is clearly expressed here.

28. *op. cit.* p. 293. *cf.* Ath.v. XVIII.2.20 and XI.1.36.

29. Muir's translation. *op. cit.* p. 293. Whitney translates this line as follows:

'The great sacrifice as it goes, with mind, I ascend after, with fervor (*tapas*) of like origin'.

30. Ṛgv. II.29.6: 'Save us ye holy from the pit and falling' and IX.73.8.9 as well as VII.104.3.17 and IV.5.5. According to L. Renou the idea of sin is frequently brought out in connection with Varuṇa 'faisant penser par moments que la théorie du *karman* s'est constituée en milieu varuṇien.' 'Hymnes ā Varuṇa': notes. *Études véd-pān.* VII. fasc. 12, p. 4, 1960.

31. *cf.* Ṛgv. IX.73.6 d: *ṛtasya panthāṃ na taranti duṣkṛtaḥ.* For a discussion of *duskṛta* see J. Gonda, *Loka,* etc. pp. 126–8. From passages in the Ṛgveda and the Atharvaveda he shows that '. . . here no distinction is made between deliverance from evil deeds and their results on the one hand and pollution on the other. The performance of evil deeds really is a sort of pollution' (p. 128). See also p. 127 for a different translation of IX.73.6 d. The opposite, *suhita* or good deeds, is according to the same author used foremost in the sense of ritual deeds or merits.

32. *op. cit.* p. 409. *cf.* also p. 572.

33. For a discussion of *sukṛtasya lokaḥ* as meaning 'the sphere of ritual and religious merit' and *sukṛtāṃ lokaḥ* as 'the sphere or condition of those who have earned the rewards of well-performed rites' see J. Gonda, *Loka,* etc. p. 130.

34. *op. cit.* p. 319.

35. *pāpāsaḥ santo anṛtāḥ asatyāḥ idaṃ padam ajanata gabhīram.* Hell is clearly the result of grave transgressions—sinners dig their own hell. According to H. von Glasenapp, *Immortality and salvation in Indian religions* (Calcutta, 1963): 'Even in the oldest Vedic Times, there is not yet any mention of a sharp differentiation of the fate of good and bad people' (p. 25).

36. Translated by Muir, *op. cit.* p. 312. *vidvān sa viśva bhuvanā 'bhi paśyati avajustan vidhyati karte avratan.*

37. *Dadāmi asmā avasānam etad yaḥ eṣa āgan mama ced abhūd iha. yamaś cikitvān prati etad āha mamaiṣa rāya upa tiṣṭhatām iha.* (Trans. J. M.) Whitney translates as follows: 'I give this release to him who hath thus come and hath become mine here—thus replies the knowing Yama—let this one approach my wealth here'. The word *rayi* demonstrates that it does not always mean earthly wealth as commonly interpreted. *Avasāna* translated as 'abode' by Muir and 'release' by Whitney means resting-place, where the horses are unharnessed. Heaven is a rest from earthly labours.

38. *lokaṃ pitṛṣu vitvā edhasva yamarājasu.*

39. This principle is found in a different way in the idea of like going to like after death. *cf.* Ṛgv. X.16.3: 'Go according to thy nature, to heaven and earth'.

40. *Eine Legende des Catapatha-Brāhmaṇa über die strafende Vergeltung nach dem Tode*, pp. 237–240, D.M.G.Z. **9.**

41. This is a mere surmise. The italics are our own.

42. This also is a surmise which does not stand examination as will be seen.

43. *On the morality of the Veda.* Translated by W.D. Whitney, pp. 344 & 345, J.A.O.S. **3** (1853)

44. W. N. Brown's translation, '*The Rigvedic Equivalent for Hell*', p. 77. J.A.O.S. **61.**

45. 'So let our foes abide in utter darkness' (Griffith's translation). If foes are to *abide* in darkness—or any other condition—there cannot be annihilation. (*andhena amitrās tamasā sacantām.* This may also be equivalent to 'suffer in blinding darkness').

46. 'I saw the maiden being led . . . alive for the dead . . . enclosed with blind darkness' (Whitney's translation).

47. *op. cit.* p. 312.

48. Whitney translates this line thus: 'come up out of death's profound black darkness'. *udehi mṛtyor gambhīrāt kṛṣṇāc cit tamasas pari.*
49. *cf.* Ṛgv. X.135.3 and Ath.v. VIII.1.8. '. . . ascend out of darkness' and 10. '. . . to that darkness, O man, do not go forth').
50. *op. cit.* p. 312.
51. It is useless to argue that psychology was not known in those early days. The greatest psychologists of ancient times were the Hindus, the finest example being the Buddha. Western psychology, by comparison with Hindu or Buddhist psychology, is only in its infancy.
For further elucidations on the whole subject see 'The Vedic concept of aṃhas' by J. Gonda, in *Indo-Iranian Journal*, **1,** pp. 33–60, 'S-Gravenhage (1957).
52. *op. cit.* p. 313. *cf.* Īśā Upaniṣad (9).

PART III
Immortality

I. IMMORTALITY, A PRIZE TO BE WON

Since hell does not necessarily imply annihilation, so heaven does not equally imply immortality. The one atrophies, the other invigorates, but there their action may stop. Indeed, if paradise were permanent, if it signified eternal life for each individual, if it were deemed equivalent to immortality, there would be no such insistent asking as is found in Ṛgv. IX.113: why those implorations *to be made immortal in heaven*?[1] 'Make me immortal in that realm where dwells the king' (8) begs the poet of Soma, after declaring 'place me in that deathless state' (7) (*amṛte loke akṣita*).

> (9) Make me immortal in that realm where they move even as they list in the third sphere of inmost heaven where lucid worlds are full of light . . .
>
> (10) Make me immortal in that realm of eager wish and strong desire . . .
>
> (11) Make me immortal in that realm where happiness and transports, where joys and felicities combine, and longing wishes are fulfilled . . . (Ṛgv. IX.113. Griffith's translation).[2]

The words cannot be mistaken: *tatra mām amṛtaṃ kṛdhi*; that realm is heaven where eternal light (*jyotir ajasram*) prevails.

What is the difference between heaven and immortality? What kind of virtues are required to win heaven, what to gain immortality?

The essential quality for the winning of heaven is expressed in the one word *tapas* which means the kindling of the inner self[3] through the sacrifice of the ego or outer self, hence the undertones of austerity, of penance. This kindling, needless to say, is also achieved in various degrees.

All the virtues stemming from *tapas* are described in Ṛgv. X.154. Here is Muir's translation:

2. Let him depart to those who, through rigorous abstraction (*tapas*) are invincible, who, through *tapas*, have gone to heaven; to those who have performed great *tapas*.
3. Let him depart to the combatants in battles, to the heroes who have there sacrificed their lives, or to those who have bestowed thousands of largesses.
4. Let him depart, Yama, to those austere ancient Fathers who have practised and promoted sacred rites.
5. Let him depart, Yama, to those austere rishis, born of rigorous abstraction, to those sages, skilled in a thousand sciences, who guard the sun.[4]

Those who sacrifice themselves in any walk of life—whether battle-field or home—will receive the blessings of heaven. There is perceptible a gradation: through self-abstraction, through self-sacrifice even unto death, through extreme generosity, through the deliberate cultivation and promotion of law, of truth, of the institution of sacred rites, the gate of heaven is open. Only finally are mentioned those *ṛṣis* who, through the inner kindling effected by *tapas*, were born through that kindling (*tapojān*), were born of *tapas*, or, as we might advance, those born of contemplation through that power are the great knowers, the great seers of old (*sahasranīthāḥ*) and the herdsmen, the hero-guardians of the sun (*ye gopāyanti sūryam*). This last verse (Ṛgv. X.154.5) hides the secret of immortality.[5]

Even though we may gather that the majority of human beings does enjoy the heaven state of bliss after death, it remains quite plain that only a few have become immortal. Heaven harbours gods, the patriarchs, and departed humans, but of these three categories only the gods and some patriarchs, e.g. the Aṅgirasaḥ and the Ṛbhus, are termed immortal. We also, indirectly, learn that originally the gods were not immortal.

What wins immortality? What is the significance of immortality as against heaven? What is the fate of those who do not win immortality?

The answer to the first question may be developed along two lines of investigation, that of the gods and that of the ancestors, both meeting in the end in the one underlying factor which points the way to a third line, that of human immortality: the necessity of personal exertion in certain directions of which the fruit is *amṛta*. The latter is by no means a free gift from heaven, as Roth would have it. The average person is not indicated as striving for this particular goal, but the *ṛṣis* obviously long for it. Prayers and incantations at death demand heaven for the dying as a reward for a good life, specific demands for *amṛta* being the prayer of the *ṛṣis*: 'Place us with the generation of immortality'.[6] 'Place us, with your help, in the state of immortality'.[7]

Western exegesis has failed to differentiate between these themes. Heaven was considered *ipso facto* as implying immortality as in Christianity and no penetrating analysis was made of those *pitṛs* who did gain *amṛta* as against the ordinary mortal who finds for himself a place in heaven.

J. Muir[8] in his discussion of Vedic thought on the after-life first shows nineteenth century scepticism with regard to the possibility of survival. Finding the evidence as to Vedic belief in the latter irrefutable he yet sees and draws no distinction between the idea of paradise and that of eternal life and whether both are equivalent.

It is true—he argues—that the Ṛibhus, on account of their artistic skill, are said, in some texts in the earlier books, to have been promised, and to have attained, immortality and divine honours . . . (Ṛgv. IV.35.3, where it is said: *atha aita Vājāḥ amṛitasya panthāṃ ganaṃ devānām Ṛibhavaḥ suhastāḥ*.

'Then, skilful Vājas, Ṛibhus, ye proceeded on the road to immortality, to the assemblage of the gods'; and verse 8 . . . 'Ye . . . O sons of Sudhanvan, have become immortal'). This, however, is a special case of deification, and would not prove that ordinary mortals were considered to survive after the termination of their earthly existence. There are, however a few other passages . . . intimating a belief in a future state of happiness.

Muir is here merely concerned with the evidence for survival. Nevertheless he does note the 'special case of deification' and without questioning the incongruity of all mortals becoming automatically immortal in paradise (whereas the Ṛbhus had to perform particular feats) passes on to the proof for survival and leaves the question here at issue not even posited.

II. PATRIARCHAL IMMORTALITY

On the strength of Ath.v. VI.41.3[9] A.A. Macdonell states:[10] 'The Fathers are immortal (Ath.v. VI.41.3) and are even spoken of as gods (Ṛgv. X.56.4).' Here a qualification is needed: Ath.v. VI.41.3 is addressed to the 'divine' *ṛṣis* (*ṛṣayo daivyāḥ*), not to all ancestors. Each individual *pitṛ* does not necessarily become a divine *ṛṣi* after death or for that matter during life. Those particular ancestors of the Vedic *ṛṣis* are a class by themselves. This is recognised by Macdonell: 'The fathers are also spoken of as a class distinct from men, having been created separately (TB. 2.3.8.2.)'[11] There are hints, even in the Ṛgveda, that they had unusual powers. Thus Ṛgv. X.56.4 declares: 'The gods have placed insight in them as gods' as translated by W. Wallis.[12] This certainly refers to the 'divine' seership so pronounced among those ancient *ṛṣis* as to lift them up to the status of gods in the eyes of their descendants. 'The *pitṛs*' thus 'have also mastered the great power of the gods, for the gods placed *kratu* in them as gods'.[13]

Those patriarchs who are directly related to the Vedic *ṛṣis* in their quality of seership are enumerated in Ṛgv. X.14.6: 'Our fathers are Aṇgirasaḥ, Navagvas, Atharvans,

Bhṛgus', all of whom were great sages who showed the way. (Ṛgv. X.15.13 admits that the Vedic bards did not know all the *pitṛs*). What can be learnt of these ancestors and what kind of deeds did they perform to win the boon of *amṛta*?

According to Macdonell and Keith the Aṅgirasaḥ are:

semi-mythical beings and no really historical character can be assigned even to those passages (Ṛgv. I.45.3; 139.9; III.31.7, etc.) which recognise a father of the race, Aṅgiras. Later, however, there were definite families of Aṅgirasaḥ, to whose ritual practices (*ayana, dvirātra*) references are made (Ath.v. XVIII.4.8).[14]

Similarly the Navagvas' ancestor,[15] as a name (*nava-gva*):

. . . occurs in several passages of the Rigveda as a man, an Aṅgiras in the highest degree (*Aṅgirastama*) [X.62.6] apparently being the type of the Navagvas [Ṛgv. I.62.4; III.39.5; V.29.12 etc.] who appear as a mystic race of olden times, coupled with, and conceived probably as related to the Aṅgirases [sic].[16]

The doubt expressed as to the historical existence of an original Aṇgiras or Navagva is obviously not shared by the Vedic poets. It is easy to infer that there were in times already remote from the Vedic age, great religious leaders or reformers somewhat in the line of Hermes, Orpheus, Zoroaster, whose impact was too powerful to be easily forgotten and around whom legend embroidered its tales. A well marked trend in the hymns not to break with tradition is reflected in the handing down from generation to generation of certain knowledge, a *paramparā* through which the *ṛṣis* would trace their line of descent to an actual figure in the past. This continuity both at the physical and spiritual levels was a proof to them of the firm foundation of their knowledge. They perpetuated this bond in the institution of the sacrifice given to them by those forefathers, e.g. the Aṅgirasah 'Not breaking the links, let us, seeking help, follow after the powers (*śaktīḥ*) of our forefathers' (Ṛgv. I.109.3). The same idea lies at the back of the following prayer: 'Through wisdom' (*vidmanā*) 'we invoke the inspired thought (*manīṣām*) that we may get in contact with the heroes of the middle region' (*antarikṣa*) (Ṛgv. I.110.6). So the Vedic seers call upon Agni 'as did Bhṛgus, Manus, Aṅgiras' in former times (Ṛgv. VIII.43.13) as 'Aurva Bhṛgu and Apnavāna used to do' (Ṛgv. VIII.102.4).[17]

What of the deeds of those ancestors? Here we are confronted with the essence of the Vedic myth which in its attempt to convey a spiritual truth exaggerates externalities and thus gives a miraculous colouring. We cannot take literally the verse which, translated by Griffith, reads:

Like a dark steed adorned with pearl the Fathers have decorated heaven with constellations. They set the light in day, in night the darkness. (Ṛgv. X.68.11).

Juxtaposed with Ṛgv. I.71.2, the stanza assumes a significance quite in harmony with the achievements of the Aṅgirasaḥ:

Our fathers, the Aṅgirasaḥ, broke open with their invocations and their clamour even the firmly fixed mountain-rock; they made for us a way to vast heaven, they found the day, the beams of dawn, hall-mark of heaven's light' (*svar ketum*). (Trans. J.M.)

Looking at the core of the myth, it is specifically stated that they made a path (*cakrur divo bṛhato gātum asme*) to heaven and found heaven's light for humanity, 'for us', (*asme*) . . . It is interesting to note that this word which is in the locative plural, but may also be dative plural, is translated by Śrī Aurobindo as 'in us',[18] this being correct from the literal translation point of view and the general intent. The breaking open of strongholds (a feat peculiar to the Aṅgirasaḥ as well as to Indra) would thus have a psychological import. 'Within us' they cut a way to heaven by rending the rock of the subconscious and yielding the light buried therein, that light which pertains to another dimension of our being generally ignored. The dawn and rising sun are constantly used as external elements in a story of internal significance. All the legends concerned with the Aṅgirasaḥ refer to this breaking of rocks or pens enclosing cows which, when set free, cause the sun to rise (*cf.* also the feats of Indra and Bṛhaspati, Ṛgv. VI.17.5, III.39.4–5, etc.). The link with vision or meditation through the verb $\sqrt{dh\bar{\imath}}$ with regard to the Aṅgirasaḥ's action is also remarkable. Thus J. Gonda[19] translates Ṛgv. VII.90.4, where it is stated that they found the wide light (*uru jyotir vividur*), as 'receiving visionary insight' (*dīdhyānāḥ*), again emphasising the psychological bearing of the whole myth. Fundamentally, the breaking open of rocky mountains, or barriers, made them 'awaken' (*bubudhānā*) to a 'heaven-allotted treasure' (*ratnaṃ dyubhaktim*) (Ṛgv. IV.1.18). Again 'they found the light' (*vidanta jyotiḥ*) (Ṛgv. IV.1.14), able to do so through their visionary insights (*dībhiḥ*). The clamour, or prayers, or singing of mantras by means of which they burst the fortresses are certainly evidence of a technique in the process of enlightenment, the secret of which they bequeathed to their descendants, the *ṛṣis* of Vedic India.[20]

Ṛgv. I.71.3 takes us a step further in the labyrinth of ancestral victory and bequest of the fruits of that victory. J. Gonda's excellent analysis throws a clear light on this difficult passage:

> In stanza 3 they [the Aṅgirasaḥ] are related to have established a special manifestation of ṛta, of the regular, normal, true, harmonious and fundamental structure and nature of the universe, underlying and determining the cosmic, mundane and ritual events, and to have started its *dhītiḥ* 'vision' . . . The Aṅgirasaḥ were credited with important functions as 'establishers'. The verb *dhā* . . . often conveys the idea of 'to establish, to institute, to create, lay down, dispose' . . . the Aṅgirasaḥ made a particular manifestation of ṛta and the intuitive-and-visionary 'sight' of it an institution.[21]

Through their meditation they realised aspects of truth which they then institutionalised by establishing an outer rite which translates into human terms of orderly action the truth conceived in the ground of being.[22] This is explained in Ṛgv. X.67.2. Borrowing J. Gonda's translation for the first half of the stanza: 'Stating the ṛta, having the right visionary insight . . . the sons of heaven, the men of the Asura', the Aṅgirasaḥ made of the wise priest an institution and thought out the original order of the sacrifice.[23] So the Aṅgirasaḥ, first invokers of Agni, born through Agni (*te Agneḥ pari jajñire* Ṛgv. X.62.5) 'first established their powers by kindling their fires through toil and good deeds'

(Ṛgv. I.83.4);[24] 'through [the power of] truth they raised the sun to heaven' (*ye ṛtena sūryam ā arohayan divi* X.62.3) and performed various other miraculous deeds. 'Anointed by their sacrifice and high gift . . . they gained immortality' (Ṛgv. X.62.1).[25]

Turning to Atharvan, we find that the Atharvans are placed on an equal footing with 'the Aṅgirasaḥ, the Ādityas, the Rudras, the Vasus, the gods in heaven, full of wisdom' (Ath.v. XI.6.13). Macdonell and Keith in their *Vedic Index*[26] consider that 'the name in the singular denotes the head of a semi-divine family of mythical priests, of whom nothing historical can be said. In the plural the family as a whole is meant.' Atharvan's son, Dadhyac is mentioned many times in the Ṛgveda. Like the Aṅgirasaḥ, Atharvan 'first laid sure foundations by means of sacrifice' (Ṛgv. X.92.10). This is repeated in a slightly different way in Ṛgv. I.83.5: 'he first laid down the paths by means of sacrifice (*yajñair atharvā prathamaḥ pathas tate*) after which was born the seer [as] a sun, upholder of ordinances' (*tataḥ sūryo vratapā vena ā ajani*).

The Ṛbhus' achievements seem, of all, the most enigmatic. Three words used in Ṛgv. III.60.2 are of particular interest in bringing out the kind of 'resources' the Ṛbhus employed to perform their miracles: *śaci*, 'mighty help or dexterity', but also 'grace' and 'eloquence'; *dhī* 'meditative or visionary thought'; *manas* 'mind'. These three words denote mental power and to this was due their great achievement as every hymn that sings of the Ṛbhus gives us to understand. They 'made fourfold the single chalice' (Ṛgv. IV.35.3 *vi akṛṇota camasaṃ caturdhā cf.* also I.110.3) and by speaking certain words 'entered upon the path of immortality' (Ṛgv. IV.35.3 *amṛtasya panthām*). Through their own endeavours and high artistry (*sukṛtyā*),[27] or skilful of hand (*suhastaḥ*) they reached godhood (*ye devāso abhavatā* Ṛgv. IV.35.8); they became immortal (*abhavata amṛtasaḥ* Ṛgv. IV.33.4). Journeying long, they even reached the home of Savitṛ (I.110.2), announcing the unconcealed one (*agohyam*) (I.110.3) with sun-eyed insight (*sūracakṣuḥ* I.110.4). Savitṛ there and then bestowed immortality on them (*amṛtatvam ā asūvat*. I.110.3). Mortal as they were, emphasises I.110.4, they won immortality, not an easy gain, and certainly not a free gift from heaven bestowed on the first mortal.[28]

However superficially different appears the achievement of each of those ancestors (selected as examples) who rose above average man and won immortality, the underlying theme is the finding of the light out of the darkness, therefore the discovery of truth of which the sun is the evident symbol and the institutionalising of that truth for the sake of coming generations. This is expressed in various ways, as 'the begetting of the dawn' (Ṛgv. VII.76.4) or the fashioning of the fourfold chalice to mirror each level of manifestation, or as the causing of the sun to rise or to shine (Ṛgv. VIII.29.10), or the finding of the fire within the wood or within the human tabernacle and the setting it up in human houses.[29] This search for the wider light of heaven, for the sun, for Agni, found present in the heart and discovered in meditation (Ṛgv. VII.90.4) underlines both godly and human or ancestral activity (*cf.* Ṛgv. IV.1.14). Both gods and human sages are path-finders.[30] Indra, the meditating (Ṛgv. X.32.1) god also found the sun hidden away in darkness (Ṛgv. III.39.5 *sūryaṃ viveda tamasi kṣiyantam*) like Atri (Ṛgv. V.40.6) and after slaying Vṛtra raised it on high.[31]

This light, as well as the means of discovering it, the *ṛṣis* received as a heirloom from their fore-fathers: 'great light has come [to us] bestowed by the fathers' (*mahi jyotiḥ pitṛbhir dattam ā agāt*) Ṛgv. X.107.1); hence their wish to perpetuate the link and to make themselves worthy recipients of its beneficent influence; hence their setting it up as a goal for men to reach.

III. GODLY IMMORTALITY

Just as the patriarchs, by their own efforts, gained the desired *amṛta*, so too, as we learn indirectly, the gods had to win immortality, though it is not actually stated in what way and at what time they did so.[32] It is only certain that originally they were not immortal and that this 'originally' belongs to a different cycle from that in which Yama became king of the dead. Keith states that 'the conception of the four ages of the world' is wholly unknown to the Vedic literature.[33] The four ages (*yuga*), *kṛta* (or *satya*) *tretā*, *dvāpara,* and *kali*, may be unknown as such, but not so the great cycles of time. The opening words of Ṛgv. X.190.3 make it clear that the manifested universe is not the first one that has come into existence, but rather that age succeeds age:

As of old (*yathā pūrvam*) so now the creator fashioned forth yonder sun and moon, and heaven and earth and the intermediate realm and the empyrean.[34]

'As before' and 'so now' cannot be mistaken. This universe is not the first one that ever came to manifestation but one in a series. An even more striking example is found in Ath.v. XI.8.7: 'The earth that was previous to this one (*itas*) which the sages indeed know, whoever may know that by name, he may think himself knowing the ancient things', in other words, he may deem himself wise in ancient lore. The doctrine of the great cycles of time is characteristic of India. The germ of alternating days and nights of Brahma of later speculation is found in Ṛgv. X.129.2: 'Death was not then or immortality, neither night's nor day's confine existed', as well as in Ṛgv. X.121.2 where immortality and death are described as but the shadow of the Lord of Creation. In Ṛgv. X.72.9 Aditi, the all enfolding mother space, approaches with her seven sons 'the former generation' (*pūrvyaṃ yugam*) or age, and offers Mārtāṇḍa, our sun, 'again' for the sake of procreation and dissolution, or bringing to birth and death (*prajāyai mṛtyave*).[35] What ancient or mortal generation or age is referred to here?[36] The myth of the churning of the ocean hinted at in Ṛgv. X.136.7 points to a previous age at the end of which, through the mighty upheaval, the *devas* extracted the essence or nectar of immortality, as the Pūraṇas were to explain later on. In its philosophical significance the myth implies the necessity of the descent into matter that the sacred beverage may be quaffed by the conquerors of matter. This is what the gods did. By the time the first man incarnated in the present cycle, this churning of the ocean was already a very remote past in the minds of the *ṛṣis* who referred to it through myths.

In the Ṛgveda three gods are intimately concerned with the granting of immortality:

Savitṛ who generates (*sū*) 'for the worthy gods the highest share (*bhāgam uttamam*), immortality' (Ṛgv. IV.54.2); Agni, Lord of abundant *amṛta* (Ṛgv. VII.4.6, *amṛtasya bhūreḥ*), who through *kratu*[37] makes the gods immortal (Ṛgv. VI.7.4);[38] and Soma whom the gods drunk for the same reason (Ṛgv. IX.106.8).[39] Similarly Soma and Pūṣan, combined in Ṛgv. II.40.1 as the exhilarating and vivifying solar power, have been made by the gods 'centre of immortality' (*devā akṛṇvan amṛtasya nābhim*) in their quality of 'protectors of the whole world' (II.40.1).[40]

It seems therefore that each of these three deities is not only regarded as a god in his own right but also as a principle active within all the gods:

Savitṛ is the lord of stimulation, the great vivifier, the life-giving principle, whose creative activity (*prasava*) is found in all nature's variegated forms.[41]

Agni is the quickening flame, the dynamic power at the core of all beings moving all forward, the ruler of thought who grants illumination and ecstasy, for 'mightiest of all is his rapture and utterly inspired his wisdom' (Ṛgv. I.127.9).[42] Of all the gods he is perhaps the most precious one both for deities and for men. So the gods having established the boon-bestowing (*draviṇodām*) Agni protect him as their own immortal state (Ṛgv. I.96.6).[43]

Soma, in his turn, the 'giver of vigour' (*vayodhāḥ*), the 'finder of light' (*svarvid*) is that urge for life in all its aspects, finding its full realisation in bliss, exhilaration, calling 'all the divine races to immortality' (Ṛgv. IX.108.3).[44] He is also the essence of the sacrifice (*cf.* Ṛgv. IX.74.4).

Examining these dynamic qualities of *vivifying*, *kindling* and *exhilarating*, embodied in each god, conducing to a state of invigoration, being set ablaze and enraptured, to joy, more life, completeness, there emerges as common denominator the power to increase what already exists potentially and therefore to grant that kind of life which is far fuller in intensity and reaching out to deeper depths than what is commonly known as life with its limitations at the physical level, or its desires, frustrations, inhibitions, at the emotional and mental levels. It is that power in the deities which, triumphing through the churning of the ocean of matter enabled them to extract from the latter the essence of 'life', making them what they are in the time of the Vedic bards, namely 'sons of immortality'. This essence of life was later to be expressed as *brahma*. The Śatapatha Brāhmaṇa (XI.2.3.6), after declaring that 'originally the gods were mortal' states 'but when by Brahma they were pervaded then did they become immortal'. Of the three ways of winning immortality mentioned there, namely either by celebrating all the forms of Prajāpati in worship and toil (X.4.3.1.ff) (sacrificial ritual as well as action), or by winning the year (*saṃvatṣaram āpur* XI.1.2.12) or becoming imbued with Brahma, the latter is the most significant as it points to the idea of the all pervading principle which when realised in full self-consciousness enables man to become immortal.

Indra himself who seems to have developed somewhat later in time than the others, is declared to have conquered the heavenly light *svar*, in his case, through the kindling of himself by *tapas* which Śrī Aurobindo explains as 'the pressure of consciousness on its own being'.[45] The Sanskrit uses a very strong expression (*tvaṃ tapaḥ paritapya ajayaḥ svaḥ* Ṛgv. X.167.1). In other words, the fervour of his meditation was so great that he was able to reach out even to the supreme light. He, the 'meditating god' (*dhiyasāna* Ṛgv. X.32.1)[46] gained *svar*–his special conquest. Is *svar* equivalent to immortality? The answer is found in Ṛgv. I.44.23 where Indra discovers the nectar of *amṛta* hidden away in the third sphere of heaven. In the triple world of heaven (*tridhātu divi*) he found hidden within its threefold splendour (*rocaneṣu triteṣu*) the longed for *amṛta*. Immortality is thus not heaven itself, but its fast concealed treasure, is something to be sought and to be won, is the goal of Indra's quest.

Furthermore, of the three gods who grant immortality,

Soma and Agni are the purifiers par excellence. But Savitṛ and all the other gods are also invoked for purification. Soma is even said to have 'three filters set within his heart (*trīṣa pavitrā hṛdi antar ā dadhe* Ṛgv. IX.73.8). In a long prayer (Ṛgv. IX.67) he is begged 'to purify us with his filter' (*naḥ pavitreṇa . . . punātu* IX.67.22). Agni is then asked to purify the singer's prayer (*brahma*) with his flame of light (*arcis*) outspread as a filter (*pavitram . . . vitatam*) that he may be exalted by it (IX.67.23 & 24).[47] The theme centers around the idea that stimulation and invigoration occur as a result of the purifying power, either of the intoxicating Soma, or of the flame of Agni whose purifying tongue makes him the conveyor of sacrifice (Ṛgv. VI.11.2 *pāvakayā juhvā vahnir*; *cf.* Ṛgv. VIII. 23.19) or simply of prayer which in the Ṛgveda is the power of the *ātman*.

Purification and sacrifice, according to Vedic tenets, are the two wings wheron man ascends to heaven and to immortality.

IV. POTENTIAL HUMAN IMMORTALITY

That which enabled the gods to attain immortality is also present within man. Man's father is heaven (*dyaus*); man's mother is earth (*pṛthivī*) (Ṛgv. I.164.33); his birthplace is Aditi the boundless (Ath.v. VI.20.2). Heaven and earth, the divine and the terrestrial, the limited and the unlimited constitute his nature. In such a creature 'both immortality and death are set together (Ath. v. X.7.15). We are told in Ṛgv. VIII.27.14 that the gods unanimously bestow their gifts to mortals.[48] These are the divine potencies or powers originally born of the gods and thus 'sons of gods' (Ath.v. XI.8.4)[49] and inherited by men. As in the same mother's womb have gods and men been nurtured, so they are of one origin.[50] The Atharvaveda gives more specific details: 'Having made the mortal a house the gods entered him' (Ath.v. XI.8.18). The same claim is made in Ath.v. XI.8.13; 'Having poured together the whole mortal the gods entered man'.[51] This confirms that the gods, apart from their cosmic existence, are also viewed as the divine powers in man. The physical body which is apparently the gods' handiwork is used as a centre and a stepping stone for the development of these potencies.

We have seen how the human constitution separates at death. Further references gathered from the Atharvaveda (X.2.29–33) clarify to a certain degree the Vedic conception of the human being and the 'vehicle' (*ratha*) into which he climbs at death (Ṛgv. X.135). The human body is the 'brahman's stronghold' (*pur*), 'eight-wheeled', 'nine-doored'[52] and 'impregnable'; therein is a 'golden vessel' (Ath.v. X.2.32) 'heaven-going', 'covered with light' (Ath.v. X.2.31), 'three-spoked, three-propped'—the *ratha* of Ṛgv. X.135.3; therein is found a *yakṣa* which we would not translate as 'soul-possessing monster' (as W. D. Whitney) but as the inner entity; this mysterious *yakṣa* 'the knowers of the brahman know'. We have thus three main constituents, the body or citadel (*pur*), the soul or heaven-going vessel covered with light, and the inner, mysterious entity, the *yakṣa*. The heaven-going, golden vessel may be taken as the intermediate link between matter (*pur*) and spirit (*yakṣa*), or citadel and occupant.

Because of this divine occupant which the knowers of *brahman* know, men are also heirs to immortality and like the gods they have to make efforts to win it. The two poles of human nature, the divine or immortal and the natural or mortal cemented within the human citadel, find their personification in the first man, Yama, who laid down his body.

1. YAMA AND THE ORIGIN OF THE HUMAN RACE

Yama is the son of Vivasvant, the sun, and Saranyu, daughter of Tvaṣṭṛ, the divine architect. His father is also said[53] to be the *gandharva*, that celestial entity whose habitation is heaven, who knows its secrets and keeps watch over the *soma*, the draught of immortality with which, in Ṛgv. IX.86.36,[54] he is identified. Is the *gandharva* the same entity as Vivasvant? To all appearances he is not. What is the meaning of such a genealogy which, within the same collection of hymns, traces Yama to both Vivasvant and the *gandharva* if the two are not identical?

No Vedic genealogy is rigidly fixed and nowhere is this more apparent than in Vivasvant and in Sūrya. Vivasvant[55] is the 'shining one'; in some myths, he is the son of Kásyapa,[56] the husband of Aditi and in Ṛgv. X.39.12 he is Sūrya, the cause of night and day.[57] Both Sūrya and Savitṛ are two facets of the one idea,[58] but how far they differ from Vivasvant is not made clear in the *saṃhitas*. In Ṛgv. I.83.5 Sūrya is both the cosmic and the human sun, the all-seer and the all-illuminator. Seer-guardian of the law (*sūrya vratapā vena*)[59] even like Agni (Ṛgv. I.1.8), Sūrya arises (*ā ajani*) after Atharvan has first laid the paths through sacrifices (Ṛgv. I.83.5). A long hymn is addressed to this 'seer' (*vena*) where he is identified with the *gandharva* (Ṛgv. X.123) who, in his turn, in Ṛgv. IX.85.12 and Ṛgv. IX.86.36[60] becomes Soma, the draught of immortality, '[Soma] co-dweller with Vivasvant' (Ṛgv. IX.26.4 *saṃvasānaṃ vivasvataḥ*).

This apparent mixture of origin and function, or lack of fixity in relationships, hints at an underlying cause, yet one usually overlooked: the constantly shifting images of myths express different layers of thought which themselves enshrine kernels of deeper insight. Sūrya-Savitṛ, the *gandharva*[61] and Soma, are aspects of one idea. They are the stimulators, vivifyers, exhilarators and granters of illumination and through the latter, immortality.[62] Their functions and attributes may be differentiated, their essence is the same. The Vedic mind is, in these myths, attempting to view from its myriad angles that divine, refulgent, immortal principle which, as the later Upaniṣads stressed, is at the root of each human being as well as of the cosmos; divine therefore angelic; refulgent, therefore solar; immortal, therefore identified with Soma, and later to be called *ātman*, but already in the Ṛgveda referred to as *aja*, the unborn and undying, as *ātman* the breath of Varuṇa, the soul of what moves and moves not (*sūrya* Ṛgv. I.115.1). Vivasvant represents exactly this idea. He sums it up in himself: he is the sun in its stimulating-illuminating activity; the angel in its divine essence, immortality in its principle of everlasting life, the sacrificer or that which offers itsel up in the human being.[63] To him goes the appeal to gran *amṛta*: 'May Vivasvant place us in immortality'.[64]

Thus through Yama, the son of Vivasvant, the humar race is directly descended from the sun, that is to say, is of solar and thus divine birth. But when the *ṛṣi* declarec 'I was born even a sun' (Ṛgv. VIII.6.10) he expressed not merely his original birth but his second birth in which he was endowed with sun-eyed perception, hence fully illumined.

The main difference then between the godly and the human race is that man is subjected to death. Savitṛ according to Ṛgv. IV.54.2 grants to the gods immortality, but to men only 'successive existences':[65]

devebhyo hi prathamaṃ
vajñiyebhyo amṛtatvaṃ
suvasi bhāgam uttamam
ād id dāmānaṃ savitar
vy ūrṇuṣe anūcīnā jīvitā
mānuṣebhyaḥ.

First thou hast bestowed upon the worthy gods the loftiest share, immortality; then for men as their share thou openest out successive existence.

Successive existences are themselves part and parcel of the great cosmic rhythm, a subjection which Yama deliberately chose (Ṛgv. X.13.4).[66]

Yama is stated to be 'the first of men to die' (Ath.v. XVIII.3.13 *yo mamāra prathamo martyānām* 'who first of mortals died'.) Literally and logically 'the first of men to die' implies that there were men before Yama and that they did not die. The human race, as we have seen, merges into the solar deity. Did Vivasvant have other offspring besides Yama and Manu and the Aśvins? Or are the Aśvins prototypes of that race of men before Yama who did not die? These are obscure points to which the texts provide no answer.[67]

In point of fact Yama does not really die if we mean by death complete cessation of consciousness, since he is found on the other side very much alive and active as the king among those who have passed beyond and the pioneer who showed the way thereto (Ṛgv. X.14.2). It appears from Ṛgv. X.13.4 that Yama deliberately chose death for the gods' sake (*devebhyaḥ kam avṛṇīta mṛtyum*). He did not choose immortality for the sake of the creatures, insists the same verse. His death means his casting off the physical body. There is no answer to the questions why did Yama choose death, why should man's body be subjected to corruption and that of the gods be spared? The gods' body (like that of the defunct) is made of the substance of light and therefore cannot decay. Man's body belongs to the earthly part of his nature and is therefore mortal.

It is easy to surmise that immortality, to the Vedic mind, may have meant life in or with the physical body, the losing of which renders man mortal. Since however the gods are immortal and with them there is no question of a physical body, there may be another meaning; death may not simply refer to the loss of the body. It may involve the temporary loss of consciousness, of one's familiar landmarks and the entering into a new state and with it oblivion of the previous one (with perhaps a later throw-back to earthly conditions if the doctrine of reincarnation was already outlined). Whereas immortality implies a permanent state of full consciousness such as that granted by Sūrya's enlightenment and Soma's exhilaration and that enjoyed by the gods who are omniscient and thus not subject to phases of unconsciousness, oblivion and ignorance.

Immortality, issued of Yama[68] is honoured with offerings. The expression may simply refer to that immortal principle inherent in Vivasvant, the luminous one, which is inherited by the separate entity Yama, and then by man, in other words, through Yama the immortal essence of Vivasvant is transmitted to man, and yet again through Yama's choice, man dies, his immortality is not complete. Ludwig interprets Ṛgv. I.83.5 as 'Seek we to win by sacrifice the immortality which has sprung from Yama'.[69]

The word *yama* (from $\sqrt{yam}$ to sustain, hold, support) has several meanings: 'rein, bridle, self-control' as in yoga; and finally 'twin'.[70] The idea of self-restraint predominates. Yama may then represent that which controls, restrains, uplifts to heaven (*cf.* Ṛgv. X.14.2) (and finally judges) immortal principle in its essence, deliberately subjecting itself to the rhythm of day and night, consciousness and unconsciousness, physical awareness and its opposite light and darkness. A later text, the Śatapatha Brāhmaṇa says Yama 'doubtless is he who shines yonder, for it is he who controls (*yam*) everything here and by him everything here is controlled'. (Śat.Br. XIV.1.3.4). Son of the sun, Yama must partake of his father's splendour, but he is also 'he who blows here' (Śat.Br. XIV.2.2.11). This identifies him with the soul or spirit of man, for the wind and the soul are often, in ancient scriptures, interchangeable (*cf.* Ṛgv. VIII.26.21), a conclusion rejected by Keith.[71] As Yama, the controller, he is born (*yamo ha jāto*), as Yama he is responsible for what is to be born (*yama janitvam* Ṛgv. I.66.8). Because of his 'birth' which implies an eventual 'death' Yama is also identified with death 'Reverence be to Yama, death, who first reached the river, spying out the road for many' (Ath.v. VI.28.3). The road of Yama is the road of death[72] and Vivasvant is asked to preserve the worshipper from death (Ath.v. XVIII.3.62, which is thus Yama's fetter (Ṛgv. X.97.16).

Slowly the grand figure of Yama with its symbolic significance fades into the picture of a rather terrifying arbiter of justice in the nether world as is found in the Pūraṇas.[73] Yet the original meaning of Yama still lingered on and is perceptible in the Kaṭha-Upaniṣad since Naciketas tells Yama: 'man is not fully satisfied with wealth; were we to desire such we should obtain it in just seeing thee. So too shall we live so long as thou rulest' (I.1.27).[74] Having beheld the son of Vivasvant, man can no longer thirst for anything else and he is assured of long life. This was the original meaning of Yama. To that Yama Naciketas begs to know the secret of immortality. To whom else but to the divine principle in man, which in the Ṛgveda has been connected with Agni[75], could man ask such a question?

2. THE TWO PATHS

Two paths are said to lead away from earth into the beyond:

dve sruti aśṛṇavaṃ pitṛṇām aham	I have heard of two pathways of the fathers,
devānām uta martyānāṃ tābhyām idaṃ	of gods and of mortals, along one of these
viśvam ejat sam eti	travel all the living
yad antarā pitaraṃ mataraṃ ca.	between the father and the mother.
(Ṛgv. X.88.15)	

Three categories of beings are enumerated but only two paths, the divine and the ancestral called elsewhere *devayāna* and *pitṛyāṇa*. Between the father and the mother, between earth and heaven, between those two fundamental principles of cosmic manifestation, the active and passive, positive and negative, the manifest and the unmanifest, lie those two paths. They are described in the next verse as bearing the pilgrim along and as being similar.[76] They are travelled upon by gods and mortals.[77] No indication is given as to what constitutes the difference between the way of the fathers and that of the gods, and between that of the fathers and that of mortals, if there be any.[78]

We have to turn to the later literature, to the Brāhmaṇas and the Upaniṣads which expound the Vedas to find the interpretation—presumably a traditional one—given to the verse. Thus in the Bṛhadāraṇyaka Upaniṣad (VI.2 = Śatapatha-brāhmaṇa XIV.8.16, also given in Chāndogya Up. V.3) the king sage asks the boy visitor what are 'the means of attaining the path which leads to the gods or that which leads to the fathers, by what act the one or the other is gained', and he quotes the Ṛgvedic verse to the point. As the boy cannot give the explanation the king in due course speaks. The path of the gods goes through the flame or 'lightning' where is found *puruṣa* who leads to Brahma whence there is no return. 'This is the way of the gods . . . They who proceed by it return not to the human condition here, yea return not'. (Chāndogya Up. 4.15.6). But those who follow the way of the fathers finally pass into the moon and 'after having remained . . . as long as there is a residue [of their good works] then by that course by which they came they return again'. (5.10.5). The descriptions of the various places where the soul abides on its way from and back to the earth are extremely odd to the modern mind. Nevertheless it is clear that the way of the gods is the way of no return, the way through the fire of purification, and that is the main difference with that of the fathers.

In the fortieth *adhyāya* or last book of the white Yajurveda (V.S.) considered an *upaniṣad* and known as the *Īśā Upaniṣad* is found a quotation (stanza 16) of a verse from Ṛgv. I.189.1[79] (also quoted in Yj.v.5.36):

> By a goodly path lead us to riches, Agni, thou god who knowest all our works and wisdom. Remove the sin that makes us stray and wander.[80]

To the expression 'goodly path', the translator, Griffith, has the following remark: 'Not by a path that leads to the abode of the Manes and subsequent transmigration, but by the fair road travelled by the gods, on which there is no returning'. To the Ṛgvedic verse itself which is here quoted, Griffith makes no such remark. Yet if both the Yajurveda and the Īśā quote this same verse they must do so for its 'authority' and 'traditional' doctrine which was never broken in India but the outlines of which can be traced back to that source book of them all, the Ṛgveda. It is difficult to believe that there could have been a complete break between the tradition of Ṛgvedic times and that prevalent when the Yajurveda was compiled. The whole history of Indian religious philosophy is against such a possibility.

The difference between godly and human attainment is reflected in the two paths, that of the *pitṛs* being under the fetter of death, and that of the gods being free from it. The word *path* is also used in the plural in the Ṛgveda.[81] The goal of mankind is cryptically expressed in one enigmatic stanza which recalls the New Testament.[82]

> Seven landmarks (*sapta maryādaḥ*) have the wise established. For one of these (*tāsām ekām*) may the troubled mortal set out (*aṅhura*). Thence liberated from the paths (*pathām visarge*—in the liberation of the paths) indeed a pillar of life (*āyor ha skambhaḥ*) he stands on firm foundations (*dharuṇeṣu taṣṭhau*) in the abode of the most high (*upamasya nīḷe*). (Ṛgv. X.5.6).

For those who had passed beyond the stage of earthly desire, for those liberated from the paths, the *ṛṣis* could offer a deeper vision, the vision of a reality experienced in the highest mystical absorption, 'the abode of the most high'.[83] The hints as to the possibility of human immortality are plentiful.

V. AGNI, LINK BETWEEN EARTH AND HEAVEN, THE IMMORTAL PRINCIPLE IN MAN

Agni, the most enigmatic and the most dynamic of Vedic deities, personifies that power inherent and active in gods and potential in men which, through due cultivation, raises the mortal to highest immortality (Ṛgv. I.31.7 *amṛtatve uttame martam*).

'Born in the loftiest heaven' (Ṛgv. VII.5.7)[84] 'head of heaven, earthly messenger' (Ṛgv. VI.7.1),[85] mediator between heaven and earth, the 'guest of men' (*atithiṃ janānām*) who dwells in earthly tenements (Ṛgv. IV.1.11) as well as in the third sphere of heaven, he pervades all spheres from the seventh abode right down to the earth, 'undeceived herdsman and guardian of *amṛta*' (Ṛgv. VI.7.7).[86] He 'knows the path of gods' (Ṛgv. I.72.7)[87] and is naturally the conductor to that thrice hidden abode, that mysterious seat where the Unborn holds dominion (Ṛgv. I.164.6), whence he descends here below to animate all things, to which he re-ascends by means of sacrifice, prayer, righteous action. Here on earth he sits 'within the house, king immortal of mortals' (Ṛgv. III.1.18)[88] he, the 'all wisdom knower' (*viśvāni kāvyāni vidvān*).

'Hidden away within Agni' (*nihitā*), as the holy ones (*yajniyāsaḥ*) discovered (*avidan*), are thrice seven seats or stations (or levels of existence?)[89] which act as guardians to the *amṛta*.[90] The latter is also 'found hidden in heaven in its triple splendour'.[91] Are these thrice seven *pada* that conceal the ambrosia comparable to the 'three earths in sixfold order' and the three heavens (Ṛgv. VII.87.5) of

Ṛgvedic lore with, crowning these three superior realms, the 'unshakable abode' of Varuṇa?[92] Do they symbolise stages (*pada* = step) on the path to immortality, deepening levels of consciousness? Does one have to rise through plane after plane, lift veil after veil to reach that ultimate boon?[93]

We are told in different passages that the nectar of immortality is stored away and deeply concealed in the third sphere of heaven where Indra discovers it (Ṛgv. VI.44.23), where according to the Atharvaveda (V.4.3) the gods won the insight (*cakṣaṇa*) of immortality; or that it is laid away in the home of *Vāta*, the wind,[94] the *ātman* of Varuṇa (Ṛgv. VII.87.2) and therefore, to all appearances, it is far away from earth and human grasp. Yet that treasure stored however far away is nonetheless within grasp; as light or enlightenment (*cf.* Ath.v. V.4.3) the insight of immortality and illumination, it is within the heart and through Agni's action it comes within reach of the human being. According to the Yajurvedic hymn 34.1–6[96] which surely is but a continuation of Vedic traditional belief, the immortal essence, without which nothing can be done (34.4) is hidden in all creatures and thus has its seat on earth and in man. Light, whether it be mental (Ṛgv. VI.9.5 & 6 & V.85.2) or spiritual (Ṛgv. X.129.4, X.177.1 & VII.33.9) perception, dwells within the heart.[96] Each *ṛṣi* meditates in his heart to find the truth. Thus with insights (*praketaiḥ*) focussed in the heart (*hṛdayasya*) the *ṛṣis* secretly repair to the thousand branched tree [of life] (Ṛgv. VII.33.9).[97] The reaching of heaven and then of immortality is not an outer space journey but an inner space travelling where levels of consciousness acting as veils have to be mastered and then cast aside.

Thus to experience the *amṛta* in its wholeness, to exteriorise that inherent power to a dynamic all sweeping flame, raising the mortal beyond himself, requires exertion in certain types of activity, as for example in meditation, of which the *ṛṣis* seem to have been masters, and in sacrifice. Its presence in man only implies potentiality but as Śrī Aurobindo hinted,[98] and as may be inferred from the tenor of the various Vedic texts, the hidden power has to be lifted out of the subconscious or dark levels of nature where it is embedded as the reflection of heaven on earth, to the realms of divine freedom where it is no longer reflection but actual being. Agni, as stated in Ṛgv. I.31.7, raises up the potential immortality hidden in matter and in man as the light divine to the loftiness of actual immortality stored away in its fullness in the highest empyrean (*amṛtatve uttame*). In his truth and splendour he is likened to the *ātman*[99] a treasure to be desired fervently. 'His fires, unaging, purifying, drive the houses forward'.[100] Taken literally this verse is meaningless. Through *tapas*, the inner kindling of the flame divine, man is moved to purification, spiritual insight and attainment.[101] Man is thus actuated by the flame of Agni which he must first kindle within himself in the 'threefold abode' (*tri ṣadhasthe* Ṛgv. V.11.2), but also by that expression of this flame which is the light of the sun,—not the mere physical light—but that wide light (*uru jyotiḥ*) which through meditation (*dīdhyānāḥ*)[102] the patriarchs did find (Ṛgv. VII.90.4), which grants that sun-eyed perception or spiritual insight and divine omniscience; and finally, by the invigorating exaltation of Soma which in the ecstasy of illumination lifts the human to godly status (*cf.* Ṛgv. I.139.2 & VIII.48.3).

Agni, Sūrya-Savitṛ and Soma, those three principles that in a former age granted immortality to the gods themselves, here too foster in the human being those very conditions that set him upon the path of attainment: fire, dynamic urge to action, that which underlies all created things; sun, vivifyer-illuminator, that without which nothing can live; Soma, stimulator, the very essence of bliss at the core of all life; these three fundamental elements which the Vedas personified as Agni, Sūrya-Savitṛ and Soma, are indeed themselves aspects of, and summed up in, the later conception of *ātman*, the eternal, unaging, unborn (*aja*) in man.

VI. THE ĀTMAN AND IMMORTALITY

Among the various attempts to fix the derivation of the word *ātman* two are noteworthy, especially in connection with the science of yoga: $\sqrt{an}$ to breathe, and *tman* the old reflexive form meaning self. Both roots point to an essence or essential self, *sāra* or *svayam*. It is this self which the priest, in the Ṛgvedic hymn addressed to the medicinal plants, is trying to recall that he might 'win back' the departing one's 'very self', *ātman*, to this life (Ṛgv. X.97.4).

As the most intimate bodily process on which life depends is breathing it is not surprising that *ātman* should have been linked with the life-breath. The close connection between, and even identification of, wind, breath and spirit is noticeable throughout antiquity as in the Greek *pneuma* and the Latin *anima*. Examining the wind first, it is called the *ātman* of Varuṇa, in the Ṛgveda: 'the wind, thy *ātman*, has sounded through the region' (Ṛgv. VII.87.2). Praises should be sung to the wind for it is the *ātman* of all (Ṛgv. X.92.13: *ātmānaṃ vasyo abhi vātam arcata*). 'The wind, *ātman* of the gods (*ātmā devānām*), seed of the world (*bhuvanasya garbho*), this god wanders according to his will. His sounds are heard, his form is not seen' (Ṛgv. X.168.4).[103] The Aśvins are enjoined to come to the sacrifice like the *ātman*, like the wind, to their own dwelling places (Ṛgv. I.34.7). Vāta's home is also the hidden place where is stored away the nectar of immortality.

What is the basis of this virtual identification of the wind with the *ātman*?[104] The subtle connection may best be understood by examining the Indian meaning of *prāṇa*, the grosser expression of it being the life-breath. Both are not identical (though one is used as a translation of the other since there is no real word in our modern languages for *prāṇa*) for breath is perceptible to the outer senses and heard like the wind, but *prāṇa* is not so obvious. But by wielding breath and achieving full control over it the yogin becomes aware of *prāṇa* and by wielding the latter he achieves mastery over his inner psychic centres.

Even without such mastery, however, in deepest absorption, such as comes about with the stilling of the mind, there is perceptible a peculiar rhythm of the whole person resulting from the prāṇic currents flowing *outwardly* as they do during the waking state. This natural rhythm is slowed down during the meditation process through the halting down of thought itself until such time as it is brought to a standstill. Then occurs its complete reversal; the vast tidal wave of prāṇic current now flows *inwardly* and with sufficient practice will eventually reach an innermost point of focus and finally that centre of all centres called *ātman*, the self. In meditative absorption sufficient *prāṇa* remains in the body to continue to animate it. But at death, the indrawing of *prāṇa* is complete and irreversible so that death supervenes when it has altogether left the physical body which becomes cold, motionless and rigid. With this prāṇic reversal (whether at death or in meditation) the consciousness, carried on the tidal wave, is removed from the physical body and so from the brain, for thought follows the ebb and flow of *prāṇa*. The opposite is also true. Both are intimately linked. Thus *prāṇa* which lies behind breath may now be viewed as the breath of the *ātman*, the rhythmic outgoing and ingoing breath analogous to the great breath of the ONE that breathed breath–less–ly by ITSELF (Ṛgv. X.129.2), hence the connection between wind, breath, *ātman*.[105]

It is characteristic that Naciketas, in the Kaṭha Upaniṣad, remains three days at the gates of death without eating or doing anything, in perfect silence and acquiescence to death, before he meets the king of the dead face to face. For the student of meditation, this myth is highly significant for it is only when perfect stillness has been attained that consciousness begins to become aware of subtler levels of activity within the human being. It may also serve as an example of the origin of the Vedic myth, i.e. a story or projected image, built up around a subjective experience of psychological import. Through the wielding of the life-breath, effected through the controlling of the *prāṇa*, through the poise of thought, the inner turning of all the senses and the complete mastery of each constituent of human nature, an entry is effected into the subtler levels of that nature; the human being is carried to that which controls all, Yama, thence to that of which Yama is the son, i.e. Vivasvant, the sun of Vedic lore, the *ātman* of the Upaniṣads, the *puruṣa*, refulgent as the sun. Let us examine this conception.

Within the human constitution, as already noticed, is a 'golden vessel' (Ath.v. X.2.32), 'heaven going, covered with light' (Ath.v. X.2.31). Into this 'resplendent, yellow, golden, unconquered stronghold, that was all surrounded with glory', 'the brahman entered' (Ath.v. X.2.33). 'Whoever indeed knoweth that brahman's stronghold covered with *amṛta*, unto him the *brahman* and the Brahmans have given sight, breath, progeny' (Ath.v. X.2.30). 'Whoever know the *brahman* in man, they know the most exalted one' (Ath.v. X.7.17).[106]

What is that *brahman* within the human stronghold? The supreme evocative power of prayer was, in the Ṛgveda, called *brahman*. This power is here identified with the exalted core within the human being, a pointer to the *ātman*. Further elucidations in this direction may be gathered from the Yajurvedic hymn (34.1–6) which is considered an *upaniṣad*. An ageless light or flame is described as that whereby 'all that was, that is and that will be is embraced' (*yena idaṃ bhūtaṃ bhuvanaṃ bhaviṣyat pari gṛhītam amṛtena sarvam* 34.4); 'which is wisdom' (*prajñāna*) as well as 'illumined-consciousness' (*cetas*)[107] and 'steadfastness' (*dhṛti*); which, as 'the unfailing light among creatures' (*jyotir antar amṛtaṃ prajāsu*) is that 'without which there can be no action' (*na karma kriyate* 34.3) and that 'within which the mind (*citta*) of creatures is established' and the whole is centred in the heart (*hṛt pratiṣṭham* 34.5 & 6). We find here once again the association of light with immortality, of consciousness with illumination, and hence the idea of sun-eyed perception already so prevalent in the Ṛgveda as the core of every being. Such ideas, without doubt, lead to the conception of the *ātman* of the Upaniṣads within which dwells the power that moves all things (*cf.* Ṛgv. I.115.1), the seed whence all the worlds develop.

The real man (*puruṣa*) is this sun, the golden āditya (*āditya varṇa*) who dwells beyond the reach of darkness (*cf.* Ṛgv. I.50.10) in the human citadel (*pur*):

vedāham etaṃ puruṣaṃ mahāntam ādityavarṇaṃ tamasaḥ parastāt tam eva viditvāti mṛtyum eti na anyaḥ panthā vidyate 'yanāya.
(Yajurveda. 31.18)

I have known this mighty puruṣa refulgent as the sun beyond darkness. Only by knowing him does one overcome death. No other way is there to go.

The shining of the sun is the divine, all radiating, illumination which equates the solar splendour (and therefore the sun) with *puruṣa*, the 'lord of immortality' (Ṛgv. X.90.2 *amṛtatvasya īśānaḥ*). Here is outlined the Vedic thought concerning the *ātman*: first, as the sun of all things, the breath, root or essence of what moves and moves not (Ṛgv. I.115.1 and IV.53.6), the all-seeing, all-illuminating life-giver (Ṛgv. IV.53.3 & 4), the bestower of insight (Ṛgv. VII.66.10), illumination, and lastly immortality (Ṛgv. IV.54.2), that solar splendour which for the races of men extends with his rays 'immortal light' (Ath.v. XII.1.15); then as the light immortal not outside but within all beings (Yj.v.34.1–8); finally as the immanent *ātman* equivalent to the transcendent Self of the Upaniṣads, already fully expressed in the Atharvaveda which makes the transition between the Ṛgvedic solar deity and the Upaniṣadic Self:

akāmo dhīro amṛtaḥ svayaṃbhū rasena tṛpto na kutaścanonaḥ, tam eva vidvān na bibhāya mṛtyor atmānaṃ dhīram ajaraṃ yuvānam.
(Ath.v. X.8.44)

Desireless, wise, immortal, self-existent, contented with the essence, lacking nothing is He. One fears not death who has known him, the ātman, serene, ageless, youthful.

Deussen remarked that this is the first and oldest passage where the *ātman* is proclaimed the world principle unreservedly.[108] We fail to agree. No specific mention is made of 'the world's all pervading principle' but rather the essential nature of the *ātman* is given in so far as the mind can grasp and define it. The 'world principle' *per se* had already been proclaimed in the Ṛgveda where the sun is called 'the *ātman* of that which moves and moves not' (Ṛgv. I.115.1 *ātmā jagatas tasthusaśca*);[109] hence the *ātman* is in the Ṛgveda proclaimed the basis of all things, even what we would call the inanimate or that which moves not. This statement is itself a remarkable link between the Ṛgvedic sun as supreme illumination, god-like insight and as the transcendent one found beyond the darkness, and the Upaniṣads.

Thus *ātman*, *puruṣa*, *Sūrya*, *brahman*, these are four specific words, apparently dissimilar in their idea and applications in so far as they are used in different contexts with various emphases, yet similar in their essential meaning and implication—the immortal principle hidden in the citadel of man (*pur* Ath.v. X.2.30), upon uniting with which one is raised from corruption to incorruption. The mighty *puruṣa* is thus the divine man who lifts the mortal to immortality, a role ascribed to Agni in the Ṛgveda; that celestial man is effulgent as the sun and the one goal to which all men finally aspire for there is ultimately 'no other way'. Here is a hint as to what the end of all things must eventually be.

The *ātman*, which as Sūrya-Savitṛ pervades, animates and vivifies the world,[110] which as Agni the 'herdsman of immortality' guards the world and is ever hither and thither travelling (Ṛgv. I.164.31), which as the flame divine 'raises the mortal to highest immortality' (Ṛgv. I.31.7) is the *puruṣa*, the original divine man, and thus innate in man, his inmost nature.[111] This is confirmed and summarised in the Maitrī Upaniṣad. 'Brahman is the ātman of the sun ... He who is in the fire and he who is here in the heart and he who is yonder in the sun, he is one'. (96.17).

We can thus reduce these ideas, images or symbols, to one single word, *ātman*. What is the nature of this *ātman*?

Two main lines of thought are perceptible in the Atharvaveda quotation (X.8.44). The many epithets lavished on the *ātman* there emphasise its perfect self-sufficiency—no desire whatsoever, a state difficult to conceive for the ordinary mortal whose life is desire itself, a state which is the very antithesis of 'heaven'—as described in Vedic literature—which is the fulfilment of all desires (Ṛgv. IX.113.7–11) and could be summed up as desire constantly fulfilling itself. The *ātman* is beyond the thrall of any desire whatsoever. It is therefore not heaven but quite beyond for desire pertains to manifestation or *māyā*. The *ātman* is also ageless, therefore out of time. The addition of the epithet 'youthful' serves to enhance the fact of timelessness—it can never grow old, stale. Those two main conceptions lift it entirely out of the domain of the conditioned, the limited, the earthly and thereby out of all relation to ordinary human life, physical, emotional, intellectual, which is a constant adding to or substracting from and thus an endless flux. Self-existent and self-sufficient, changeless, timeless, these adjectives endeavour to express a state of divine being which has nothing in common with habitual human states of consciousness.

A difference, implied in the quotation, may be drawn between the human who has 'known' that *ātman*, and one who has not: the 'one fears not death who has known him', the other does. The one has won dominion over death for he has entered the realm of self-sufficiency, of wisdom, of agelessness wherein abides the *ātman*, beyond the mind and its limiting, crippling categories, in short the state of immortality.

Again, the whole process of yoga is implied in this knowledge. That the science of yoga, that the practice of *prāṇāyāma* may have already been known in Ṛgvedic times, may be inferred from the hints scattered in various hymns, especially Ṛgv. X.136. There Vāyu, the Lord of life, stirs up (*amanthat*) and grinds (*piṇaṣṭi*) the 'unbendable' (*kunamnamā*). Upon the course of the wind ascend the ascetics (*vātasya anu dhrājiṃ yanti*) when the gods have penetrated them (*yad devāso avikṣata*).[112] Have we here a figure of speech which would specifically describe the inward wielding of the prāṇic currents?

What does to have 'known' mean? This special knowledge[113] is referred to in both the Atharvaveda (X.8.44) and the Yajurveda (31.18) quotations; these thereby make it clear that it is this knowledge of the *ātman* which alone allows the human to transcend death. To have known the *ātman* is to have merged into that highest or deepest centre in which Agni is concealed and which men in deep meditation discover (Ṛgv. I.67.2),[114] that centre where the sun is found beyond darkness (Ṛgv. I.50.10, V.40.6), that centre of fullness where bliss is experienced. 'Bliss' and 'light' always characterise descriptions of ātman realisation. Both Soma and Sūrya are expressive of states of consciousness beyond the ordinary. Bliss, exaltation and insight are summed up in Soma. In their enthusiasm, after drinking the soma, the *ṛṣis* cry out: 'we have become immortal; we have gone to the light; we have found the gods' (Ṛgv. VIII.45.3). Here are brought together the elements of joy, light, divinity and immortality, that is, freedom from shackles or any constricting influence, hence the rapture, that rapture being the hall-mark of ātman knowledge. The difference drawn between the visible plant or juice and that for which it stands is made plain in Ṛgv. IX.85.3 and 4.[115]

The probable intoxicating effect of the plant has its hidden meaning. It points to something much deeper than mere intoxication. As *brahman* in the Ṛgveda means prayer or meditative absorption and the power released thereby, and *brāhmaṇas* are therefore those who practise such contemplation and show such power, the verse implies that only those who enter into deep absorption can know the true significance of Soma—the everlasting bliss of the *ātman*. Mere brain consciousness can know nothing of this, mere intoxication neither, hence 'those who dwell on earth do not taste of thee'.

Furthermore, Soma, the *ātman* or essence of the sacrifice (Ṛgv. IX.6.8: *ātmā yajñasya*; IX.2.10: *ātmā yajñasya pūrvyaḥ*) through the human being's sacrificial life sublimates all human endeavours, attunes the whole nature to its higher principle, and sets it upon the path of truth.[116] For Śrī Aurobindo, it is 'the divine delight hidden in all existence which, once manifest, supports all life's crowning activities and is the force that finally immortalises the mortal, the amṛtam, ambrosia of the gods'.[117]

Having tasted of this, the *ṛṣi* knows the immortal state, the divine ecstasy (Ṛgv. VIII.48.3). Similarly, having known the *ātman*, he has risen beyond death (Ath.v. X.8.44) and knows there is no other way to go (Yj.v.31.18). When consciousness has reached such a state of refulgent bliss, the solar splendour of Vedic lore, death has no more meaning, holds out no fear. It is transcended. This is supreme *samādhi*, this is ātman realisation.

NOTES

1. *cf.* A. Bergaigne, *La Religion Védique* (tome I, 1878): 'Ce séjour ... est celui ou l'homme *espère* devenir immortel' (p. 85). The italic is our own. Also J. Gonda, *Loka*, etc. 'This loka which is said to be in heaven (*div*), and where one hopes to be "immortal" or safeguarded against death, is the object of the poet's desire' (p. 65).

2. 9. *yatra anukāmaṃ caraṇaṃ trināke tridive divaḥ*
lokā yatra jyotiṣmantas tatra mām amṛtaṃ kṛdhi ...

10. *yatra kāmā nikāmāś ca yatra bradhnasya viṣṭapaṃ*
svadhā ca yatra tṛptiś ca tatra mām amṛtaṃ kṛdhi ...

11. *yatra ānandāś ca modāś ca mudaḥ pramuda āsate*
kāmasya yatra āptāḥ kāmās tatra mām amṛtaṃ kṛdhi ...

3. Śrī Aurobindo, *On the Veda*, p. 302 (Pondicherry, 1964), describes *tapas* thus: '... the pressure of consciousness on its own being'.

4. *op. cit.* p. 310. This hymn has been interpreted in purely materialistic terms because of the word *dakṣiṇa*. *cf.* also Ṛgv. X.107.2 and Ath.v. XIX.26.1, 'the gold born out of the fire'.

5. *cf.* also Ṛgv. I.125.5. 'There are suns for them in heaven; they attain immortality'.

6. Ṛgv. VII.57.6: *dadāta no amṛtasya prajāyai.*

7. *uto asmān amṛtatve dadhātana*, Ṛgv. V.55.4. *cf.* also Ṛgv. V.63.2. 'We pray for rain and immortality, your bounty'. *vṛṣṭiṃ vāṃ rādho amṛtatvam īmahe.*

8. *op. cit.* p. 284.

9. Whitney translates Ath.v. VI.41.3 as follows: 'Let not the seers who are of the gods leave us ... O immortal ones, attach yourselves to us mortals.'

10. *op. cit.* p. 171.

11. *op. cit.* p. 171.

12. *The Cosmology of the Rigveda*, p. 73 (London, 1887).

13. Ṛgv. X.56.4 *mahimna eṣāṃ pitaraś cana īśire, devā deveṣu adadhur api kratum.* Wallis has the following note: 'For this bold application of the name *deva* to the sacrificers compare III.7.7, 54.17, IV.2.17, VIII.48.3.' *cf.* also St. John X.11. 'Is it not written in your law, I said, ye are gods'—gods in the making, a doctrine which runs through the Vedas to reach its epitome in the Upaniṣad injunction 'become what thou art'. 'Thou are That.'

14. A. A. Mcdonell and A. B. Keith, *Vedic Index of names and subjects*, p. 11 (London, 1912). *cf.* also A. Bergaigne, *La Religion Védique*, tome II, pp. 307–26 (1883).

15. *cf.* IX.108.3. Through Soma, Dadhyac Navagva opened closed doors and the sages won the glories (*śravānsy ānaśuḥ*) of cherished immortality (*amṛtasya cāruno*).

16. *op. cit.* p. 437.
17. *cf.* also Ṛgv. I.80.16, IV.16.20, VIII.6.11, etc.
18. *On the Veda*, p. 212 (Pondicherry, 1964).
19. *The Vision of the Vedic Poets*, p. 205 (The Hague, 1963).
20. *cf.* Ṛgv. IV.5.3 and I.67.2 where men, meditating, *dhiyamdhāḥ* when they have pronounced their mantras which they make in their heart (*hṛdā yat taṣṭān*) find Agni, the divine flame, securely hidden away).
21. *op. cit.* p. 174.
22. J. Gonda's explanation takes us right back to the central idea of Jung's and Kerenyī's thesis that myth is grounded in the depth of the *psyche*.
23. J. Gonda's translation of the second part of the stanza is as follows: 'instituting (creating) the inspired sage and (sacred) word imagined the first form of worship (the sacrifice)' (*op. cit.* p. 206), *ṛtaṃ śaṃsanta ṛju dīdhyānā divas putrāso asurasya vīrāḥ vipraṃ padam aṅgiraso dadhānā vajñasya dhāma prathamaṃ mananta*.
24. *prathamaṃ dadhire vaya iddhāgnayaḥ śamyā ye sukṛtyayā*.
25. *ye yajñena dakṣiṇayā samaktā . . . amṛtatvam ānaśa*.
26. *op. cit.* p. 17.
27. For *sukṛt* see J. Gonda's *Loka. World and Heaven in the Veda* (Amsterdam, 1966) p. 120. J. Gonda is of the opinion that *sukṛt* refers to their '. . . ability, not to their "piety"'. Also p. 129: 'In connection with the Ṛbhus . . . it [*sukṛtyā*] reads in Ṛgv. I.20.8 that they acquired, among the gods, a share in the sacrifice by their sukṛtyā "skill" (not "good or righteous act, virtuous action", Monier-Williams)'.
28. For further comments on the Ṛbhus in the light of their feats see G. Feuerstein and J. Miller, *A Reappraisal of Yoga*, pp. 138–43 (London, 1971).
29. *cf.* also Ṛgv. VI.15.2; IV.1.13; I.148.1; VI.16.13, etc.
30. *cf.* Ṛgv. I.105.15 'To him the path-finder [or knower] *gātuvidam*, Varuṇa, we turn'.
31. Ṛgv. I.51.4 & I.52.8 etc.
32. The gods were once bound by a curse as one may gather from Ṛgv. VII.13.2. Since they originally were not immortal, this curse may be the same as that which binds men: birth, growth, decay. Agni set them free, as he does men.
33. *op. cit.* vol. 31, p. 82.
34. *Sūrya ā candram asau dhātā yathā pūrvam akalpayat*
divaṃ ca pṛthiviṃ ca antarikṣam atho svaḥ.
35. *prajāyai mṛtyave tvat punar mārtāṇḍam ā abharat*. For the sake of generation and dissolution (or birth and death) she again (*punar*) brought forth Mārtāṇḍa.
36. *cf.* also Ṛgv. X.97.1.
37. Explained by Śrī Aurobindo as 'power . . . effective of action'. *On the Veda*, p. 67 (Pondicherry, 1964).
38. *tava kratubhir amṛtatvam āyan cf.* also V.3.4 and III.17.4, the gods made Agni centre of immortality—*akṛṇvan amṛtasya nābhim*.
39. *tvaṃ devāso amṛtāye kaṃ papuḥ*.
40. *cf.* also Ṛgv. III.17.4 and V.81.5.
41. *cf.* Ṛgv. V.47.2 where the paths going on all sides reach the centre of immortality (*amṛtasya nābhim*). *cf.* also Bhagavad Gitā 4:11.
42. *śuṣmintamo . . . mado dyumnintama uta kratuḥ*.
43. *amṛtatvaṃ rakṣamāṇāsa enaṃ devā*.
44. *daivyā . . . janimāni . . . amṛtatvāya*.
45. *On the Veda*, p. 302 (Pondicherry, 1964). *cf.* A. C. Bose's definition: 'Not self-mortification, but self-awakening by activising the spiritual power within oneself'. *Hymns from the Vedas*, p. 8 (London, 1966).

46. This is a clear hint that the practice of *tapas* leads to enlightenment and that this kind of contemplation was known in Ṛgvedic times.

The Atharvaveda, as translated by Whitney, states:

'By Vedic studentship, by fervor, the gods smote away death; Indra by Vedic studentship brought heaven for the gods' (Ath.v. XI.5.19). *brahmacaryeṇa tapasā devā mṛtyum apāghnata, indro ha brahmacaryeṇa devebhyaḥ suar ā abharat.* This verse is thus translated by J. Muir (O.S.T. V, p. 401): 'By self-restraint and *tapas* the gods destroyed death. By self-restraint Indra acquired heaven from [or for] the gods'. Here again the factors responsible for bringing about conquest over death are self-mastery and spiritual exertion which originally applied to the gods, as it does now to men. *cf.* Patañjali's Yoga-sūtra II.1 & 32. *cf.* Rgv. X.154, Muir's translation of verses 2–5 being given on p. 152. *cf.* also Rgv. X.129.3 where through the flame power of spiritual contemplation the universe was made manifest.

47. Ṛgv. IX.67.24: *arcivad agne tena punīhi naḥ brahmasavaiḥ punīhi naḥ.* For further discussions of these stanzas (Ṛgv. IX.67.22.24) the reader is referred to J. Gonda's *The vision of the Vedic poets*, p. 105 (The Hague, 1963).

48. *devāso hi ṣmā manave samanyavo viśve sākam sarātayah.*

49. *cf.* Ath.v. XI.8.3,10,26,29,30,31,32.

50. Ṛgv. VIII.83.8. *cf.* also Ṛgv. I.164.30 & 38.

51. *cf.* Ṛgv. IV.1.18: 'Now all the gods are in all their dwellings'. This was the discovery made by the Aṅgirasaḥ on awakening to the light of the higher spheres. *cf.* Śrī Aurobindo's remark: 'In proportion as we learn to subjugate the ego and compel it to bow down in every act to the universal being and to serve consciously in its least movements the supreme will . . . Agni himself takes form in us . . . Thus is it that man can be said to form by his toil the great gods'. *op. cit.* p. 295. *cf.* also Ath.v. XI.8.31: *sūryaś cakṣur vātaḥ prāṇaṃ puruṣasya vi bhejire.* 'The sun, the wind, shared (respectively) the eye, the breath of man'. (Whitney's trans.) *cf.* also Ath.v. XI.8.32: all deities are seated in man as cows in a cow-stall.

52. The 'nine-doored' citadel is, in this particular instance, the male body as against the female ten-doored citadel. *cf.* Ath.v. X.8.43: 'The lotus-flower of nine doors, covered with three strands.'

53. Ṛgv. X.10.4.

54. *apāṃ gandharvaṃ divyaṃ nṛcakṣasaṃ Somam.*

55. from *vi* +$\sqrt{vas}$ to shine.

56. Name of a sage who belongs to the distant past. *cf.* Rgv. IX.114.2.

57. In Ṛgv. VIII.26.21 Vāyu is said to be Tvaṣṭṛ's son-in-law. Is Vāyu another aspect of Vivasvant?

58. See previous section on Vedic meditation.

59. For the translation of *vena* see J. Gonda, *The Vision of the Vedic Poets* (The Hague, 1963) pp. 349–358.

60. *cf.* Ṛgv. IX.66.8.

61. The Vedic *gandharva* is the angel of ancient lore, not the solar orb, or sun-ray or rainbow (Von Roth and Grassman), or thunder-cloud (Wilson), these being the various attempts by scholars at finding a physical basis for a non-physical entity. In both Ṛgv. IX.86.36 and Ṛgv. IX.85.12 where the *gandharva* seems identified with the sun, Griffith identifies it with the moon through Soma, in the latter instance following Hillebrandt (V.M.I. 429). In the Ṛgveda only the sun 'beholds' all creatures, not the moon. See Griffith's note to Ṛgv. X.123.7.

62. In Ṛgv. X.139.6 the *gandharva* instructs Indra as to the hiding-place of the *amṛta.* He is the guardian of Soma and thus the knower of immortality. (*cf.* Ṛgv. IX.83.4).

63. One may then view Vivasvant specifically as the divine Head at the origin of mankind and Sūrya-Savitṛ, the bestower of illumination, as kin to the godly race. Their functions, however, merge just as the human and the godly race originally were of one common birth and presumably will finally merge once more.

64. Ath.v. XVIII.3.62: *vivasvān no amṛtatve dadhātu.* J. Gonda has an interesting remark which lends weight to the present contention:

'Whether we are inclined to see in Vivasvant nothing more or less than a "deification" of the first sacrificer, to believe with Bergaigne that Agni alone is responsible for the character of this figure, or to lay, with Keith and others, special stress upon his relations with the (rising) sun, the power inherent in this figure—which elsewhere (I.139.1) is called a *nābhi*—"navel", i.e. a mystic centre and point of contact with the high and indispensable powers—becomes manifest, is re-actualized, at the place called his "seat".' *cf.* Ṛgv. I.53.1; III.34.7. *op. cit.* p. 179–180.

Vivasvant represents just that 'mystic centre and point of contact' which, present in man, acts as a link between the human and divine nature and is thus the 'navel' or centre of both earth and man, the place *sada* where the sacrificial exchange occurs, each giving of its self to the other. So songs (*giraḥ*) are offered to Indra in Vivasvant's dwelling (*sadane*). (Ṛgv. I.53.1 and III.34.7.)

65. *anūcīna*, from *anvañc* 'coming after, successive', thus *anūcīnāham* = on successive days. *anūcīna* coupled with *jīvita* (pp. of $\sqrt{jīv}$) can but mean successive existences. This could refer to repeated embodiments if we take *jīvita* as meaning embodied life. However, scholars refuse to admit any trace of belief in reincarnation in the Vedas. The examples brought forward and critically discussed by Keith, for example, (*op. cit.* vol. 32, pp. 570–584. Ṛgv. I.164.30,38; X.14.4; VII.33 and IV.27.1) are no proof of such a belief and in this respect are not worth discussing. Ṛgv. I.164.31 might be regarded as referring to repeated births. Keith adds in a note 'Ṛgv. IX.113 is not good evidence' (p. 571). It is, like Ath.v. VI.120.2, only indirect evidence. *cf.* Sukumari Bhattacharji, *The Indian Theogony* p. 75 (Cambridge, 1970). *cf.* also Macdonell *Vedic Mythology*, 'There is no indication in the Vedas of the later doctrine of transmigration' (p. 166).

66. *devebhyaḥ kam avṛṇīta mṛtyuṃ prajāyāi kam amṛtaṃ na avṛṇīta.*

67. *cf.* Old Testament, Genesis, ch. 4 where Cain the son of the first couple goes to a nearby land and marries (4.16 & 17). If Adam and Eve were the original man and woman there could be no one else on earth beside their offsprings Cain and Abel. Similarly, Cain's son Enoch eventually marries, whom? and builds a city, for whom?

68. not 'Yama's deathless birth' as translated by Griffith, Ṛgv. I.83.5, a contradiction in terms: *yamasya jātam amṛtaṃ yajāmahe.*

69. Quoted in R. T. H. Griffith's *The Hymns of the Rigveda*, second ed., vol. 1, p. 106 (Benares, 1896).

70. *cf.* E. W. Hopkins, *The Religions of India* (Boston, U.S.A. 1895). 'Etymologically his name means Twin and this is probably the real meaning, for his twin sister Yamī is also a Vedic personage' (p. 130).

71. Keith writes: 'The effort to remove Yamī from the tradition and to see in Yama the alter ego of the living man, his soul, is clearly contrary to the whole of the Vedic and the Avestan evidence' (*op. cit.* p. 408). Yama and Yamī may represent the positive and negative poles of the human being, the active, positive and the receptive, passive principles, the outward and the inward going tendencies, the extravertive and introspective, manifesting not simultaneously but according to a peculiar rhythm which again recalls the cosmic rhythm. Keith views the Vedic religion as static. Each personage, each myth, however, each symbol

represents various aspects of ideas in constant fluctuation. So Yama and Yamī also stand for the two sexes once man has become a physical entity.

72. *cf.* Ṛgv. I.38.5, X.97.16 and Ath.v. XVIII.3.62.

73. The Vedic idea was perhaps closer to that enjoined upon the dying in the *Tibetan Book of the Dead.* (W. Y. Evans-Wentz): 'Apart from one's own hallucinations, in reality there are no such things existing outside oneself as Lord of Death, or god, or demon, or the Bull-headed Spirit of Death', p. 167 (New York, Oxford U.P., 1971). (According to Lāma Kazi Dawa-Samdup's English rendering). In other words, all these personifications are dramatic representations set up by the mind. The Ṛgveda, as compared to the Pūraṇas, is singularly free of these.

74. *Na vittena tarpaṇiyo manuṣyo lapsyāmahe vittam adrākṣma cet tvā jīviṣyāmo yāvad iśiṣyasi tvaṃ varas tu me varaṇiyaḥ sa eva.*

75. *cf.* Ṛgv. I.163.2, X.51.3, X.21.5 for Yama's link with Agni. In X.21.5 Agni is both the beloved friend of Yama (*yamasya kāmyo*) and the messenger of Vivasvant (*dūto vivasvato*). *cf.* also Ath.v. II.12.7, XII.2.8 *cf.* also Ṛgv. X.15.13 & 14 and Yj.v. (vs) 19.60.

76. *dve samīcī bibhṛtaś carantam.*

77. *cf.* Jacob's ladder in the Old Testament.

78. Keith finds a difference in the path of the gods and that of the fathers '... since it is described as *pravat*, which may denote either a downward path as of a stream, or, at any rate, a path forward to the horizon, rather than one rising erect to the heaven' (*op. cit.* vol. 32, p. 411) and he mentions Ṛgv. X.14.1, Ath.v. VI.28.3, XVIII.4.7. On p. 571 he explains the two ways as referring merely to 'day and night'.

79. Ṛgv. I.189.1: *agne naya supathā rāye asmān viśvāni deva vayunāni vidvān yuyodhy śmaj juhurāṇam eno bhūyiṣṭhāṃ te nama uktiṃ vidhema.*

80. *The Texts of the white Yajurveda.* Translated by R. T. H. Griffith (Benares, 1899).

81. *cf.* also Ṛgv. V.47.2.

82. The resemblance with Revelation should be noted: 'Him that overcometh will I make a pillar in the temple of my God, and he shall go no more out; and I will write upon him the name of my God', etc. Rev. III.12.

83. *cf.* Ṛgv. XI.164.21: *ino viśvasya bhuvanasya gopāḥ sa mā dhīraḥ pākam atra ā viveśa.* The question of a higher vision known to the *ṛṣis* of Vedic times has been an object of doubt to Western scholars. However, the relevant references are examined in the chapter on Vedic Meditation.

84. *sa jāyamānaḥ parame vyoman.*

85. *mūrdhānaṃ divo aratiṃ pṛthivyā.*

86. *adabdho gopā amṛtasya rakṣitā. cf.* also Ṛgv. VI.9.4 and I.44.5.

87. *vidvān adhvano devayānām.*

88. *ni duroṇe amṛto martyānāṃ rājā sasāda.*

89. Ṛgv. I.72.6: *triḥ sapta yad guhyāni tve it padā.*

90. Ṛgv. I.72.6: *tebhī rakṣante amṛtaṃ sajoṣāḥ.*

91. Ṛgv. VI.44.23: *divi rocaneṣu triteṣu.*

92. Ṛgv. VIII.41.9: *dhruvaṃ sadaḥ. cf.* also Ṛgv. I.164.6.

93. *cf.* the 'dividing threefold' of the after death state in Ath.v. XI.8.33 which is commented upon on p. 134.

94. *cf.* 'Yonder O Vāta, in thy dwelling is placed the store of *amṛta*, give us of it that we may live' *yad ado vāta te gṛhe amṛtasya nidhir hitaḥ tato no dehi jīvase.* Ṛgv. X.186.3.

95. Yajurveda, Vājasaneyi saṃhitā. This hymn will be examined further on.

96. *cf.* Ṛgv. X.5.1: 'the one ocean, the foundation of riches ... shines forth

from our hearts'.

97. *cf.* J. Gonda's 'They penetrate into the mystery by the perceptions of their heart' *ta in ninyam hṛdayasya praketaiḥ . . . abhi saṃ caranti, op. cit.* p. 277. *cf.* also Ṛgv. I.105.15; V.4.10; IV.24.4; X.64.2; 123.6; 177.1.

98. *On the Veda.* See pp. 295–6 and p. 127 (Pondicherry, 1964).

99. Ṛgv. I.73.2: *ātmā iva śevo didhisāyyo bhut.*

100. Ṛgv. X.46.7: *asya ajarāso damām aritrā . . . agnayo pāvakāḥ.*

101. *cf.* Ṛgv. X.154 quoted on p. 170, and X.167.1.

102. J. Gonda translates this word as 'receiving visionary insight'. *op. cit.* p. 205.

103. *cf.* N. T. John 3:8: 'The wind bloweth where it listeth' etc.

104. A. B. Keith summarises the data concerning the *ātman* thus:

'. . . Without pretending that the problems of the relation of Ātman and Tman is [sic] easy, or that the etymology is certain, the fact remains that the word does mean "wind" in the Rigveda, that the normal use of it there is "breath of life", and that the meaning "wind" is harder to deduce from "breath", than *vice versa*, and that to deduce either "wind" or "breath" from the conception of "this I" is extremely difficult.

The real history of Ātman seems then to be that from the meaning "wind" sprang early up that of "the breath"; thence came the meaning "self", as when it is said of Sūrya that he is the self of that which stands and moves. Then we have the use of the self as a reflexive pronoun, and the use as meaning the body an idea which is clearly intended when it is contrasted with Prāṇa, "the breath" . . . But the sense of "breath" or "self" is also capable of being understood in more abstract ways, and we, therefore, find Ātman used to denote the essential nature of a thing. This use is already found in the Rigveda'. *op. cit.* p. 451.

105. A. B. Keith in his comments on *prāṇa* shows his failure to grasp the difference between *prāṇa* and breath and between *prāṇa* and *ātman*. *See 'The Philosophy of the Veda and the Upanishads'* (vol. 32, pp. 453–4) of which the concluding remarks are as follows:

> 'Nor are there lacking evidences of efforts to make Prāṇa the one reality, as Ātman was so made: Prāṇa is identified with Prajāpati, and also the Ātman, but these views are late and isolated.'

In the light of the above explanation it should be clear that *prāṇa* is that which underlies breath and therefore life and therefore pervades all things. Without it there is no life.

Practical, experimental yoga shows that there is no need of an 'effort' to 'make prāṇa the one reality'. That which underlies all biological life may, in that sense, be regarded as the one reality, but only at that particular level. Far beyond that level is the one, supreme reality. Such is the meaning of the Vedic texts.

cf. J. Gonda, *Some observations on the Relations between 'Gods' and 'Powers' in the Veda*, p. 73–4 ('S-Gravenhage, 1957).

106. Whitney's translation. *Atharva-Veda Saṃhitā* (Cambridge, Mass. 1905).

107. *cetas* means splendour as well as consciousness, intelligence—obviously the illumined awareness which characterises the sage.

Whether this passage belongs to the later period of the Brāhmaṇa epoch does not alter the general line of development of the Vedic divine principle within and without man and descriptions thereof, such a development being fully traceable from the Ṛgveda to the Upaniṣads and indirectly pointing to a science of yoga. For Keith 'Of other expressions of the inner nature of man, the Puruṣa is of no very serious importance for the philosophy of this epoch'. *op. cit.* p. 452. The importance, not seen by Keith, is that it links the Ṛgvedic solar concept with the Upaniṣadic Self. J. Gonda sums this up with examples from the Upaniṣads: 'The same identification was used to explain the character of the puruṣa, "Man" or the Person as soul and original soul of the universe, and the personal and animating principle in men. SV. Up. 3.12 "the puruṣa is a great lord (*prabhuḥ*) the instigator of existence ... he is light (*jyotiḥ*), imperishable". He is of the colour of the sun, beyond darkness (st. 8)'. *op. cit.* p. 270. This shows beyond doubt that *puruṣa* is another word for *ātman* and that *puruṣa* and the solar deity are one since *puruṣa* is of the colour of the sun beyond darkness (*cf.* Ṛgv. I.50.10). J. Gonda goes on: 'In Bar Up. 4,3 it is explained that the light (*jyotiḥ*) which a living being has here is the sun' (p. 270).

108. *Geschichte* I.1.334. Quoted in W. D. Whitney, *Atharva-Veda Saṃhitā*, vol. 8, p. 601 (Cambridge, Mass. 1905).

A. B. Keith has a similar view: 'AV. X.8.44 recognises Ātman as the world soul probably for the first time' although on p. 451 he refers to Sūrya as 'the self of that which stands and moves'. *op. cit.* p. 450. *cf.* fn. 4.

109. Savitṛ, the alter ego of Sūrya, is also 'he who controls the world, what moves not and what moves' (Ṛgv. IV.53.6).

110. Savitṛ assumes all forms (Ṛgv. V.81.2) i.e. manifests through all forms: *viśvā rūpāṇi prati munchate. cf.* Ṛgv. I.115.1.

111. A. B. Keith does not see the inner connection between Puruṣa and Ātman: 'The development of the meaning of Ātman was accompanied by the development of the conception of the relation of the Ātman of the universe and the Ātman of the individual ... In the case of Puruṣa ... under that name we do not find that the conception of his Ātman was developed: of the individual man we have the question asked, later at least, what is left after his members are dispersed by death; but, though it might have been expected that this problem would have been posed in the case of Puruṣa, there is no evidence that this was ever done'. *op. cit.*, p. 452. Puruṣa is the *ātman* as is seen in the famous *puruṣa sūkta*. The Vedas expressed by various means and therefore various words the central idea of the one divine spark, be it Agni, Sūrya, puruṣa, brahman, pervading all creation, and these were finally merged in the *ātman* of the Upaniṣads.

112. For further comments on this subject see G. Feuerstein and J. Miller, *A Reappraisal of Yoga* (London, 1971).

113. The Ṛgveda also hints at a certain secret knowledge vouchsafed to the genuine enquirer. Thus '... He the god granted this grace to me the mortal, to me the simple, he the wise, the immortal ... he has proclaimed to me this hidden wisdom (*apagūḷhaṃ manīṣām*, Ṛgv. IV.5. 2 & 3).

114. *cf.* also Ṛgv. I.146.4, X.37.5; Śvet. Up. 3.20 & 4.17. & 20; Maitrī Up. 6.34 & 7.7; Kaṭha Up. 2.12.

115. *somaṃ manyate papivān yat saṃpinṣanty oṣadhiṃ*
somaṃ yaṃ brahmāṇo vidur na tasya aśnāti kaś cana

> 'Whoso has brayed the plant thinks that he has drunk the Soma's juice.
> That Soma which Brahmans know, of that no one has ever tasted'.

na te aśnāti pārthivaḥ.

> 'Who dwells on earth tastes not of thee'. (Ṛgv. IX.3 & 4.)

116. *cf.* Ṛgv. VIII.12.3: *panthām ṛtasya yātave tam īmahe.*

117. *On the Veda*, p. 196 (Pondicherry, 1964).

SECTION IV

Selected Hymns which Illustrate Subjects Discussed

Ṛgv. I.1

Oṃ agnim īḷe purohitaṃ yajñasya devam-ṛtvijam hotāraṃ ratnadhātamaṃ
agniḥ pūrvebhir-ṛṣibhir-īḷyo nūtanair uta sa devān ā-iha vakṣati
agninā rayim-aśnavat-poṣam-eva dive-dive yaśasaṃ vīravattamaṃ
agne yaṃ yajñam-adhvaraṃ viśvataḥ paribhūr-asi sa id-deveṣu gachati
agnir-hotā kavi-kratuḥ satyaś-citraśravastamaḥ devo devebhir-ā gamat
yad-aṅga dāśuṣe tvam-agne bhadraṃ kariṣyasi tava-it-tat-satyam-aṅgiraḥ
upa tvā-agne dive-dive doṣāvastar dhiyā vayaṃ namo bharanta ā-imasi
rājantam-adhvarāṇāṃ gopām-ṛtasya dīdiviṃ vardhamānaṃ sve dame
sa naḥ pitā-iva sūnave 'gne su-upāyano bhava sacasvā naḥ svastaye.

Agni I glorify, foremost, divine ministrant of sacrifice, invoker, best treasure-bestower.

May Agni worthy to be praised by past and present sages bring the gods hither.

Through Agni may riches be daily obtained, even so abundance, glorious, with highest heroic power.

Agni, that worship and sacrificial rite which thou encompassest in all directions reaches out even to the gods.

May Agni, the invoker, the seer-will, the true, of marvellous renown, god among gods, come!

Whatever good thou wilt do to the worshipper, Agni, that indeed is thy truth, O Son of Fire!

To thee, Agni, day after day, obscured or illumined, do we come, with thought bearing homage.

Thou, Lord of sacrifices, radiant guardian of truth, thriving in thine own sphere

As father to son, Agni, be thou of open approach to us! Abide with us for our weal!

I.77

Kathā dāśema-agnaye kā-asmai devajuṣṭā-ucyate bhāmine gīḥ
yo martyeṣv-amṛta ṛtāvā hotā yajiṣṭha it kṛṇoti devān.

yo adhvareṣu śaṃtama ṛtāvā hotā tam-ū namobhir-ā kṛṇudhvaṃ
agnir-yad-ver-martāya devānt-sa cā bodhāti manasā yajāti

sa hi kratuḥ sa maryaḥ sa sādhur-mitro na bhūd-adbhutasya rathīḥ
taṃ medheṣu prathamaṃ devayantīr-viśa upa bruvate dasmam ārīḥ.

sa no nṛṇāṃ nṛtamo risādā agnir-giro 'vasā vetu dhītiṃ
tanā ca ye maghavānaḥ śaviṣṭhā vāja-prasūtā iṣayanta manma.

eva-agnir-gotamebhir-ṛtāvā viprebhir-astoṣṭa jātavedāḥ
sa eṣu dyumnaṃ pīpayat sa vājaṃ sa puṣṭiṃ yāti joṣam-ā cikitvān.

In what way shall we pay homage to Agni? What song divinely acceptable shall be uttered for that refulgent one? Who, immortal in mortals, truth bearer, worthiest invoker, makes the gods [manifest].

Amidst oblations most beneficent, truth bearer, invoker, him make ye indeed manifest through your obeisance!

When Agni seeks out the gods on behalf of the mortal, then does he awaken and send offerings through the mind.

For he is creative-power, he the wooer, he the holy; he like a Friend has become the vehicle of the transcendent. Him, the foremost, the marvellous, pious people, God-seekers, invoke in their offerings.

May Agni, manliest among men, foe-devourer, look upon our songs, our visions, with favour. So may the bounteous, the mighty ones, courage-fosterers, acknowledge our thought.

Thus has Agni the truth bearer, knower of births, been glorified by the Gotama seers. Let him foster among them resplendence and vigour, for he comes into abundance, contentment, he the wise.

Ṛgv. VII.88

pra śundhyuvaṃ varuṇāya preṣṭhāṃ matiṃ vasiṣṭha mīḷhuṣe bharasva
ya īm-arvāñcaṃ karate yajatraṃ sahasrā-maghaṃ vṛṣaṇaṃ bṛhantaṃ

adhā nv-asya samdṛśaṃ jaganvān-agner-anīkaṃ varuṇasya mansi
svar-yad-aśmann-adhipā u andho'bhi mā vapur-dṛśaye ninīyāt

ā yad-ruhāva varuṇaś-ca nāvaṃ pra yat-samudram-īrayāva madhyaṃ
adhi yad-apāṃ snubhiś-carāva pra preṇkha īnkhayāvahai śubhe kaṃ

vasiṣṭhaṃ ha varuṇo nāvy-ā-adhād-ṛṣiṃ cakāra svapā mahobhiḥ
stotāraṃ vipraḥ sudinatve ahnāṃ yān-nu dyāvas-tatanan-yād-uṣāsaḥ

kva tyāni nau sakhyā babhūvuḥ sacāvahe yad-avṛkaṃ purā cit bṛhantaṃ mānaṃ varuṇa svadhāvaḥ sahasradvāraṃ jagamā gṛhaṃ te

ya āpir-nityo varuṇa priyaḥ san-tvām-āgāṃsí kṛṇavat-sakhā te
mā ta enasvanto yakṣin-bhujema yandhi ṣmā vipraḥ stuvate varūthaṃ

dhruvāsu tvā-āsu kṣitiṣu kṣiyanto vy'smat-pāśaṃ varuṇo mumocat
avo vanvānā aditer-upasthād-yūyaṃ pāta svastibhiḥ sadā naḥ.

Convey O Vasiṣṭha, thy purified, most cherished thought to generous Varuṇa who directs [to us] the mighty bull of the thousand treasures worthy of worship.

When just now going into the presence of that Varuṇa I contemplated the face of fire. So may the sovereign of light and darkness take me to the firmament to behold its beauty.

When Varuṇa and I ascend and drive forward our boat upon the middle of the ocean then do we move over the ridges of the billows, swaying indeed with the swinging waves.

For Varuṇa placed Vasiṣṭha into the boat and with his skill and powers made him a seer. In auspicious days, so long as the enlightened one made him a singer, the heavens and the dawns were outspread.

And now what has become of our friendship of old when we two kept unhindered company? O Varuṇa, law-abiding, I went into thy mighty mansion, thy thousand-gated home!

Though he, thy cherished, devoted boon companion, has transgressed against thee, yet he is thy friend. O living-god, [though], sinners, let us not be disheartened by thee. O wise one, verily extend thy protection over the worshipper!

Abiding in these abodes made firm by thee, may Varuṇa

loosen our tie as we gain favour from the lap of Aditi. Protect us ye [gods] for ever with your blessings!

Ṛgv. III.38

abhi taṣṭā-iva dīdhayā manīṣām-atyo na vājī sudhuro jihānaḥ
abhi priyāṇi marmṛśat-parāṇi kavīnr-ichāmi saṃdṛśe sumedhāḥ

inā-uta pṛcha janimā kavīnām manodhṛtaḥ sukṛtas-takṣata dyām
imā u te praṇyo vardhamānā manovātā adha nu dharmaṇi gman

ni ṣīm-id-atra guhyā dadhānā uta kṣatrāya rodasī samaṃjan
saṃ mātrābhir-mamire yemur-urvī antar-mahī samṛte dhāyase dhuḥ

ā-tiṣṭhantaṃ pari viśve abhūṣañ-chriyo vasānaś-carati svarociḥ
mahat-tad-vṛṣṇo asurasya nāmā viśvarūpo amṛtāni tasthau

asūta pūrvo vṛṣabho jyāyān imā asya śurudhaḥ santi pūrvīḥ
divo napātā vidathasya dhībhiḥ kṣatraṃ rājānā pradivo dadhāthe

trīṇi rājānā vidathe purūṇi pari viśvāni bhūṣathaḥ sadāṃsi
apaśyam-atra manasā jaganvān-vrate gandharvān api vāyukeśān.

tad-in-nv-asya vṛṣabhasya dhenor-ā nāmabhir-mamire sakmyaṃ goḥ
anyad-anyad-asuryaṃ vasānā ni māyino mamire rūpam-asmin

tad-in-nv-asya savitur-nakir-me hiraṇyayīm-amatiṃ yām-aśiśret
ā suṣṭutī rodasī viśvaminve apa-iva yoṣā janimāni vavre

yuvaṃ pratnasya sādhatho maho yad-daivī svastiḥ pari ṇaḥ syātaṃ
gopājihvasya tasthuṣo virūpā viśve paśyanti māyinaḥ kṛtāni

śunaṃ huvema maghavānam-indram-asmin-bhare nṛtamaṃ vājasātāu śṛṇvantam-ugram-ūtaye samatsu ghnaṇtaṃ vṛtrāṇi saṃjitaṃ dhanānāṃ.

As a carpenter have I been absorbed in meditation, proceeding like a spirited well-yoked steed. Brooding upon desirable and lofty matters I yearn to commune with inspired sages.

Enquire of the glorious generations of sages [who] with concentrated minds, devoutly orientated, have fashioned the heaven. Such guidances as are for thee exalting and desirable will certainly reach thee in [accordance with] the law.

Keeping here-below their secret [abodes] they have anointed both worlds for dominion; measured them out at equal distance; established and checked both wide expanses to hold firm the mighty ones in their point of contact.

All attended on him as he ascended, splendour clad; self-illumed he wanders. This might of the asura stallion he, omniform, has established as his immortal names.

The primeval one, the elder, the mighty one, created; these are his ancient draughts. Ye grandsons of heaven, ye kings, from of old ye exerted your sway over the council by means of your visions.

Three seats in the council, many, all, do ye attend, O kings. I saw from near, going thither in my mind, the angels in their realms, with wind-blown hair.

So now have they marked out by their obeisances that essence of that mighty one and the milch cow. Donning one [garb] or other, the skilful ones adjusted on him a celestial form.

No one has ever assumed for me the golden brightness which is Savitr's. With lofty-praise he displays both all-pervading worlds even as a woman her offsprings.

Of the ancient one ye two promote the might which as celestial welfare ye spread around us. All the skilful ones behold the manifold deeds of him who stands-unmoved with shepherd's tongue.

Let us invoke Indra, the auspicious, the bounteous one, most heroic in that battle where prize is won, him the powerful who gives heed to [pleas for] aid in conflicts, remover of obstacles, conquerer of riches!

Ṛgv. V.81

yuñjate mana uta yuñjate dhiyo viprā viprasya bṛhato vipaścitaḥ
vi hotrā dadhe vayunāvid-eka in-mahī devasya savituḥ pariṣṭutiḥ

viśvā rūpāṇi prati muncate kaviḥ pra-asāvīd-bhadraṃ dvi-pade catuṣpade
vi nākam-akhyat-savitā vareṇyo'nu prayāṇam uṣaso vi rājati.

yasya prayāṇam-anv-anya id-yayur-devā devasya mahi-mānam-ojasā
yaḥ pārthivāni vimame sa etaśo rajāṃsi devaḥ savitā mahitvanā

uta yāsi savitas-trīṇi rocanā-uta sūryasya raśmibhiḥ sam-ucyasi
uta rātrīm-ubhayataḥ pari-īyasa uta mitro bhavasi deva dharmabhiḥ

uta-īśiṣe prasavasya tvam-eka id-uta pūṣā bhavasi deva yāmabhiḥ
uta-idaṃ viśvaṃ bhuvanaṃ vi rājasi śyāvāśvas-te savitaḥ stomam-ānaśe.

They harness their minds, they harness their visions, the seers of the vast seer, the inspired one. He alone versed in ordinances, allots the priestly functions. Mighty is the praise of godly Savitṛ.

The divine-poet assumes all forms; for men and animals he fosters auspicious-days. Most blessed Savitṛ has revealed the heaven's vault and rules resplendent after the vanishing of the dawn.

By his power the other deities follow in the wake of this god's journeying and mightiness. By his greatness he measured out the earthly realms, he, the godly stallion, Savitṛ.

To the three luminous spheres thou proceedest, Savitṛ, investing thyself with Sūrya's rays. On both sides thou spannest the night. Through thy statutes thou art the godly Friend.

Thou art sole Lord of generation; thou art the increaser, O god, by thy wanderings. Over all this world thou rulest. Śyāvāśva has brought his praise to thee Savitṛ.

Ṛgv. X.177

pataṅgam aktam asurasya māyayā hṛdā paśyanti manasā vipaścitaḥ
samudre antaḥ kavayo-vi cakṣate marīcīnāṃ padam-ichanti vedhasaḥ

pataṅgo vācaṃ manasā bibharti tāṃ gandharvo 'vadad-garbhe antaḥ
tāṃ dyotamānāṃ svaryaṃ manīṣām ṛtasya pade kavayo-ni pānti

apaśyaṃ gopām-anipadyamānam-ā ca parā ca pathibhiś carantaṃ
sa sadhricīḥ sa viṣūcīr-vasāna ā varīvarti bhuvaneṣv antaḥ.

The sages with heart and mind behold the winged one anointed with the Asura's magic-power. The inspired ones gaze upon him in the oceans' depths. The wise ones yearn for the centre of his rays.

Within the mind the winged one bears the word ere the angel pronounces it within the womb. That lightning flash of celestial intuition the poets safeguard in the seat of truth.

I saw the herdsman, the unflagging one, approaching and withdrawing by the pathways. Invested with the outgoing and ingoing-forces, he continually revolves within the worlds.

Ṛgv. VI.9

ahaś-ca kṛṣṇam-ahar-arjunaṃ ca vi vartete rajasī vedyābhiḥ
vaiśvānaro jāyamāno na rājā-ava-atiraj-jyotiṣā-agnis-tamāṃsi

na-ahaṃ tantuṃ na vi jānāmy-otuṃ na yaṃ vayanti samare 'tamānāḥ
kasya svit-putra iha vaktvāni paro vadāty-avareṇa pitrā

sa it-tantuṃ sa vi jānāty-otuṃ sa vaktvāny-ṛtuthā vadāti
ya īṃ ciketad-amṛtasya gopā avaś-caran-paro anyena paśyan

ayaṃ hotā prathamaḥ paśyata-imam-idaṃ jyotir-amṛtaṃ martyeṣu
ayaṃ sa jajñe dhruva ā niṣatto 'martyas-tanvā vardhamānaḥ

dhruvaṃ jyotir-nihitaṃ dṛśaye kaṃ mano javiṣṭhaṃ patayatsv-antaḥ
viśve devāḥ samanasaḥ saketā ekaṃ kratum-abhi vi yanti sādhu

vi me karṇā patayato vi cakṣur-vi-idaṃ jyotir-hṛdaya āhitaṃ yat
vi me manaś-carati dūra-ādhīḥ kiṃ svid-vakṣyāmi kim-u nū maniṣye

viśve devā anamasyan-bhiyānās-tvām-agne tamasi tasthivāṃsaṃ
vaiśvānaro 'vatu-ūtaye no- 'martyo 'vatu ūtaye naḥ.

[One half of] day is dark [the other half of] day is bright and of their own accord revolve both spheres. Agni, who belongs to all men, manifesting as sovereign ruler, with his light dispels the darkness.

I know neither warp nor woof nor what they weave

when in the encounter they press-forward. Whose son can here, without his father behind him, pronounce what should be pronounced?

Such indeed knows the warp and woof, such in due course pronounces what should be pronounced. Herdsman of immortality proceeding hitherward, who-so-ever beholds him, he understands beyond any-other!

He is the high-priest, the primeval one! Behold him, that light immortal 'midst mortals! He took his birth firmly established as an immortal with ever-waxing self.

Unflickering the light set up [that we may] see. 'Midst flying creatures the mind is swiftest. All gods, one-minded, one-intentioned, unerringly proceed to the one intelligent-awareness.

My ears, my eyes speed after this light lodged here within my heart. With far-off thought wanders my mind. What indeed shall I utter? O what shall I think?

All gods in awe of thee, Agni, paid homage to thee when thou didst stand in darkness. O thou who-belongest-to-all-men! Favour us with thy help, O immortal one, favour us with thy help!

Ṛgv. X.129

na-asad-āsīn-no sad-āsīt-tadānīṃ na-āsīd-rajo no vyomā paro yat
kim-ā-avarīvaḥ kuha kasya śarmann-ambhaḥ kim-āsīd-gahanaṃ gabhīram

na mṛtyur-āsīd-amṛtaṃ na tarhi na rātryā ahna āsīt-praketaḥ
ānīd-avātaṃ svadhayā tad-ekaṃ tasmād-ha-anyan-na paraḥ kiṃ cana-āsa

tama āsīt-tamasā gūḷham-agre 'praketaṃ salilaṃ sarvam ā idam
tuchyena-ābhv-apihitaṃ yad-āsīt-tapasas-tan-mahinā-ajāyata-ekaṃ

kāmas-tad-agre sam-avartata-adhi manaso retaḥ prathamaṃ yad-āsīt
sato bandhum-asati nir-avindan-hṛdi pratīṣyā kavayo manīṣā

tiraścīno vitato raśmir-eṣām-adhaḥ svid-āsīd-upari svid-āsīt
retodhā āsan-mahimāna āsant-svadhā avastāt-prayatiḥ parastāt

ko addhā veda ka iha pra vocat-kuta ājātā kuta iyaṃ visṛṣṭiḥ
arvāg-devā asya visarjanena-athā ko veda yata ābabhūva

iyaṃ visṛṣṭir-yata ābabhūva yadi vā dadhe yadi vā na
yo āsya-adhyakṣaḥ parame vyomant-so aṅga veda yadi vā na veda.

The Unmanifest was not then, or the Manifest; spatial depths or heaven beyond were not. What encompassed, where, who nurtured it? What ocean, profound, unfathomable, pervaded?

Death was not then or immortality. Neither night's nor day's confine existed. Undisturbed, self-moved, pulsated the One alone. And beyond that, other than that, was naught.

Darkness there was; at first hidden in darkness this all was undifferentiated depth. Enwrapped in voidness, that which flame-power kindled to existence emerged.

Desire, primordial seed of mind, in the beginning, arose in That. Seers, searching in their heart's wisdom, discovered the kinship of the created with the uncreate.

Their vision's rays stretched afar. There was indeed a below, there was indeed an above. Seed-bearers there were, mighty powers there were. Energy below, will above.

Who knows the truth, who can here proclaim whence this birth, whence this projection? The gods appeared later in this world's creation. Who then knows how it all came into being?

Whence this creation originated; whether He caused it

to be or not, He who in the highest empyrean surveys it, He alone knows, or else, even He knows not!

X.121

hiraṇyagarbhaḥ sam-avartata-agre bhūtasya jātaḥ patir-eka āsīt
sa dādhāra pṛthivīṃ dyām-uta-imāṃ kasmai devāya haviṣā vidhema

ya ātmadā baladā yasya viśva upāsate praśiṣaṃ yasya devāḥ
yasya chāyā-amṛtaṃ yasya mṛtyuḥ kasmai devāya haviṣā vidhema

yaḥ prāṇato nimiṣato mahitvā-eka id-rājā jagato bubhūva
ya īśe asya dvipadaś-catuṣpadaḥ kasmai devāya haviṣā vidhema

yasya-ime himavanto mahitvā yasya samudraṃ rasayā saha-āhuḥ
yasya-imāḥ pradiśo yasya bāhū kasmai devāya haviṣā vidhema

yena dyaur-ugrā pṛthivī ca dṛḷhā yena svaḥ stabhitaṃ yena nākaḥ
yo antarikse rajaso vimānaḥ kasmai devāya haviṣā vidhema

yaṃ krandasī avasā tastabhāne abhy-aikṣetāṃ manasā rejamāne
yatra-adhi sūra udito vibhāti kasmai devāya haviṣā vidhema

āpo ha yad-bṛhatīr-viśvam-āyan-garbhaṃ dadhānā janayantīr-agniṃ
tato devānāṃ sam-avartata-asur-ekaḥ kasmai devāya haviṣā vidhema

yaś-cid-āpo mahinā pary-apaśyad-dakṣaṃ dadhānā janayantīr-yajñaṃ
yo deveṣv-adhi deva eka āsīt kasmai devāya haviṣā vidhema

mā no hiṃsīj-janitā yaḥ pṛthivyā yo vā divaṃ satyadharmā jajāna yaś-ca-apaś-candrā bṛhatīr-jajāna kasmai devāya haviṣā vidhema

prajāpate na tvadetānyanyo viśvā jātāni pari tā babhūva yat-kāmās-te juhumastanno astu vayaṃ syāma patayo rayīṇāṃ.

In the beginning was evolved the effulgent matrix and the Lord of beings manifested; the One that was. He established this earthly and heavenly world. Which divinity shall we worship with oblations?

Self-bestower, might-bestower, He, whose command all acknowledge, the gods also; He, whose shadow is immortality, whose shadow is death. Which divinity shall we worship with oblations?

He who by his might has become sole ruler of the world, of the living and the slumbering; He who is lord of both its men and beasts. Which divinity shall we worship with oblations?

His are yon snow-clad heights, by his might, his the ocean-deep together with its nectar, so they say; his these dominions which his arms [encompass]. Which divinity shall we worship with oblations?

Through whom the sky and earth, the mighty, were firmly fixed; by whom heaven and its canopy were sustained; He who has measured out the intermediate realms. Which divinity shall we worship with oblations?

To whom look up both hosts with shaken mind propped up by his support, there where the risen sun shines forth from above. Which divinity shall we worship with oblations?

When indeed unfurled the mighty waters that generated the universal matrix conceiving fire; thence was that one life-breath of the gods breathed forth. Which divinity shall we worship with oblations?

He who by his greatness surveyed the waters establishing creative Intelligence (*Dakṣa*), originating sacrifice; who above the gods has been the one God. Which divinity shall we worship with oblations?

He who is earth's procreator may never harm us nor he who through his righteous law gave birth to heaven, gave birth to the refulgent, mighty waters. Which divinity shall we worship with oblations?

Lord of creatures, none other save thou encompassest all these generations. May our desires find fulfilment through these our invocations. We would be lords of prosperity.

X.81

ya imā viśvā bhuvanāni juhvad-ṛṣir-hotā ny-asīdat-pitā naḥ
sa āśiṣā draviṇam - ichamānaḥ prathamachad-avarān ā viveśa

kim svid-āsīd-adhi-ṣṭhānam-ārambhaṇaṃ katamat-svit-kathā-āsīt
yato bhūmiṃ janayan-viśva-karmā vi dyām-aurṇn-mahinā viśva-cakṣāḥ

viśvataś-cakṣur-uta viśvato-mukho viśvato-bāhur-uta viśva-tas-pāt
saṃ bāhubhyāṃ dhamati saṃ patatrair-dyāvābhūmī janayan-deva ekaḥ

kiṃ svid-vanaṃ ka u sa vṛkṣa āsa yato dyāvāpṛthivī niṣṭat-akṣuḥ
manīṣiṇo manasā pṛchata-id-u tad-yad-adhy-atiṣṭhadbhu-vanani dhārayan

yā te dhāmāni paramāṇi yā-avamā yā madhyamā viśvakar-mann-uta-imā
śikṣā sakhibhyo haviṣi svadhāvaḥ svayaṃ yajasva tanvaṃ vṛdhānaḥ

viśvakarman-haviṣā vāvṛdhānaḥ svayaṃ yajasva pṛthivīm-uta dyāṃ
muhyantv-anye abhito janāsa iha-asmākaṃ maghavā sūrir-astu

vācas-patiṃ viśvakarmāṇam-ūtaye manojuvaṃ vāje adyā huvema
sa no viśvāni havanāni joṣad-viśvaśambhūr-avase sādhu-karmā.

Our Father who, as priestly sage, sat down offering up all these worlds, he, desiring substantiality, by means of prayer veiling his original self, pervaded the lower forms.

What point was it from which He took his stand, indeed where was it, whence the all-creator, the all-seer, by his might, brought forth the earth and uncovered the heaven.

All-seeing, all-facing, all-embracing ['all-armed'], all pervading ['all-feet'], with his arms, with his wings altogether he whirled forth, generating heaven and earth, he the One God.

What indeed was the wood, what indeed was the tree wherewith heaven and earth were fashioned? The wise searched in their mind on what did He take his stand to prop up the worlds.

Those highest and lowest and midmost realms, O All-Creator, and those here, open thou to thy friends loyal to the sacrificial rite, sacrifice thyself for thine own exaltation.

Exalted by the sacrifice, O All-Creator, offer up for thyself both heaven and earth. Let other men around be perplexed, but for us here let the Wise One be our blessed Lord.

The Lord of speech, the thought-swift all-creator, let us invoke today for our help, for our strengthening. Let him favour our invocations, He whose actions for our safeguard are all bounteous and unerring.

X.82

cakṣuṣaḥ pitā manasā hi dhīro ghṛtam-ene ajanan-namna-māne
yadā-id-antā adadṛhanta pūrva ād-id-dyāvā-pṛthivī apra-thetām

viśvakarmā vimanā ād-vihāyā dhātā vidhātā paramā-uta saṃdṛk
teṣām-iṣṭāni sam-iṣā madanti yatrā sapta-ṛṣīn-para ekam-āhuḥ

yo naḥ pitā janitā yo vidhātā dhāmāni veda bhuvanāni viśvā
yo devānāṃ nāmadhā eka eva taṃ saṃpraśnaṃ bhuvanā yanty-anyā

ta ā-ayajanta draviṇaṃ sam asmā ṛṣayaḥ pūrve jaritāro na bhūnā
asūrte sūrte rajasi ni-ṣatte ye bhūtāni sam-akṛṇvann imāni

paro divā para enā pṛthivyā paro devebhir-asurair-yad-asti
kaṃ svid-garbhaṃ prathamaṃ dadhra āpo yatra devāḥ sam-apaśyanta viśve

tam-id garbhaṃ prathamaṃ dadhra āpo yatra devāḥ sam-agachanta viśve
ajasya nābhāv-adhy-ekam-arpitaṃ yasmin-viśvāni bhuvanāni tasthuḥ

na taṃ vidātha ya imā jajāna-anyad-yuṣmākam-antaraṃ babhūva
nīhāreṇa prāvṛtā jalpyā ca-asutṛpa ukthaśāsaś-caranti.

The Lord of Vision with wise insight created these two worlds moulding them as ghee; and when the original poles were firmly fastened, then did heaven and earth extend afar.

The all-creator, all-knower and almighty, preserver, dispenser, loftiest Overseer! Beyond the seven sages, where they rejoice together in the fruit of their offerings, they speak of the One.

Who is our Father, our creator, who as dispenser of realms knows all beings, who bestowed names upon the gods, even to that only One, other beings go for enquiry.

Together to Him they consecrated their treasure, the sages of old, like invokers in their multitude, who, seated in familiar and unfamiliar realms fashioned out these worlds.

Earlier than the heaven, earlier than this earth, earlier than the gods and the archangels, That indeed is. What seed primeval the ocean-deeps conceived wherein all the gods appeared together?

That seed primeval the ocean-deeps conceived, wherein all the gods gathered together; the One, projected from the core of the Unborn, wherein all the worlds have their being.

That which generated these things you will not find; something else has emerged to being from amongst you. Veiled in mist and inarticulate, hymn-chanters wander life-intoxicated.

Ṛgv. I.159

Pra dyāvā yajñaiḥ pṛthivī ṛtāvṛdhā mahī stuṣe vidatheṣu pracetasā
devebhir-ye devaputre sudaṃsasā-itthā dhiyā vāryāṇi prabhūṣataḥ

uta manye pitur-adruho mano mātur-mahi svatavas-tad-havīmabhiḥ
suretasā pitarā bhūma cakratur-uru prajāyā amṛtaṃ varīmabhiḥ

te sūnavaḥ svapasaḥ sudaṃsaso mahī jagñur-mātarā pūrvacittaye
sthātuś-ca satyaṃ jagataś-ca dharmaṇi putrasya pāthaḥ padam-advayāvinaḥ

te māyino mamire supracetaso jāmī sayonī mithunā sam-okasā
navyaṃ-navyaṃ tantum-ā tanvate divi samudre antaḥ kavayaḥ sudītayaḥ

tad rādho adya savitur-vareṇyaṃ vayaṃ devasya prasave manāmahe
asmabhyaṃ dyāvāpṛthivī sucetunā rayiṃ dhattaṃ vasuman-taṃ śatagvinaṃ.

Loudly do I praise with offerings in our gatherings

Heaven and Earth, the mighty and wise whose growth accords with the law, whose offspring are gods, who with the gods, just by means of their accomplishment and their vision proffer their blessings.

And with invocations I brood upon the genial Father's mind and on the Mother's valiant might. With their immensities [these] prolific parents created [this] vast multitude and for their progeny [gave] immortality.

These your offsprings, industrious, highly accomplished, forthwith gave birth to the two great mothers. The laws of that which stands and moves ye keep as truth, as the seat of your son, the pure.

The highly skilled, the deeply wise, have measured out the pair as of one common origin and one home. The flame-bright sages outspread the ever renewed warp within the sky, within the ocean.

On such priceless munificence of the shining Savitṛ do we meditate today. On us let bounteous Heaven and Earth graciously bestow a hundredfold their wealth.

Ṛgv. X.72

devānāṃ nu vayaṃ jānā pra vocāma vipanyayā
ukthesu śasyamānesu yaḥ paśyād-uttare yuge

brahmaṇaspatir-etā saṃ karmāra iva-adhamat devānāṃ pūrvye yuge 'sataḥ sad-ajāyata

devanaṃ yuge prathame 'sataḥ sad-ajāyata tad-āśā anv-ajāyanta tad-uttānapadas-pari

bhūr-jagña uttānapado bhuva āśā ajāyanta
aditer-dakṣo ajāyata dakṣādv-aditiḥ pari

aditir-hy-ajaniṣṭa dakṣa yā duhitā tava tāṃ devā anv-ajāyanta bhadrā amṛta-bandhavaḥ

yad-devā adaḥ salile susamrabdhā atiṣṭhata
atrā vo nṛtyatām-iva tīvro reṇur-apa-āyata

yad devā yatayo yathā bhuvanāny-apinvata atrā samudra
ā gūḷham-ā sūryam-ajabhartana

aṣṭau putrāso aditer-ye jātās-tanvas-pari
devān upa pra et saptabhiḥ parā mārtāṇḍam-āsyat

saptabhiḥ putrair-aditir-upa pra et pūrvyaṃ yugaṃ prajāyai
mṛtyave tvat punar-mārtāṇḍam-ā-abharat.

The birth of the gods! Let us now joyfully proclaim it that in the ages to come it may be visioned in these exalting utterances.

The Lord of prayer, even like a smith, forged these [worlds] together, in the primeval age of the gods, as Being emerged from non-Being.

In the primeval age of the gods Being emerged from non-Being. Thence did divisions follow into existence, thence this [all] from the creative power.

From the creative power the earth emerged, from the earth divisions were formed; from the Infinite Intelligence was born and again from Intelligence the Infinite.

Yea, Aditi (the Infinite) was born of Dakṣa (Intelligence), that daughter of thine; following her were the gods begotten, blessed in the kinship of immortality.

When in yon billowy-deeps ye gods stood closely-clasped, then from ye as though from dancers hot dust was whirled away.

Even like devotees O gods, when ye filled up the worlds, then did ye bring forth the sun till then concealed in billowy-deeps.

Eight were the sons of Aditi born from herself. With seven she approached the gods, Mārtāṇḍa she cast away.

With seven sons Aditi went forth towards the former generation. Mārtāṇḍa she again brought forth for the sake of generation and dissolution.

Ṛgv. X.14

pareyivāṃsaṃ pravato mahīr-anu bahubhyaḥ panthām-anupaspaśānaṃ
vaivasvataṃ saṃgamanaṃ janānāṃ yamaṃ rājānaṃ haviṣā duvasya

yamo no gātuṃ prathamo viveda na-eṣā gavyūtir-apabhartavā u
yatrā naḥ pūrve pitaraḥ parā-īyur-enā jajñānāḥ pathyā anu svāḥ

mātali kavyair-yamo aṅgirobhir-bṛhaspatir-ṛkvabhirvāvṛdhānaḥ
yāṃś-ca devā vāvṛdhur-ye ca devānt-svāhā-anye svadhayā-anye madanti

imaṃ yama prastaram-ā hi sīda-aṅgirobhiḥ pitṛbhiḥ saṃvidānaḥ
ā tvā mantrāḥ kaviśastā vahantv-enā rājan-haviṣā mādayasva

aṅgirobhir-ā gahi yajñiyebhir-yama vairūpair-iha mādayasva
vivasvantaṃ huve yaḥ pitā te' smin-yajñe barhiṣy-ā niṣadya

aṅgiraso naḥ pitaro navagvā atharvāṇo bhṛgavaḥ somyāsaḥ
teṣāṃ vayaṃ sumatau yajñiyānām-api bhadre saumanase syāma

pra-ihi pra-ihi pathibhiḥ pūrvyebhir yatrā naḥ pūrve pitaraḥ parā-īyuḥ

ubhā rājānā svadhayā madantā yamaṃ paśyāsi varuṇaṃ ca devam

saṃ gachasva pitṛbhiḥ saṃ yamena-iṣṭāpūrtena parame vyoman
hitvāya-avadyaṃ punar-astam-ā-ihi saṃ gachasva tanvā suvarcāḥ

apa-ita vi-ita vi ca sarpata-ato' smā etaṃ pitaro lokam-akran
ahobhir-adbhir-aktubhir-vyaktaṃ yamo dadāty avasānam-asmai

ati drava sārameyau śvānau caturakṣau śabalau sādhunā pathā

athā pitṛn-suvidatrān upa-ihi yamena ye sadhamādaṃ madanti

yau te śvānau yama rakṣitārau caturakṣau pathirakṣī nṛcakṣasau
tābhyām-enaṃ pari dehi rājant-svasti ca-asmā anamīvaṃ ca dhehi

urūṇasāv-asutṛpā udumbalau yamasya dūtau carato janān anu
tāv-asmabhyaṃ dṛśaye sūryāya punar-dātām-asum-adya-iha bhadram

yamāya somaṃ sunuta yamāya juhutā haviḥ
yamaṃ ha yajño gachaty-agni-dūto araṃkṛtaḥ

yamāya ghṛtavad-havir juhota pra ca tiṣṭhata
sa no devaṣv-ā yamad dīrgham-āyuḥ pra jīvase

yamāya madhumattamaṃ rājñe havyaṃ juhotana
idaṃ nama ṛṣibhyaḥ pūrvajebhyaḥ pūrvebhyaḥ pathikṛd-bhyaḥ

trikadrukebhiḥ patati ṣaḷ-urvīr-ekam-id-bṛhat
triṣṭub-gāyatrī chandāṃsi sarvā tā yama ā-hitā

Honour with oblation king Yama who has passed away along the mighty heights, exploring the path for the many, son of Vivasvant, convener of mankind.

Yama first discovered the way for us, such a pasture as may not be taken away from us. There did our ancient parents pass away and thither those born hereafter, each along his own path.

Mātalī thrives with the Kavyas, Yama with the Aṅgirasaḥ, Bṛhaspati with the Ṛkvans; these the gods exalt and they the gods. The ones rejoice in the sacrificial call *svāhā*, the others in the sacrificial offering.

Sit thee down upon this strewn-grass O Yama, together with our ancestors the Aṅgirasaḥ. May the mantras intoned by the seers bring thee here! Exult O king in this oblation!

Come hither Yama with the holy Aṅgirasaḥ, rejoice here with the sons of Virūpa! I invoke Vivasvant thy father that he may sit upon the grass at this sacrificial-rite!

Our forebears [are] the Aṅgirasaḥ, the Navagvas, the Atharvans, the Bhṛgus, the Soma-lovers. In the good-will, the auspicious favours of these holy ones, we would remain!

Go forth, go forth, by the ancient paths whereon our ancient forebears did pass away. Both kings, Yama and godly Varuṇa, rejoicing in the sacrificial offering, thou shalt behold.

Unite with the patriarchs, unite with Yama, with the rewards-of-thy-good-works in the highest heaven. Leaving transgression, again go home! Unite with thy splendid self.

[Addressed to evil spirits:]

Off with ye, disperse, slink away! For him have the patriarchs prepared that place. To him has Yama given a resting-place anointed with the days and the waters and the nights.

Run by the fair path past the two dogs of Saramā, four-eyed, powerful. Thence approach the benevolent fathers who together with Yama revel at the same festival.

To those two dogs of thine, Yama, the watchers, the four-eyed, protectors of the path, observers of men, hand him over, and on him extend well being and health.

Broad-nosed, life-taking, copper-coloured, Yama's two messengers roam about 'midst mankind. May these two, that we may see the sun, grant us again this day blessed life!

For Yama's sake press ye the Soma. For Yama's sake offer ye the oblation! For to Yama speeds the sacrifice, suitably prepared, with Agni as the envoy.

To Yama offer the buttered oblation and step forward! May he bring us to the gods that we may live a long life!

To king Yama offer up the mellowest oblation! This homage [is meant] for the sages born of old, for the ancient path-makers!

From the three Soma vessels it soars. Six are the broad ones, one is the vast one! *Triṣṭub*, *gāyatrī*, the metres, all these are placed in Yama!

Index

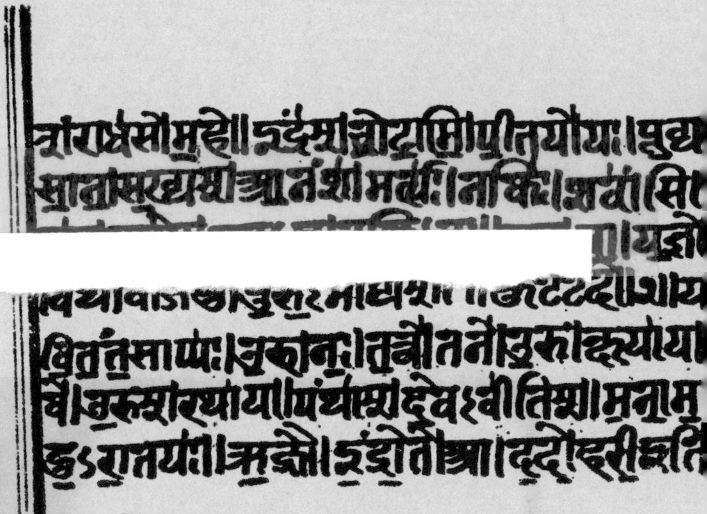

Ṛgveda *above:* Page of a sixteenth-century manuscript

below: Page of a fifteenth-century manuscript
Courtesy of The British Library Board

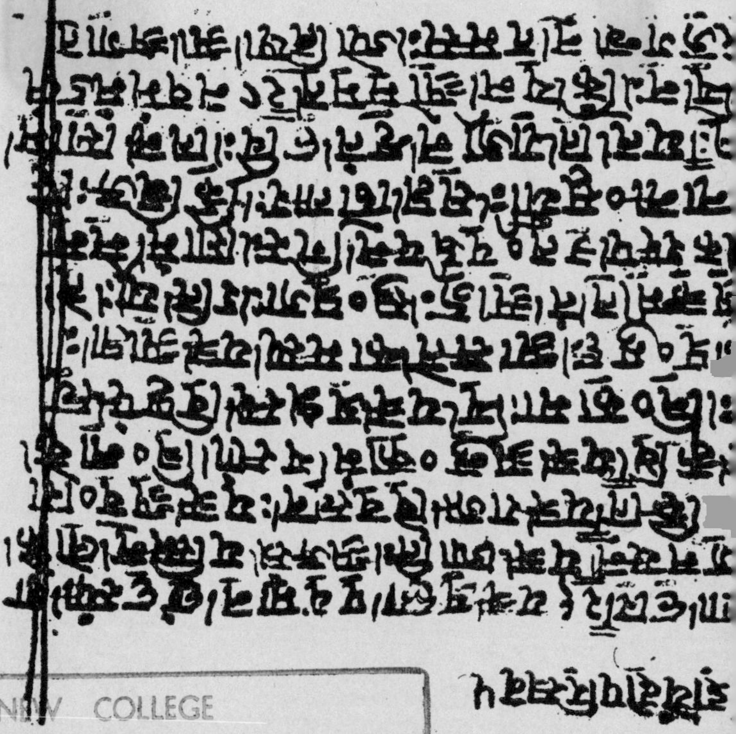